INTIMATIONS OF GLOBAL LAW

A strain of law reaching beyond any bounded international or transnational remit to assert a global jurisdiction has recently acquired a new prominence. *Intimations of Global Law* detects this strain in structures of international law claiming a planetary scope independent of state consent, in new threads of global constitutional law, administrative law and human rights, and in revived notions of *ius gentium* and the global rule of law. It is also visible in the legal pursuit of functionally differentiated global public goods, general conflict rules, norms of 'legal pluralism' and new legal hybrids such as the global law of peace and humanity law.

The coming of global law affects how law manifests itself in a global age and alters the shape of our legal-ethical horizons. Global law presents a diverse, unsettled and sometimes conflicted legal category, and one which challenges our very understanding of the rudiments of legal authority.

NEIL WALKER holds the Regius Chair of Public Law and the Law of Nature and Nations at the University of Edinburgh.

D1610011

GLOBAL LAW SERIES

The series provides unique perspectives on the way globalisation is radically altering the study, discipline and practice of law. Featuring innovative books in this growing field, the series explores those bodies of law which are becoming global in their application, and the newly emerging interdependency and interaction of different legal systems. It covers all major branches of the law and includes work on legal theory, history and the methodology of legal practice and jurisprudence under conditions of globalisation. Offering a major platform on global law, these books provide essential reading for students and scholars of comparative, international and transnational law.

INTIMATIONS OF GLOBAL LAW

NEIL WALKER

CAMBRIDGE
UNIVERSITY PRESS

CAMBRIDGE
UNIVERSITY PRESS

University Printing House, Cambridge CB2 8BS, United Kingdom

Cambridge University Press is part of the University of Cambridge.

It furthers the University's mission by disseminating knowledge in the pursuit of education, learning and research at the highest international levels of excellence.

www.cambridge.org
Information on this title: www.cambridge.org/9781107091627

© Neil Walker 2015

First published 2015

Printed in the United Kingdom by Clays, St Ives plc

A catalogue record for this publication is available from the British Library

Library of Congress Cataloguing in Publication data
Walker, Neil, 1960– author.
Intimations of global law / Neil Walker.
pages   cm – (Global law series)
ISBN 978-1-107-09162-7 (hardback)
1. International law.   2. Globalization.   3. International cooperation.
4. Global Governance.   I. Title.
KZ1321.W35 2014
341–dc23
2014032236

ISBN 978-1-107-09162-7 Hardback
ISBN 978-1-107-46378-3 Paperback

For Gillian

CONTENTS

ACKNOWLEDGMENTS

This book began as the Montesquieu Lecture, delivered at Tilburg University in June 2012 on the occasion of the inauguration of the new Law Schools Global League. That, of course, was just the kind of event a book looking out for 'Intimations of Global Law' ought to be taking a close interest in. My first thanks, then, are due to my Tilburg hosts, Willem Witteveen, Randall Lesaffer and Morag Goodwin, both for providing me with a platform for developing the outline of the book and for taking an initiative that helped me make proper sense of my subject matter.

The passage from lecture to book was made much easier, and much more enjoyable, by a number of other generous invitations to try out my ideas. I learned much from lecture audiences and seminar participants at the Universities of Amsterdam, Durham, Helsinki, Southampton and Tilburg (again), at the European University Institute in Florence, at University College London, at the Católica Global School of Law in Lisbon, and at the iCourts Institute of the University of Copenhagen. I am grateful to my hosts at all of these institutions. I also owe a special debt of gratitude to my own Edinburgh colleagues at the Law School, the Centre for Law and Society and the Global Justice Institute, who together organised what proved to be a stimulating – and, for me, invaluable – full-day discussion of an early draft of the manuscript.

Many people have engaged with my ideas on global law in ways that have been extremely helpful. They include Daniel Augenstein, Loïc Azoulai, Christine Bell, Oren Ben-Dor, Nehal Bhuta, Dan Carr, Emilios Christodoulidis, Carlos Closa, Sharon Cowan, Marise Cremona, Deirdre Curtin, Gráinne de Búrca, Bruno de Witte, Luis Duarte d'Almeida, Navraj Ghaleigh, Alun Gibbs, Marco Goldoni, Morag Goodwin, Jane Holder, Claire Kilpatrick, Mattias Kumm, Randall Lesaffer, Cormac MacAmhlaigh, Euan MacDonald, Daithí Mac Síthigh, Miguel Maduro, Ruth Rubio Marin, Joana Mendez, Claudio Michelon, Hans Micklitz, Elisa Morgera, Steve Neff, André Nollkaemper, Aiofe O'Donoghue, Dennis Patterson, George Pavlakos, Ulli Petersmann, Haris Psarris, Gonçalo de Almeida Ribeiro, Paolo

Sandro, Giovanni Sartor, Martin Scheinin, Robert Schütze, Kathryn Sikkink, Mark Telford, Stephen Tierney, Jim Tully, Kaarlo Tuori, Bert van Roermund, Marlene Wind, Jonathan Zeitlin and Peer Zumbansen. A very special mention is due to Zenon Bankowski, Hans Lindahl, Martin Loughlin, Gianluigi Palombella, Alec Stone Sweet and William Twining, each of whom took the considerable trouble of reading and commenting on the entire manuscript.

Thanks, too, to Finola O'Sullivan at Cambridge University Press, who met all reasonable expectations, not to mention quite a few unreasonable ones. And also to Tom Daly, who proved to be a quite brilliant editorial assistant in the early stages of pulling the manuscript together. And last but never least, I have my family to be thankful for. Even more so than most books, this one was written in the early mornings, late at night, and at weekends. To Emilia, Lewis and Ross, and particularly to Gillian, many thanks for your constant patience, support and love. The book would never have seen the light of day without you.

1

Why global law?

This is a book about how we might fruitfully think about global law. Few terms are more topical in the transnational legal literature. Yet there has been little serious discussion – and little agreement where there has been discussion – on what is meant by 'global law', if, indeed, it means anything of note at all. In what follows, I suggest that we *can* nonetheless arrive at a core sense of global law as an emergent idea and practice, and that our so doing is key to any proper appreciation of the ways in which law is affected by, and is responding to, the contemporary wave of globalisation. The elucidation of that core sense will not, of course, tell us how law – global or otherwise – *should* be (re)shaped, and how it ought to be deployed to tackle the problems of global justice. Conceptual analysis and empirical inquiry alone can never solve normative problems. Yet they can help us to understand these problems more clearly, and to provide a better route map through the moral and political maze. The hope is that the reader will emerge with a sharper sense of the complexity of the global legal environment, and of the vital forces underwriting that complexity, and so with a keener appreciation of why and how the contemporary legal world has evolved as it is has and what it would take to change it.

But what of the view that, far from supplying an explanatory touchstone, stripped of its superficial glamour 'global law' is simply the wrong place to start in accounting for changes in the contemporary legal condition? It is with that most basic objection, and the serious concerns about 'global' thinking in general that stand behind it, that we begin.

1.1   The perils and promise of global analysis

1.1.1   Don't mention the word

In his voluminous writings William Twining[1] has been relentlessly curious and uniquely informative about the processes, practices,

---

[1]   A recent predecessor as the Montesquieu Lecturer; published as *Globalisation and Legal Scholarship: Montesquieu Lecture 2009* (Nijmegen: Wolf Legal Publishers, 2011).

institutions, doctrines, values and aspirations through which law becomes less centred upon the jurisdiction and less dependent on the organs of the modern state, and instead gradually comes to assume a 'global' significance.[2] Yet he has little time for catch-all labels such as 'global law'. Twining has always been wary of any umbrella term that purports to capture in full the legal dimension of so-called 'globalisation', just as he prefers to hold the generic concept itself at arm's length. So much so, indeed, that he has long cultivated the habit of banning the 'g' word in all its varieties from the seminar room.[3] Such language, he says, has at best limited added value. It may even, in the particular case of 'global law', possess negative value; and this for two reasons.

In the first place, there is a tendency towards the indiscriminate use, and so also the *overuse*, of what remains a radically ambiguous and open-ended label.[4] Whether talking about a body of doctrine, an emergent conception of legal order, a set of institutional capacities, a form of professional legal practice and culture, an academic discipline, a research programme or a teaching template, or about any combination of these, we might be tempted to make vague or overstated claims about the prevalence of something that goes under the banner of 'global law'. The danger is not just that the general label will not necessarily add anything to our understanding of the richly disparate set of activities and processes through which legal doctrine and other legal phenomena are spreading further and more thickly across the globe than before. More than that, its invocation may have a misleadingly reductive effect, implying false unity, coherence or settlement. In its neat singularity, a term like 'global law' may suggest identity where there is multiplicity, uniformity where there is diversity, closure where there is opening, simplicity where there is complexity, order where there is disarray, agreement where there is conflict, achievement where there is aspiration. Most dangerously seductive of all, the notion of global law as a singular phenomenon or prospect might invite us to imagine a false normative ideal – a sense of there being 'one best way' of 'global law', or even 'one best global way' of 'law'.

In the second place, inasmuch as the global label, as Twining advises,[5] might tolerably be employed in a more discriminating fashion to refer to

---

[2] W. Twining, *Globalisation and Legal Theory* (Cambridge University Press, 2000); *Globalisation and Legal Scholarship, ibid.*; and *General Jurisprudence: Understanding Law from a Global Perspective* (Cambridge University Press, 2009).
[3] Twining, *General Jurisprudence, ibid.*, p. 14.
[4] Twining, *Globalisation and Legal Scholarship*, n. 1 above, pp. 17–28.   [5] *Ibid.*, p. 24.

legal institutions organised on a global level and legal activity occurring on a worldwide scale, this may nevertheless be too narrow a perspective, and too mean a dividend, where the first-mentioned reference of 'global law' is too broad and too generous. For a focus on global law as the spatially specific category of planetary law, he argues, misses out a lot of what is most interesting about the intense contemporary flow of legal phenomena beyond the confines of the state.[6] Instead, much of that movement actually takes place at more limited levels, whether international, private transnational, regional or sub-state. What is more, the resulting dense layering and interweaving of regulatory activity is far from being 'nested in a single vertical hierarchy'[7] in which the planetary level has pride of place at the authoritative apex.

We must acknowledge the force of William Twining's scepticism. So much so, indeed, that we should begin our exploration of the case for a more central understanding of the place of something called 'global law' in the scheme of legal things by investigating the more general methodological concerns that underlie his own reservations. For unless and until certain basic difficulties with the keystone concept of 'globalisation' are addressed – difficulties signalled by the breadth of his terminological embargo – we cannot hope to make headway with the particular case of global law. These methodological concerns go to the very question of the kind of explanatory activity we are engaged in when we use the generic 'g' word. Indeed, they even challenge whether and on what terms the study of something called 'globalisation', still less global law, might be a coherent undertaking at all. Yet, as I will argue, an exploration of these concerns can also point us towards a more productive way of thinking about global law.

1.1.2 Globalisation as process

Whatever our mature theoretical misgivings, our gut fascination with the notion of globalisation is neither surprising nor misconceived. It derives from, and is sustained by, the widespread belief that there is a strong trend away from 'the local' and the territorially confined, and in particular the state-confined, as the main point of reference for many areas of human organisation, and that this trend represents a defining and deepening feature of the contemporary age. Naturally enough, we are also interested in the deep roots and preconditions of globalisation so understood. If

[6] *Ibid.*, p. 24.   [7] *Ibid.*, pp. 24–5.

globalisation is such a definitive feature of today, how, we are bound to ask ourselves, did it come about, and how did we get to this point?

The inquiry into causes yields different answers, and supplies countless shades of emphasis. For some, globalisation is a movement that has extended or recurred across the ages: from the economic and cultural pull of Ancient Greece, through various 'archaic'[8] phases of imperial influence – Roman, Islamic and Mongol – to the so-called 'proto-globalisation'[9] of the first European overseas empires of the fifteenth and sixteenth centuries. For others, globalisation is essentially a modern phenomenon: beginning with early nineteenth-century industrialisation, rapid population growth and the development of new consumer markets, and with the mutual encouragement of these trends through deepening channels of trade and investment and accelerating avenues of communication between Europe's competing imperial powers, their colonies and the United States. And while the two World Wars of the first half of the twentieth century interrupted the long march of nineteenth-century globalisation, the years since 1945 have undoubtedly witnessed a new globalising wave. Yet beneath the basic consensus of that modern narrative, much disagreement persists. Opinions differ sharply over the distinctiveness, phasing and intensity of the dynamic triggered by the new political and economic institutions of the post-war years – in particular, the United Nations system and the so-called Bretton Woods institutions[10] – and, later, by the end of Cold War bipolarity in 1989.[11]

However, while excavation of historical roots remains an important – and much contested – part of any account of contemporary globalisation, it can by no means be the whole story. What is more, it may even compromise or curtail efforts to seek out and tell the rest of the story. This danger arises because an inquiry into underlying causes implies that we already have a firm grasp of what the 'it' is that is in need of explanation. That impression, in turn, may contribute to the *reification* of our object of inquiry. For to the extent that efforts are concentrated on

---

[8] See e.g. L. Martell, *The Sociology of Globalization* (Cambridge: Polity Press, 2010) p. 45; and A. G. Frank, *ReOrient: Global Economy in the Asian Age* (Berkeley: University of California Press, 1998).

[9] See e.g. A. G. Hopkins (ed.), *Globalization in World History*, 2nd edn (London: Pimlico, 2011) p. 6.

[10] Namely, the World Bank and the International Monetary Fund; both set up at a meeting of forty-three states in Bretton Woods, New Hampshire in July 1944.

[11] See e.g. D. Held and A. McGrew (eds.), *Globalisation Theory: Approaches and Controversy* (Cambridge: Polity Press, 2007).

working out how and why globalisation came about, this may reflect assumptions about globalisation's concretely self-evident quality; or, at least, it may nurture the proclivity to try to 'pin it down' and label it as an identifiable 'thing'. Here, then, Twining's concern about the compromised quality of the very language of globalisation finds its mark. For we can see how the 'g' *signifier*, in its seductive singularity, reflects and may come to reinforce an understanding of what *is signified* in equally singular terms.

The sustained prominence of the globalisation agenda of debate over the last quarter century reinforces the reifying tendency. The sheer intensity and persistence of our contemporary preoccupation with globalisation creates its own atmosphere of distortion. The saturation coverage that globalisation has received in the academy and in media commentary, think tanks, government policy units and other key contexts of public opinion formation in recent decades itself helps to foster or reinforce a perception of the subject matter of our curiosity as somehow palpable – its very familiarity lending it a certain tangibility and sense of distinct identity.[12]

The reifying inclination gives rise to a twofold methodological danger, anticipating Twining's more specific concerns about 'global law'. On the one hand, we might surmise, as many commentators do,[13] that globalisation has a wide referential range, embracing a complex, mutually dependent mix of economic, technological, cultural and political factors. The deployment of a capsule term to grasp our explanatory object may nevertheless reflect and encourage a readiness to impute to these diverse phenomena a discrete and distinctive quality-in-the-round they do not possess. We may be led to assume that whatever the 'it' of globalisation is, it possesses a definitive character – referring to an 'achieved' condition that is reducible to a singular abstract form and clearly distinguishable from what came before. On the other hand, we might, as other commentators do, take a more substantial, and so more obvious, approach to the apparently 'thing-like' quality of globalisation. We may focus on only one particular feature within the broader menu of candidate factors and treat that feature as globalisation's key dimension of cause and effect.

---

[12] See e.g. T. Bewes, *Reification, or the Anxiety of Late Capitalism* (London: Verso, 2002).

[13] See e.g. A. Giddens, *The Consequences of Modernity* (Stanford University Press, 1990); and D. Held (ed.), *Global Transformations: Politics, Economics and Culture* (Stanford University Press, 1999).

This may be, and often is, 'economic liberalisation', or, in a more cultural vein, it may be 'Westernisation' or 'Americanisation', or, in a technological vein, the 'Internet Revolution'.[14] In our pursuit of globalisation's hard core by any of these narrow means, however, we are bound to exclude or downgrade other aspects of the wider mix by definitional fiat.

Any and all such seductive tendencies should give us cause for concern because, however we understand its origins, and whether and in whatever fashion we might seek to organise the elements of globalisation into core and peripheral, it is clear that much of what is of *continuing* significance in globalisation requires us to look elsewhere. For globalisation refers not – or not merely – to a discrete and settled historical accomplishment – whether multidimensional or dominated by a single dimension – and its causal preconditions, but also to an ongoing and widely ramified process. Whatever else remains at issue, much thinking on globalisation rightly tends to emphasise consequences as well as foundations, incremental as well as exponential change, ripple effects as much as discrete causal chains, flow as much as accomplishment. Crudely put, if globalisation is a defining feature of the contemporary age, it is not a state of affairs preserved in aspic, but something that is constantly evolving.

What are the telling features of this other slant of inquiry, with its focus upon currents rather than – or in addition to – causes and effects? To begin with, a common theme in much of this literature is its concentration on those manifestations or indices of globalisation that refer less to distinct episodes and events or to disjunctive movements and more to the gradual accumulation of various forces and tendencies in an unfinished dynamic stretching back to the early modern period. In particular, we see this more fluid understanding of globalisation in the repeated emphasis on the gradual deterritorialisation and disembedding of the basic setting of social organisation,[15] from the telegram to the video-link and from the exceptional Congress of Vienna of 1815 to the permanent United Nations after 1945; or in the stress upon the cumulative growth and intensification of social interconnectedness across previous geographical divisions, from the bilateral trade routes and reciprocal patterns of seasonal migration of the nineteenth century to the global reach

---

[14] W. Scheuerman, 'Globalization', *Stanford Encyclopedia of Philosophy*, available at http://plato.stanford.edu/entries/globalization/.

[15] See e.g. J. A. Scholte, *Globalization: A Critical Introduction*, 2nd edn (New York: Palgrave Macmillan, 2005).

of the multinational corporation, the worldwide financial market and the budget airline;[16] and, to take a final key index, in the increased velocity of many of our circuits of social action and exchange, from the high-speed railway and the cinema newsreel to the internet and the twenty-four-hour news cycle, and the sense these bring of a global environment of simultaneous worldwide action and reception.[17]

Secondly, for all that these globalising appearances and tendencies are attended by many forms of resistance and counter-tendency – to which we return shortly – the overall graph of the evolutionary process indicates acceleration, concentration and augmentation. This can be widely illustrated. International capital finds new forms of collaboration and new routes of mobility, which supply a platform for yet more versatile forms of flow. New modes of virtual communication proliferate and prompt further technological innovation. Global access to local markets and local cultural sensibilities and preferences fosters the formation of global cultural sensibilities and preferences, which reinforces global access to local markets. New transnational political institutions attract transnational clients with transnational agendas and foster a transnational political class, all of which feeds the development of a denser institutional architecture. Global social movements in one policy area provide both a practical example and a legitimating backdrop for the development of global social movements in other policy areas.

Thirdly, this dynamic of intensification also operates across and between different domains. Again, examples are legion. Technological development enables economic growth and facilitates widespread cultural dissemination; cultural convergence stimulates new global markets, and so on. Economic development provokes new institutional and regulatory responses by coalitions of winners and losers alike; new institutional capacity frames new forms of common political culture and attracts new types of social movements, and so forth.

Fourthly, the increasing cross-domain intensity of processes of social disembedding, of the generation of new forms of interconnectedness, and of the compression of time and space, creates new alignments of capacities, interests and values as well as new cleavages, tensions and oppositions associated with these new alignments. On the one hand, the

---

[16] See e.g. Held, n. 13 above, ch. 1.
[17] See T. H. Eriksen, *Tyranny of the Moment: Fast and Slow Time in the Information Age* (London: Pluto Press, 2001); and D. Harvey, *Justice, Nature, and the Geography of Difference* (Oxford: Blackwell, 1996).

practices of globalisation reflect and reinforce the material conditions under which economically, militarily and politically powerful global actors and structures can exert greater transnational influence, thereby reinforcing existing differences and creating and pursuing new conflicts of interest as well as facilitating – or imposing – new kinds of common-alities of expectations, appetites, experiences and values. On the other hand, these objective changes supply the conditions under which, on the cultural level, territorially concentrated societies across the globe as well as new transnationally connected communities of interest and practice become more exposed to, and more aware of, both their mutual differ-ences and their mutual similarities. Crudely, then, in the 'compression chamber' of globalisation similarities and differences of life-chances and experiences alike are amplified, as are perceptions of what is valuable or otherwise in the common standards to which we aspire and the different conceptions of the good life we inherit and pursue. Newly dispersed forms and newly dislocated lines of concurrence and antagonism of interest, of co-operation and conflict, of association and dissociation, of identity and difference, of social solidarity and tension, all proliferate, each the condition, consequence and reinforcing cause of the other.[18]

Globalisation, therefore, on this process-centred understanding, is an inclination with its own momentum, its own self-explanatory dynamic, its own multi-domain and open-ended remit, and – highly pertinent to our later discussion of the different species of global law[19] – its own ceaseless mutual production and stimulation of new forms of conver-gence and divergence of interests, outlooks and affinities. And – crucial to the case for the distinctiveness of global law within the 'global' lexicon – the trajectory of globalisation involves not only a dense set of connections between the various sectors or dimensions, but also a sig-nificant degree of autonomy within each. For our very sense of the irreducibility of globalisation to any particular key, or to any particular set of historical causes or drives, demands that no one sector or dimen-sion should be seen as entirely dominant and that none should be seen as merely subordinate. Instead, each dimension should possess its own developmental logic, and each its own trajectory, with all connected through circuits of mutual influence rather than lines of unilateral determination.

---

[18] See e.g. R. Robertson, *Globalization: Social Theory and Global Culture* (London: Sage, 1992).
[19] See Chapter 3 below.

If we bring these insights back to the use-value of the global law concept, we gain a deeper appreciation of Twining's misgivings. His reservations about global law as a closed category derive from and reflect a more general set of reservations about globalisation as a closed category. Just as the combination of globalising forces produces a shifting, unresolved and unpredictable state of affairs, so too each dimension within that combination displays the same open horizon of development. In particular, we can see how the idea that each sector, in the absence of any overarching logic of convergence or of causal priority, must follow its own *relatively autonomous*,[20] uncharted course, informs Twining's research agenda. It supports his conclusion that any consideration of the field of global law in the broadest (and, from his perspective, loosest and 'best left unnamed') sense, should begin in critical and inquiring mode. Its point of departure should be the inadequacy of the received model of modern law – the state-centred law-world – to our circumstances of intensifying 'global' interdependence, rather than any definitive attempt to capture or foretell what is taking its place.[21] It should, therefore, start from a conviction of the increasing inappropriateness of the high modern view of legal statehood as a largely self-contained and so largely globally insulated 'black box'[22] of doctrine, institutions, culture and education. And it should proceed under a general commitment to re-situate the state on a multipolar and densely connected legal map in a complex relationship with other economic, political and cultural globalising forces, and not from any firm preconception or narrow conviction about the shape of things emergent or to come.

1.2   Reconceptualising global law

While I endorse the general tenor of Twining's research agenda, and take heed of his warning as to the distractions and distortions of 'g' speak, let me reiterate my intention to pursue a different tack. Rather than dismiss the use of the 'global law' label for the analytical sloppiness or normative presumption of an over-inclusive global-as-everything-post-national reading, or caution against the one-dimensional literalism and misleading focus of an under-inclusive global-as-planetary reading, I

---

[20] We return to and explore a key aspect of the relative autonomy of global law in Chapter 6.4 below.

[21] Twining, *General Jurisprudence*, n. 2 above, ch. 1.

[22] Twining, *Globalisation and Legal Theory*, n. 2 above, p. 8.

want to make stronger claims for the term, now endowed with a somewhat different meaning to those of which Twining is critical. The dangers of which Twining speaks are genuine, but they do not provide a definitive case against the use of the language of global law. On the contrary, if we are prepared to acknowledge the methodological hazards discussed above, then the importance of recognising and of exploring the relative autonomy of law in the process of globalisation can work in favour of the retention and development of a domain-specific conceptual language of legal globalisation. For if we succeed in fashioning a sense of global law that illuminates rather than denies the open horizons of the legal domain, and clarifies rather than obscures law's distinctive trajectory in the overall flow of global forces, then we will have turned a potential liability into an asset.

Our case for pursuing the idea of global law against the sceptical grain rests upon three arguments. Or rather, it is based upon one argument comprising three layers – rhetorical, structural and epistemic. In a nutshell, we should take the idea of global law seriously: first, because of the increased 'real world' currency of global law talk; secondly, because such talk echoes an underlying series of changes in the pattern of formation, distribution and circulation of law; and, thirdly, because that objective trend, and the language in which it is articulated, both reflects and encourages an important shift at the margins in the very way that we think about legal authority and strive to refashion law on the basis of that knowledge.

1.2.1   Taking 'global law' talk seriously

As our cue, and at the outer layer of inquiry, there is the bare question of language and its use, and of the pattern of thought and conceptualisation that this expresses. However tempting it might be to seek refuge, with Twining, from the cacophony of global talk, we cannot simply assume that no cost to our understanding is incurred by ignoring or sidelining it. We should not lightly disregard the crude fact that 'global law',[23] along with kindred terms such as 'world law',[24]

---

[23] The special issue of the *Tilburg Law Review* on 'Global Law' provides an excellent snapshot of the sheer variety of contemporary uses of the 'global law' concept, containing twenty-four articles each exploring a different disciplinary theme or theoretical perspective. See *Tilburg Law Review* vol. 17, no. 2, 2012.

[24] H. Berman, 'World Law: An Ecumenical Jurisprudence of the Holy Spirit' 63 *Theology Today* 365 (2006).

'universal law',[25] 'common law',[26] *jus gentium*[27] or even 'earth jurisprudence',[28] are today invoked and applied with markedly increased frequency. Even if we are initially hesitant, or at least agnostic, about the value of the 'global law' concept as a general category in explaining the changing shape and texture of the contemporary legal world, we must remain alert to its increasingly regular circulation in the world that provides the very object of any such explanatory account. The proliferation of the discourse of global law and global legality, then, should at the very least give us pause for thought.

This may seem a superficial starting point, but if we follow its lead we discover the outline of a basic structural shift in the generation and mobility of law with which the emergence of a general category of global law is aligned. As our detailed examination of 'global law' talk will make clear, it is a language that is in fact cultivated in a wide range of contexts.[29] Yet its most significant appearance has been at the cutting edge of new manifestations of legal order and doctrine. Here too, however, as we shall see, the byword is difference, with the various treatments of global law *as* law displaying a striking diversity.[30]

What, if anything, is there about the intense recurrence of the global theme across many arenas and from such a wide range of perspectives to suggest that these very different manifestations nevertheless have something important in common? Again it may be useful to begin with Twining, and his reasons for keeping global language at arm's length. For him, to recall, the effects of globalisation upon law are first and foremost to be understood negatively, as requiring us to take note of the limited and limiting purview of a state-centred framework of legal thought, organisation and practice, and so to acknowledge what non-state-centred law in its blossoming variety is *not*. But might we not turn Twining's reasoning on its head? Rather than treating the strength and diversity of the general movement of legal phenomena beyond a state-centred framework, and its well-stocked arsenal of understandings, assumptions and techniques, as

---

[25] See J. Jemielniak and P. Miklaszewicz (eds.), *Interpretation of Law in the Global World: From Particularism to a Universal Approach* (Heidelberg: Springer, 2010). Occasionally this expression is also used by the courts: see *Riggs* v. *Palmer* 115 NY 506 (1889).

[26] H. P. Glenn, *On Common Laws* (Oxford University Press, 2007).

[27] J. Waldron, *'Partly Laws Common to All Mankind': Foreign Law in American Courts* (New Haven, CT: Yale University Press, 2012).

[28] See, for example, the activities of the Center for Earth Jurisprudence: www.barry.edu/law/future-students/academic-program/center-earth-jurisprudence.html.

[29] See Chapter 2 below. [30] See Chapter 3 below.

grounds for eschewing a common language in accounting for law's global transformation, we may contemplate the opposite conclusion. For, argu- ably, as we propose below, the common ground of the various new artic- ulations of global law lies precisely in their each and all being in *response* to just that powerful diversity of movement of law beyond the state.

1.2.2   An excursus on global governance

In order to pursue our thoughts on global law in this direction we must delve once more into the broader debate on globalisation. For if we want to understand the structural shift that has affected legal phenomena in the face of globalisation, and appreciate how that shift affects our conceptualisation of these phenomena, an instructive analogy can be drawn with the rather more developed debate on 'global governance' in the closely related discipline of international relations. Here, as a basic starting point, a strategy of definition by negative contrast with the *ancien régime* can be observed, reminiscent of Twining's in the legal domain. The key contrast drawn by the sponsors of the new global approach is with a state-sovereigntist way of looking at the 'world' of governing forms and of governing practices that is defined and delimited in a very particular way in terms of its overall scope and, within that overall scope, compartmentalised into various specific domains.

More specifically, the new paradigm of global governance signals an overcoming of the 'great divide'[31] in modern political understanding between the 'international' and 'national', conceived of as spheres of action, structures of authority and forms of normativity that are distinct and different, but which together 'contain' our sense of the logic and limits of the construction of the world as an object of authoritative intervention. The 'great divide' was in fact a 'triple divide'. On the one hand, it comprised the broader division between the sphere of internal sovereignty considered as a whole and the limited external expression of that sovereignty in international forms of exchange (the *internal–external* division), as well as the further sub-division of the internal 'national' sphere into its different state parts and the mutually exclusive claims of these 'black box' states to comprehensive authority over their respective internal affairs (the *internal–internal* division). On the other hand, it covered the 'external' limits of external sovereignty – the restriction of

---

[31] I. Clark, *Globalization and International Relations Theory* (Oxford University Press, 1999).

external sovereignty to relations among sovereign states (the *external–external* division).

Of course, this set of neat demarcations has always represented a heavily stylised vision, one that spoke to relations within and between the imperial powers of Europe at the metropolitan centre, but certainly not to the relations between the various metropolitan centres and the subaltern peoples of empire.[32] Yet that is no reason to discount the historical importance of this state-sovereigntist world-view. It has undoubtedly supplied a powerful and self-reinforcing grid for thinking about the Western centre of the political world throughout the modern age.[33] And, paradoxically, the force of its insistence on equality – or, at least, equivalence – of sovereign authority has depended in no small part on its selectivity; on the ability of certain nation states to exploit the resources of empire, and so on the continued subjugation of non-sovereign peoples.[34]

If we look beyond this so-called Westphalian scheme of reference, governance today, with its growth of international regimes, its denser forms of transnational regulation, and its greater involvement of non-state bodies in the administration of large-scale transnational practices, becomes more 'global' in two related senses. This implies the weakening of each of the forms of division set out above. First, global *governance* suggests a thickened and extended regulatory fabric whose relevant spheres of interest, action, institutionalisation and normativity should be better understood as a densely interconnected continuity than as a set of discrete domains. That involves the blurring of the general (*internal–external*) divide between the exercise of internal state sovereignty and external state sovereignty, with states increasingly pooling their capacity in international organisations, which in turn undermines the (*internal–internal*) sense of their uniformly comprehensive and mutually exclusively divided internal sovereignty.[35] Secondly, the idea of *global* governance suggests a range of governance activities that are not in any case restricted to the limited (*external–external*) horizon of interests, actions, institutions and

---

[32] See e.g. J. Tully, *Public Philosophy in a New Key: Volume II, Imperialism and Civic Freedom* (Cambridge University Press, 2008).

[33] See e.g. R. Jackson, *Sovereignty: The Evolution of an Idea* (Cambridge: Polity Press, 2007).

[34] See e.g. Tully, n. 32 above, ch. 7.

[35] See e.g. N. MacCormick, 'Beyond the Sovereign State' 56 *Modern Law Review* 1 (1993); N. Walker, 'Late Sovereignty in the European Union' in N. Walker (ed.), *Sovereignty in Transition: Essays in European Law* (Oxford: Hart, 2003) pp. 3–30.

norms of merely national and inter-national (i.e. inter-state) provenance or focus that we traditionally associate with external sovereignty.

Even with the aid of a post-Westphalian perspective, however, the precise definition of global governance remains unresolved, and depends upon which of these dividing lines provides the analytical focus. One influential strand takes a highly inclusive approach.[36] It embraces everything that cuts across the old division separating intra-state from inter-state. Global governance, on this view, is the entire interdependent domain of multi-level governance extending beyond the state, covering every kind of institutional arrangement and regulatory strand that helps 'join up' the globe beyond the compartmentalised domain of the state. Another definitional strand concentrates instead on the external edge of global governmental arrangements and is more limited in range. It concerns all and only these governance institutions and activities claiming 'global' or planetary reach and significance, however this may precisely be construed. It refers, variously, to the United Nations and the World Bank, and also, on some definitions, to more specialist regimes, coalitions of interested nations and even individual nations, but only where such entities 'act globally' in terms of purpose and scope.[37] As such, this more focused (but still fuzzy) definition includes only one subset of the activities covered by the broader definition of global governance, and does not extend to local, regional or other transnational regimes whose remit is not globally embracing.

---

[36] See, for instance, James Rosenau's often-quoted definition of global governance as including 'systems of rule at all levels of human activity – from the family to the international organization – in which the pursuit of goals has transnational repercussions': J. N. Rosenau, 'Governance in the Twenty-First Century' 1 *Global Governance* 13 (1995) at 13. See also the Commission on Global Governance's (1995) definition of global governance as 'the sum of many ways individuals and institutions, public and private, manage their common affairs. It is a continuing process through which conflicting or diverse interests may be accommodated and co-operative action taken. It includes formal institutions and regimes empowered to enforce compliance, as well as informal arrangements that people and institutions either have agreed to or perceive to be in their interest': Global Governance Commission, *Our Global Neighborhood: The Report of the Commission on Global Governance* (Oxford University Press, 1995) p. 4.

[37] A typical definition of this second type is as follows: 'the government, management and administration capabilities of the United Nations, World Bank and other international organizations, various regimes, coalitions of interested nations and individual nations when they act globally to address to various issues that emerge beyond national borders, such as development, the environment, human rights, infectious diseases and international terrorism': Y. Yokota, keynote lecture: 'What is Global Governance?', NIRA International Forum, 'Global Governance – In Pursuit of a New International Order' 12–13 July 2004, available at www.nira.or.jp/past/newse/paper/globalg/en-08.html.

Clearly, however, for all that they are distinct, the more encompassing sense and the more limiting sense of global governance are also closely linked, both conceptually and causally. Conceptually, as we have seen, governance institutions and processes of global reach are only the most expansively conceived part of the much broader domain of multi-level governance extending across and beyond the 'great divide'. Causally, the narrow range of globally projected institutions and the wider network of other post-national institutions of governance stand in a relationship of mutual irrigation. For notwithstanding the many particular conflicts and tensions that may arise between different governance regimes, as the stress upon the dynamic of intensification in the general theory of globalisation suggests, in any overall assessment the various levels tend to support, sustain and reinforce each other through the emergence of networks of knowledge and power and in the development and realisation of horizons of interest and value that stretch beyond the self-referential framework of the state.[38]

1.2.3   Defining global law

1.2.3.1   Beyond transnational law

An appreciation of what is distinctive about 'global law' also requires us to set aside a regulatory map marked by fixed compartmentalisation of the legal world into the domains of internal and external sovereignty. Just like global governance more generally, the idea of global law demands that we reach beyond the old 'Westphalian duo'[39] of national and international – in this case the domestic law of the state and its citizens and denizens on the one hand, and international law as traditionally confined to relations between states on the other. We do so, moreover, in a way that involves overcoming the same kind of highly stylised and territorially reductive[40] 'triple divide' that the idea of global

---

[38]   See Held, n. 13 above.

[39]   Twining, *Globalisation and Legal Scholarship*, n. 1 above, p. 39.

[40]   Hans Lindahl's work in critical legal phenomenology has done as much as anyone's to demonstrate the (socially and politically prevalent) fallacy of a territorially reductive understanding of what joins and divides legal orders in the contemporary age, and to warn against a simplistic assessment of the disjunctive legal consequences of the contemporary phase of globalisation. For Lindahl, borders are but 'one specific kind of spatial boundary, rather than its paradigm, and . . . spatial boundaries are but one of the four kinds of boundaries that legal orders put in place to regulate behaviour' (p. 43). In Lindahl's view, legal boundaries join and separate 'places' more generally – not just

governance has sought to overcome. We should comprehend legal space
not as a series of self-contained and clearly demarcated jurisdictions both
between different states and their respective municipal laws (*internal–
internal*) and between this general domain of national law and an international law (*internal–external*) whose own horizons are limited to the statist
point of view (*external–external*), but as a pattern of heavily overlapping,
mutually connected and openly extended institutions, norms and
processes.

   On this view, the national level remains important; in fact, *the* most
important source of law within the global mosaic. It can be no part of any
serious analysis of law's global condition to suggest otherwise.[41]
Crucially, however, national law and the actors of the national legal
system are less and less self-contained and self-reliant. They are increasingly unlikely to operate in isolation, without the catalyst, guidance,
support, moderation or challenge of regulatory forms situated beyond
the national jurisdiction or otherwise not coterminous with the national
jurisdiction, or without effects on destinations situated beyond or otherwise not coterminous with the national jurisdiction, whether these be
legal rule-making sites or decision-taking forums.

   Again, however, as with global governance, this reframing yields no
settled conception of the domain of global law. Rather, it offers us more
or less expansive alternatives, depending upon whether the emphasis is
upon overcoming the division between the domestic and the non-
domestic of the received state-centred understanding or upon overcoming a restricted reading of the non-domestic.

   On the one side, there is an inclusive option that covers all forms and
levels of 'state-uncontained' law and their interdependencies against a
backdrop of an increasingly porous division between state and non-state

---

borders and other locations – but also times, subjects and act-contents. No legal order,
he argues, is conceivable which does not routinely discriminate in terms of these four
dimensions of normativity and which is not also limited by them. Any argument about
what is 'new' in law and globalisation, such as mine, therefore, must remain mindful of
the ways in which, however we comprehend their territorial borders, legal orders in
general necessarily maintain boundaries but in so doing treat them in fluid, multidimensional terms. Any such argument must instead find what is interesting and distinctive in
the contemporary phase of globalisation in more specific trends and developments. See
H. Lindahl, *Fault Lines of Globalization: Legal Order and the Politics of A-Legality*
(Oxford University Press, 2013).

[41] See e.g. H. P. Glenn, *The Cosmopolitan State* (Oxford University Press, 2013); and
M. Shaw, *Theory of the Global State: Globality as an Unfinished Revolution*
(Cambridge University Press, 2000).

law[42] and between the myriad forms of non-state law. Such a definition, however, surely falls foul of Twining's criticism of over-inclusiveness. Indeed, it is the most egregious case of such over-inclusiveness. If global law covers every form of law that extends beyond the state in terms of source, jurisdiction or significant effect, then it becomes a protean concept. In fact, we can no longer even plausibly claim semantic unity in terms of the conventional label attached to many of the phenomena under scrutiny. These forms of law would include, for example, the legal framework of regional polities such as the EU, of more limited economic unions such as NAFTA and MERCOSUR, other confederal arrangements such as the Nordic Union, regional human rights charters in Europe, America and Africa, as well as more or less formally conceived transnational but not global jurisgenerative structures ranging from Islamic law[43] to *Jus Publicum Europaeum*[44] and 'commonwealth constitutionalism'.[45] They would also include a myriad of sub-state legal forms and of connections between these legal forms – from the EU's Committee of the Regions, the Council of Europe's Committee on Local Government, and the development, as self-consciously mobile movements, of various ideas of sub-state 'sovereignty' or First Nation recognition,[46] to the various forums and substantive provisions for the representation and protection of national minorities.[47] And they would include much privately generated or hybrid public/private forms of normative order – from the Common Frame of Reference for European Private Law to the International Institution for the Unification of Private

---

[42] Such definitions either tend to be used rhetorically, as part of an insider discourse within global 'law-craft' (see Chapter 2.3.4 below), or, if applied in academic vein, tend to be adopted casually, as loose descriptive terms (often in volume or paper titles or as key words in research projects or conference labels) – as covers with little or no analytical purchase. See Twining, *Globalisation and Legal Scholarship*, n. 1 above, pp. 21–5.

[43] See e.g. W. F. Menski, *Comparative Law in a Global Context: The Legal Systems of Asia and Africa*, 2nd edn (Cambridge University Press, 2006); and Waldron, n. 27 above, pp. 212–14.

[44] See e.g. A. von Bogdandy and J. Bast (eds.), *Principles of European Constitutional Law*, rev. edn (Oxford: Hart, 2010). See also J. E. K. Murkens, *From Empire to Union: Conceptions of German Constitutional Law Since 1871* (Oxford University Press, 2013) pp. 112–36.

[45] S. Gardbaum, *The New Commonwealth Model of Constitutionalism: Theory and Practice* (Cambridge University Press, 2013).

[46] See e.g. E. Fox-Decent, *Sovereignty's Promise: The State as Fiduciary* (Oxford University Press, 2011) on the idea of trustee constitutionalism. See also J. Tully, *Strange Multiplicity: Constitutionalism in an Age of Diversity* (Cambridge University Press, 1995).

[47] T. A. Molloy, *National Minority Rights in Europe* (Oxford University Press, 2005); and P. Alston (ed.), *Peoples' Rights* (Oxford University Press, 2001).

Law (UNIDROIT), and from the rule-making of market-driven global governance networks of international standard-setting bodies and business and trade associations[48] to the adjudication of various international arbitration centres.[49]

Not only does 'global law' fail to 'add value' to our understanding of this complex and extensive field, but it also threatens to usurp an existing term of greater aptness. For much, perhaps all, of this wide legal expanse falls under the appropriately supple and now broadly endorsed label of 'transnational law'[50]– a term coined by Philip Jessup almost sixty years ago precisely so as to convey the sheer range, interconnectedness and mutability of law that 'transcends national frontiers'.[51] It is a term that was consciously and far-sightedly designed not just to capture the blurring of the conventional non-domestic categories of public and private international law but also to embrace newly emergent forms of non-state ordering irreducible to any familiar legal type.

1.2.3.2   Key terms

What we seek to define and to explore as global law in the present study is not this notion of transnational law in the round but the much less commodious category of law which operates at the external 'global' edge of the transnational domain. By this is intended something more than the narrow category of planetary law for which Twining was prepared to concede the global label without, in his view, conceding very much. Rather, what qualifies law as global law, and what all forms of global law have in common, *is a practical endorsement of or commitment to the universal or otherwise global-in-general warrant of some laws or some dimensions of law.*

So specified, global law is far from an entirely new category. Indeed, it is *not* new in two quite distinct but equally important senses. First,

---

[48] See e.g. G.-P. Calliess and P. Zumbansen, *Rough Consensus and Running Code: A Theory of Transnational Private Law* (Oxford: Hart, 2010); and ch. 3, 'The Organizational Field of Global Forest Governance: Interplay of the Governance Generating Networks' in M. S. Tysiachniouk, *Transnational Governance Through Private Authority: The Case of the Forest Stewardship Council Certification in Russia* (Wageningen University Press, 2012).

[49] See e.g. M. L. Moses, *The Principles and Practice of International Commercial Arbitration*, 2nd edn (Cambridge University Press, 2012).

[50] P. Jessup, *Transnational Law* (New Haven, CT: Yale University Press, 1956) p. 136.

[51] The full definition is 'all law which regulates actions or events that transcend national frontiers. Both public and private international laws are included, as are other rules which do not wholly fit into such standard categories.' Jessup, *ibid.*, p. 136.

conceptually, it does not seek to offer a novel definition of law-in-general. *Global* law is an adjectival rather than a nominal category. In folding 'laws' or 'dimensions of law' within its own terms it takes for granted existing legal forms and their defining criteria and merely supplements or modifies them as circumstantially appropriate with reference to the notion of a 'universal or otherwise global-in-general warrant'. Global law, therefore, supplies a selectively applicable variation on a theme, rather than a complete departure from familiar understandings of law. Secondly, empirically, the referential object of global law is far from unprecedented. As we shall see,[52] the idea of a law that is not bound to a particular territorial jurisdiction is a recurrent theme in the history of the legal imagination and its efforts to shape and reshape the regulatory environment. And this past record, as we shall also see, is far from irrelevant in accounting for current developments. What *is* unprecedented, however, like so much under the broad umbrella of contemporary globalisation, is the extent and intensity of the contemporary movement towards global law, whether implicitly understood or explicitly styled as such, and the convergence of that movement from so many different quarters and perspectives.

What, then, are the salient features of our key terms? We should start with a key silence. The new global law does *not* specify any particular source or pedigree, and so may account for itself in many different ways and may claim or assume authority on many different grounds. Certainly, the practical endorsement of, or commitment to, universality or generality may be a product of the rarified 'level' or site at which the law is promulgated or applied. And this would include Twining's idea of global law as law that emanates from a planetary source such as the United Nations, although it would also embrace those institutionally non-specific rules of international law, in particular *jus cogens*, which are commonly understood to apply globally without exception. But universal or global warrant can also be a matter of the global generality of reach of a law that is claimed from a particular local site, as in the category of legal system-specific promotions of the idea of universal jurisdiction of national and other courts for the prosecution of serious crimes under international law[53] or for the pursuit

---

[52] See Chapter 3.2 below.

[53] The literature on universal criminal jurisdiction has grown exponentially in recent years, reflecting the development of the doctrine both in national courts and within the jurisdiction of international criminal tribunals, notably the Rome Statute of the International Criminal Court (see preamble, Rome Statute of the International

of civil tort claims.[54] Or, more commonly, the authoritative basis for global relevance and resonance may not be understood and articulated in terms of specific source or pedigree *at all*, whether located at the planetary or at the local level. For global law also refers to the emergence or to the prospect of the emergence of a trans-systemic and often explicitly *inter*-systemically engaged *common sense and practice* of recognition and development of jurisdictionally unrestricted common ground on particular rules, case precedents, doctrines or principles, or even with regard to background legal orientations. This is typically achieved or approached piecemeal, both through unilateral invocations or assumptions of a general category of universal legal concepts and doctrine in local or transnational practice and through the building of consensus, conventions of approximation,[55] or other forms of transfer or exchange across different legal sites, whether horizontally between national sites or vertically 'top-down' or 'bottom-up' between higher or lower levels, or in more complicated patterns or trajectories. Here different systems, national or otherwise, all continue to operate within their own confined jurisdiction; but each also, through self-standing claims or assumptions as to the universal or global warrant of its specific legal norms or its general conception of legality, as well as through cross-systemic persuasion, reciprocation,

---

Criminal Court, UN Doc. A/CONF.183/9). See e.g. L. Reydams, *Universal Jurisdiction: International and Municipal Legal Perspectives* (Oxford University Press, 2004); and S. Macedo, *Universal Jurisdiction: National Courts and the Prosecution of Serious Crimes under International Law* (Philadelphia: University of Pennsylvania Press, 2006). The *Pinochet* case, concerning the indictment by a Spanish court of former Chilean dictator Augusto Pinochet for human rights violations under his rule, and which involved his arrest in London and legal battle against extradition to Spain, remains the most notable example of the application of universal jurisdiction in the criminal context: see X v. *Bow Street Metropolitan Stipendiary Magistrate, ex parte Pinochet Ugarte (No. 3)* [1999] 2 All ER 97, [1999] 2 WLR 827 (HL). See also R. Wedgwood, 'Augusto Pinochet and International Law' 46 *McGill Law Journal* 241 (2000).

[54] See in particular the Alien Tort Claims Act (ATCA) of 1789 (28 USC § 1350). For a recent and significant decision on the scope of the Act, see the United States Supreme Court judgment in *Kiobel* v. *Royal Dutch Petroleum Co.*, 133 S Ct 1659 (2013).

[55] An example is the 'margin of appreciation' doctrine developed by the European Court of Human Rights to permit some latitude to national authorities in the implementation of the European Convention on Human Rights, but now applied in a wider range of contexts. See Y. Shany, 'Towards a General Margin of Appreciation Doctrine in International Law?' 16 *European Journal of International Law* 907 (2005); and P. Schiff Berman, *Global Legal Pluralism: A Jurisprudence of Law Beyond Borders* (Cambridge University Press, 2012) pp. 161–3.

dialogue, inspiration or emulation, self-consciously comes to refer to, and to subscribe to, some of the same legal rules or understandings.[56]

So, to recap, the universality or generality of global law may be a matter of the more or less explicit 'sourcing' of law in globally extensive institutions or protocols or conventions of rule formation. Or it may involve the local-site-specific endorsement of a universal legal domain. Or it may be found in the cross-site acknowledgment and development of a shared body of doctrine or general legal world-view. What is more, these are by no means sealed categories, and often we will find that they interact, combine and build upon one another.[57]

In the notion of a universal or otherwise global-in-general 'warrant', however, what *is* captured, as a crucial definitional minimum, is a double sense of the global *appeal* of global law. In the first place, the global scale of global law is indicated by its destination rather than its source. The reference to the global applicability of the law's warrant or writ indicates the exhaustive reach or unbounded ambition of its embrace. Global law, whether emanating from a single source or present across and between a range of sites, purports to cover all actors and activities relevant to its remit across the globe. No a-priori territorial limitation to its domain of application can be contemplated under global law, therefore, whether imposed directly as a restricted geographical jurisdiction or indirectly through limiting the category of legal subjects by reference to their association with and connection to a particular territorial polity (e.g. citizens, nationals). Instead, the only permissible limitations are those that flow from the material scope of jurisdiction, reflecting the necessarily limiting frame of the basic purpose and remit of the law, legal regime or background legal orientation in question.[58]

---

[56] For example, the increased exchange and circulation of ideas between national Constitutional Courts and Supreme Courts in the development of a more general constitutional jurisprudence works in this way. See Chapter 3.3.1.3 below.

[57] For example, human rights law operates through such complex patterns. Global, regional and national catalogues and common law or customary sources influence each other, but there is also 'borrowing' between national courts, between transnational courts, and even between national and transnational courts in different territorial domains. There is also significant cross-fertilisation at the legislative level, including at the level of national constitutional enactment. See e.g. D. S. Law and M. Versteeg, 'The Evolution and Ideology of Global Constitutionalism' 99 *California Law Review* 1163 (2011). On the pattern of movement of human rights law, with particular reference to the trend of holding political leaders criminally accountable for serious human rights violations, see K. Sikkink, *The Justice Cascade* (New York: W. W. Norton & Company, 2011). See also Chapter 3.2.3.1 below.

[58] These material limitations may also, of course, affect the personal and temporal scope of the law: see Lindahl, n. 40 above, ch. 1.

Secondly, global law claims a global warrant and makes a global appeal in the sense of claiming or assuming a universal or globally pervasive justification for its application. Whether this is based upon the established authority of its global sourcing and institutionalisation, or whether more general considerations of consent, shared purpose, common political morality or commonly beneficial outcomes are invoked or implied, global law's global reach is grounded in the claim or assumption that there are globally defensible good reasons for its invocation. In other words, its unbounded appeal to all relevant global actors requires that it be globally *appealing*. The promise or ambition of global law is expressed in the symmetry of subject and object. It is, or should be, applicable to all who might be covered by its material terms regardless of location or association with a particular polity, because it is justifiable to all who might be covered by those material terms, or so it is claimed or assumed.[59]

If we turn to other elements of the core definition, additional important characteristics and other key variables of global law emerge, all of which will be the subject of close attention in later chapters. To begin with, there may be significant differences both in the manner in which and in the extent to which any particular claim to universality or global generality is already realised: hence the reference in our definition to either the 'endorsement' of an existing legal formation or a 'commitment' towards its (re)construction or extension; and hence, too, the regular slippage in the language and practice of global law between ambition and its satisfaction. There are, however, equally significant limits to this range. The 'law-ness' of global law requires that the objects it refers to be the product of an intended participation in, and contribution to, the shaping of global law. There must, therefore, be a performative dimension to the endorsement or commitment alike, something beyond detached approval or pure aspiration. As our key terms demand, the approval must somehow register as a 'practical' endorsement, the ambition be pursued and channelled as a 'practical' commitment. Indeed, as we shall see,[60] situated somewhere on the spectrum between settled doctrine on the one hand and disengaged observation or speculation on the other, global law's distinguishing feature *as* law lies precisely in its location in the active domain of constructive discovery or creative projection.

Equally, and closely related to this more or less under-realised quality, there may be variation over how concrete or abstract, sector-specific or transversal, rule-like or more remotely norm-shaping the manifestation

---

[59] On the variety of such claims, see Chapter 3 below.   [60] See Chapter 5 below.

of law's universal or global-in-general strain may be. This accounts for the reference both to discrete 'laws', or units of law, and to non-disaggregable 'dimensions' or aspects of 'the law'. Some of the more powerful instances of global law, indeed, are of the pre-positive or non-positive variety.[61]

And finally, there may be variation as to whether the relevant law or strain of law is claimed to be properly universal in its perspective, and so applicable to all conceivable contexts, all possible worlds of interaction and common involvement, or whether it is tailored to the particular and contingent needs and circumstances of *this* world at this particular juncture: hence the reference both to an in-principle limitless 'universal' and to a more focused 'global-in-general'. Importantly, however, it is in the apparently more modest category of the global-in-general that many of the more significant recent developments in global law have taken hold. A central theme of contemporary globalisation itself, as we have seen, is a widening and deepening experience, or at least awareness, of the world *as* a globally extensive entity. And, while the legacy of in-principle universalism remains selectively strong, for the most part it is the tangible sense of a law that can or should spread across the globe regardless of its universal credentials which is animating contemporary global law.[62] This contrasts with earlier ages and 'world-views' where the claim to law's global compass, whether associated with natural law or other and often religiously conceived universal moral codes, was typically pitched at a metaphysical level, while just as typically originating in and confined to a narrow civilisational centre, and indifferent to the prospect, remote from the calculation or ignorant of the detail of actual worldwide spread.[63]

In introducing our key terms we stressed that global law was an adjectival rather than a nominal category. Global law, we insisted, modifies rather than replaces law's canonical forms, and does so only in certain 'globally warranted' circumstances. This allows us to introduce one further defining feature of global law. For however differentiated they are in accordance with our various criteria, what all manifestations of global law have in common is their contemplation of law as capable of possessing and operating according to a kind of *double normativity*.[64]

---

[61] See Chapter 3.2.3.2 below.   [62] See Chapter 3 and Chapter 5.3 below.

[63] See e.g. R. Domingo, *The New Global Law* (Cambridge University Press, 2010) esp. pp. 44–52, and see Chapter 3.2.3.2 below. See also A. Pagden, *The Enlightenment and Why It Still Matters* (Oxford University Press, 2013) chs. 1 and 2.

[64] See further, Chapter 4.2 and Chapter 5.2.4 below.

Crucial to our understanding of the quotidian operation and invocation of global law, all versions join in the view that contemporary law, considered as a whole, should have a globally extensive and globally justifiable strain, as well as many particular strains; that contemporary law should in some respects apply equally to all implicated parties in any and all relevant globally entangled contexts, while in other respects these same globally entangled contexts should continue to invite and exhibit diversity. What is more, there is a shared sense across all versions of global law that law in its global manifestation is closely intertwined with more particular laws, and, indeed, *cannot* stand apart from more particular laws. Rather, where global law is at issue and where global law is invoked it is always in close connection with the operation of more particular legal norms.

1.2.4   *Global law and global governance: common analytical themes*

Now that we have set out the key general terms in which we understand global law, we can point to some additional ways in which the analysis of global law can be instructively compared to that of global governance. Just as the two understandings of global governance – wide and narrow – are linked both conceptually and causally, so also are the wide and narrow versions of globally extended law. Conceptually, the limited category of universally applicable or globally general law that we intend to investigate under the banner of global law is largely absorbed within the much broader ambit of transnational law. We should, however, note that our more refined category of global law is flexible enough to embrace movement, in accordance with a 'universalising' logic of identification or a 'generalising' logic of influence or exchange, between national sites. Not only does this emphasise the seamless interdependence of the evolving legal world – the permeability of all boundaries (including the *internal–internal* boundary) – but in so doing it also reinforces the continuing importance and, in some respects, even extended significance of state law. Global law, we are saying, is sometimes mobilised and developed as global law in the movement between national sites with little or no intermediation at transnational sites.

What this, in turn, alerts us to is an additional and complementary inflection of meaning in the thematisation of the globalisation of law. For the idea of the globalisation of law indicates more than the increasing density of institutions, norms and connections in transnational legal space, and so more than the broad category of 'transnational law' and our own narrower category of 'global law'. Additionally, in another influential strain of recent usage, it refers to the ever-extending importance of the domestic Rule of Law in countries throughout the world.[65] The globalisation of law broadly conceived, in other words, is about the global spread of law in general as well as the spread of specifically transnational and global law. It is as much about how law has become a more prominent medium of authority in the governance of state polities 'across the globe', so to speak, and even in the construction of some state polities, as it is about law's colonisation of the spaces below, across and in-between state polities. It is also, of course, about the connection between these two forms of expansion; about how the development of the law-state on the one side, and the development of a type of law that may implicate many state citizens and institutions but is not an exercise of the state's internal or external sovereign authority, on the other side, go hand in hand. It is about how their interwoven production speaks to a broader dynamic of legalisation, or legal normalisation, in which the coding of social and political relations in legal terms becomes an expanding and self-reproductive pattern across the planet.[66]

And causally, the connections between the wide definition and our preferred narrow definition of global law are also robust. In and across areas as diverse as human rights, trade law, labour law, migration law, criminal law and environmental law, and at and between different territorial levels or tiers of regulation, we can locate very strong circuits of mutual support and dependence and wide channels and flows of influence between more limited forms of normativity and the universal or general forms in which we are primarily interested. There is, however, one aspect of this causal connection that is of particular interest and importance to us in deepening our appreciation of what is common to global law. As we shall see, all species of what we are calling global law purport, more or less modestly, to frame and embrace something of the kaleidoscope variety and interactivity of national and transnational law, and so to impose some kind of new pattern and order on a legal world of increasingly porous internal boundaries and deepening and more

---

[65] G. G. Bryant, 'The Globalisation of the Law' in K. E. Whittington, R. D. Kelemen and G. A. Caldeira (eds.), *The Oxford Handbook of Law and Politics* (Oxford University Press, 2010) pp. 245–66.

[66] See e.g. J. Goldstein, M. Kahler, R. O. Keohane and A.-M. Slaughter (eds.), *Legalization and World Politics* (Cambridge, MA: MIT Press, 2001).

complex diversity. The very impulse towards global law as general or universal law, in other words, is always predicated upon that complex legal diversity and the myriad problems, challenges and openings deemed to be associated with it, and seeks to respond to that diversity by somehow grasping and 'containing' it from the perspective of a globally unbounded jurisdiction.[67]

1.3   The coming of global law

This brings us, finally, to the third and deepest layer of our argument, and a further key sense in which 'global law' so defined provides added explanatory value. Global law is not simply a trendy label, nor a tidy term for all or some aspects of the structural realignment of legal phenomena in a less state-centred age. It is not only about the language in which law describes itself in its canonical representations or about where and how it is required to resituate itself in response to planetary developments in the underlying topography of regulation. It is, to repeat, not only *rhetorical* and *structural* in its manifestations and effects, but also *epistemic*. For it also speaks to a shift in how we think about and seek to develop and present law's basic credentials *as* law. Global law, understood as universal or general law in the sense introduced above, is a development that questions many of our state-centric or otherwise jurisdiction-centric premises about law as a settled form and about the grounds of its authority and legitimacy. Global law as universal or global-in-general law, as already previewed and as will be developed at length, is typically projected and incompletely realised, only obliquely present and of unsettled authority. Yet it is also seemingly inexorable in its infiltration of our ways of comprehending and addressing transnationally connected law. In other words, and to introduce the title of the book,[68] global law reveals itself through its various 'intimations', including the strongly 'intimated' sense of its own irreversibility. In light of this, the very way in which we think about the law as a whole, and how we elaborate, interpret and act upon particular laws in light of the way we think of law as a whole, undergoes change as we confront a global horizon and as we fashion the various new species of global law. Indeed, not only does what registers as a legally relevant argument alter under the auspices of the emergent

---

[67] This relationship of global law to particular diversity is already implied and anticipated in the idea of 'double normativity' introduced in section 1.2.3 above.
[68] See in particular Chapter 5 below.

global law, but even what kind of material *counts as law* is subject to modification.

Global law, then, indicates a new mood. It registers as a state of contestable becoming rather than corrigible achievement. This alteration in mood, as we shall see, is partly in consequence of the many types of actors that appear on the global legal stage and the fluid intermingling of their roles – legislators, judges, litigants, clients, lawyers, activists and, of no little significance, law teachers and legal academics.[69] Equally and conversely, however, as we shall also observe, the less rigid division of functions and less restrictive allocation of jurisgenerative influence in the transnational domain of legal craftsmanship, and the increased prominence of the academic voice in particular, are also products of the inherent unsettlement and contestability of the new global law.[70]

It should be apparent by now how, as anticipated on the first page, the claims made for global law in this study are predominantly empirical and explanatory rather than normative and predictive. Our first and foremost concern is to diagnose the condition of law in a globalising age. It is to chart and understand what is a highly complex contemporary movement in how law is conceived and how it is perceived, rather than to make a claim for global law as either a generally beneficial or generally detrimental development, far less to declare support for or opposition to any particular conception of global law. As should become clear, however, it is an empirical and explanatory thesis with profound implications for our legal and political morality. For the conditions that promote global law also act against other visions of law, and so affect the authoritative grounds and the normative grammar in terms of which we might contemplate and justify any project for containing or changing the world through law.

In what follows, we explore and develop each of these levels of argument in turn. We begin in Chapter 2 with rhetoric and practice – with the development of new global horizons in areas of professional orientation and development, and of education and research, that stand at one remove from, but remain closely related to, legal doctrine and its underpinning conceptions of legal order. In the long Chapter 3 – the descriptive heart of the book – we move on to examine the emergence of new images and new species of law and legal order in the face of the structural forces of globalisation, and how these developments both reflect and

---

[69] See Chapter 2 below. [70] See Chapter 5 below.

reinforce the territorially unconfined quality of global law. In Chapter 4 we contemplate how the different conceptions and species of the emergent global law relate to each other in a manner that is both mutually accommodating and mutually challenging. In Chapter 5 we turn our attention to the profoundly epistemic dimension of global law. We assess how the peculiarities of the 'intimated' quality of global law are modifying our very conception of law as it is shaped by and reshapes its global environment, affecting how we think and talk about the possibilities of influencing the world through law. And in the concluding Chapter 6, we look at some of the challenges and objections faced by this new strain of law and ask whether, and on what terms, it might address these.

Taking law to the world

2.1   Introduction

Let us recall from our introductory discussion of the multifaceted character of globalisation that the globalisation of law, just like the globalisation of politics, or the economy, or culture, or any other dimension of
social life, follows a relatively autonomous course. Law interacts closely
with all these other dimensions. And when we come in Chapter 3 to
discuss some of the wider globalising impulses that have infiltrated our
imagination of legal order and affected our conceptions of legal doctrine,
so feeding the various new species of global law, we will observe a wide
range of causal influences acting upon law from the outside. But if we are
to take the relative autonomy of legal globalisation seriously, we must
also attend to the reasons why and the ways in which it follows a
distinctive path and makes a distinctive contribution. One part of the
answer has to do with historical features of legal ordering and legal
dogmatics. Many areas of modern social organisation, even against the
backdrop of increasing access to a global range of lifestyles and practices,
continue to be deeply recursive, exploiting past experience and tried and
tested knowledge and taking advantage of embedded conventions of
behaviour and existing patterns of consensus or acquiescence.[1] Given
that the very validity of law *as* law has always also been closely bound to
its settled pre-existence and so to its past embeddedness, however, the
historical record of law remains a particularly significant resource in
accounting for its global articulation.[2] Conversely, however, global law is
equally distinctive – equally tied to its own peculiar logic and autonomous of outside forces – in its emphasis on future projection, and in how
it grasps the present as part of that projection.

---

[1] See e.g. U. Beck, A. Giddens and S. Lash, *Reflexive Modernization: Politics, Tradition and Aesthetics in the Modern Social Order* (Cambridge: Polity Press, 1994).
[2] See e.g. M. Krygier, 'Law as Tradition' 5 *Law and Philosophy* 237 (1986).

The matter of global law's peculiar relationship to time, and how this is reflected in its 'intimated' quality, is one we will also return to and develop in some depth.[3] In the present chapter, however, we will focus not upon the deep past or upon the near future of law, but on another element that accounts for its relatively autonomous globalising trajectory: namely, the 'inside world' of contemporary professional and academic practice. The language of global law may be something with which we are growing more familiar today in the specification of legal doctrine and the characterisation of legal order more generally – and that is the main object of our attention[4] – yet global discourse is perhaps even more present, and a global orientation more obviously prevalent, in legal practice and professional organisation and culture, as well as in legal education and teaching. Legal professionals and legal academics are connected in fast-growing numbers to self-proclaimed 'global' or otherwise transnationally extended law firms, associations, networks and law schools, and through these new links they have become more able and more willing to think and to act outside the state box. In so doing, they have both relied upon and stretched some of the ties that have traditionally bound law to the state at the level of quotidian organisation and operation. These trends are sketched below and their broader significance assessed. We try to show how these internal shifts in occupational culture and practice have laid some of the groundwork for the growth and sustenance of the various new conceptions of globality in the law itself.

In summary, the emergence of a global theme in professional practice and in educational and academic contexts stands as an important influence on the development of global law due to the conjunction of the following factors. First, the profession and the academy have supplied increasingly open and receptive environments for the forging of new transnational connections and for thinking about law in a global context, while remaining very much organised and identified on a national basis and legitimated by their national standing. Secondly, the professional and academic contribution has typically manifested itself in forms of collaboration between relatively close-knit transnational elites with convergent world-views and an extensive sphere of influence. Thirdly, these elite organisations, collaborations and networks tend to hold and perpetuate the view that the increasingly global mobility of legal practice, and the increasingly global relevance of legal knowledge, is inevitable as

---

[3] See Chapter 5 below.   [4] See Chapter 1.2.3 above.

well as desirable. Pulling these strands together, we can discern the emergence of a continuum of global 'law-craft': a new and cumulative fluidity and flexibility in the way in which the various practices associated with lawyering reach out to a global horizon, in so doing softening or overcoming a range of old demarcation lines in the professional division of labour. In turn, this new mutability feeds into the very process of the generation and production of global law. Professional and academic elites have progressively come to function and to perceive themselves as functioning not merely as sources of expertise and learning in the emergent global law and as instruments of its application, but also as active players in the fashioning and shaping of global law.

In charting the development of global 'law-craft' along these lines, our aim is first and foremost descriptive and explanatory. Just as with global law itself, there is much to be concerned about and much to be critical of, but also much else that may be judged more positively in the emergence of law's global professional communities. We will return to some of these evaluative questions in the final chapter, but for now the priority is simply to give an account of the various facets of what is a diversely inspired, multifaceted and morally complex phenomenon.

2.2   Going global

The very fact that so much has been written about global law firms and other forms of practitioner and judicial collaboration in recent years, as well as global education and research, is itself a crude indicator of the increasing intensity and importance of such activity.[5] Where, until the last years of the twentieth century, socio-legal research on 'soft' cultural

---

[5] For an excellent overview, see W. Twining, *General Jurisprudence: Understanding Law from a Global Perspective* (Cambridge University Press, 2009) ch. 8, 'Empirical Dimensions of Law and Justice', particularly pp. 242–66. Twining uses the Law and Society Association Conference in Berlin in 2007, with over 2,300 participants and a significant emphasis on 'law and globalisation' research, as a telling snapshot of the academic trend (pp. 237–8). The Chicago-based Center on Law and Globalization (www.lexglobal.org), especially its 'smart library on globalization', and the *Indiana Journal of Global Legal Studies*, first published in 1993 (http://ijgls.indiana.edu), also supply key resources in this field, as well as telling examples of the globalising trend – and the American influence – in the organisation of legal research. Other useful overviews include S. Cassese, 'The Globalization of Law' 37 *New York University Journal of Law and Politics* 973 (2005); M. Shapiro, 'The Globalization of Law' 1 *Indiana Journal of Global Legal Studies* 37 (1993); and, most recently, the special issue of the *Tilburg Law Review* on Global Law: vol. 17, no. 2, 2012.

and 'hard' operational aspects of the legal habitus was predominantly national or sub-national in focus, today it is increasingly concerned with connections across borders and non-state sites.[6]

Until the 1980s, there was very little evidence of law firms developing an international presence, whether by acquisition or by 'greenfield'[7] development. Since then, growth has been exponential, predominately in corporate mergers and acquisitions and in the capital markets sectors. It has been led by the United States and, to a lesser extent, the United Kingdom; though in recent years there has been some spread to other developed capitalist systems. Numerically, globally connected lawyers remain a small minority worldwide, which helps account for the persistence of a relatively low public profile, but in terms of commercial scale the global sector increasingly stands at the forefront. The *American Lawyer*'s list of the world's top 100 law firms by annual revenue, for example, has been for some years dominated by those which have a significant global presence in terms of office reach, and, increasingly, multi-jurisdictional expertise,[8] with all but four in the 2013 list based in the United States, the United Kingdom or other anglophone and common law jurisdictions. Global expansion has also taken place through other routes. These include the growth of in-house counsel in multinational corporations and the consequent dissemination of uniform corporate values over groups of lawyers with very different national backgrounds.[9] They also include the evolution of practitioner networks such as Lex Mundi, which has provided a professional services and information exchange, again predominantly in the commercial sector,

---

[6] Compare, for example, Lawrence Friedman in 1996, stating that transnational socio-legal studies were still in a state of infancy, with his much more affirmative assessment a mere decade later: L. M. Friedman, 'Borders: On the Emerging Sociology of Transnational Law' 32 *Stanford Journal of International Law* 65 (1996); and L. M. Friedman, 'Coming of Age: Law and Society Enters an Exclusive Club' 1 *Annual Review of Law and Social Science* 1 (2005). For one of many representative collections in recent years, see e.g. A. Brysk (ed.), *The Politics of the Globalization of Law: Getting from Rights to Justice* (New York: Routledge, 2013).

[7] D. D. Sokol, 'Globalization of Law Firms: A Survey of the Literature and a Research Agenda for Further Study' 14 *Indiana Journal of Global Legal Studies* 5 (2007) at 12.

[8] See 'The Global 100 – Most Revenue' in *The American Lawyer*, 1 October 2013, available at www.americanlawyer.com/id=1380020616898; 95 out of 100 in 2013 were classified as 'international' rather than 'national' in terms of revenue source. See also J. Flood and F. Sosa, 'Lawyers, Law Firms, and the Stabilization of Transnational Business' 28 *Northwestern Journal of International Law and Business* 489 (2008); and J. Flood, 'Institutional Bridging: How Large Law Firms Engage in Globalization' 54 *Boston College Law Review* 1087 (2013).

[9] P. Le Golf, 'Global Law: A Legal Phenomenon Emerging from the Process of Globalization' 14 *Indiana Journal of Global Legal Studies* 119 (2007) at 139.

since 1989, and today numbers some 160 member firms boasting 21,000 attorneys.[10] And alongside these market-led initiatives, there is an increasing depth and formalisation of international professional organisation – global and regional, general and sectoral. At the top of this pyramid stands the International Bar Association, founded in 1947 and today with a membership of over 50,000 lawyers and over 200 national bar associations and law societies. As well as providing an expertise network, it sees itself as 'the global voice of the legal profession',[11] engaged in the development and pursuit of common positions and understandings on matters of 'public and professional interest'.[12]

This points to a general feature of legal practice as a reflection and expression of law's diverse content and resource set. Like their state-centred colleagues, transnational lawyers are not merely the 'hired guns' of big business, though that is a significant part of the work of many and the defining function of some. They also possess a more versatile remit as a 'common carrier'[13] of the wider range of client and broader constituency interests in regulation and litigation. The involvement of lawyers in transnational processes is not simply an expression of professional economic interest and power in globally expanded markets, therefore, but also speaks to their relationship to wider questions of public policy and social justice. Globally connected lawyers are involved and influential in transnational advocacy networks across a diverse range of civil, political and social rights, as well as in areas such as environmental justice, international criminal law, telecommunications, media and intellectual property law. As litigators, as subject experts, as witnesses and monitors, as navigators of national and transnational political processes, as professionally respected spokespersons and campaigners, as moral entrepreneurs for Rule of Law values and practices, as honest brokers in conflict management and resolution, as advisers and drafters of instruments, agreements, industry codes and standards, lawyers are important operators in the labyrinthine and fluidly developing processes of international governance and civil society.[14]

---

[10] See the Lex Mundi website: www.lexmundi.com/lexmundi/default.asp.

[11] See the International Bar Association website: www.ibanet.org.

[12] Through its Public and Professional Interest Division: see www.ibanet.org/Committees/Divisions/Public_Professional_Interest_Div/home.aspx.

[13] See e.g. R. Gordon, 'Why Lawyers Can't Just Be Hired Guns' in D. L. Rhode (ed.), *Ethics in Practice: Lawyers' Roles, Responsibilities, and Regulation* (Oxford University Press, 2000); and W. W. Bradley, 'Lawyers as Quasi-Public Actors' 45 *Alberta Law Review* 83 (2008).

[14] See the wide-ranging studies in Y. Dezalay and B. Garth (eds.), *Lawyers and the Rule of Law in an Era of Globalization* (Oxford: Routledge, 2011); and Y. Dezalay and B. Garth (eds.), *Lawyers and the Construction of Transnational Justice* (Oxford: Routledge, 2012).

The growth of judicial networks paints an even more vivid scene of intense collaboration within the professional elite. Some might have criticised Anne-Marie Slaughter's well-known thesis of the evolution of a 'global community of courts'[15] as overstated and unduly sanguine,[16] but there is no doubt that the last thirty years have witnessed a much greater openness to mutual information and dialogue between different judiciaries and the development of an intricate web of personal and institutional relations. Much of this development is horizontal, linking various national judiciaries.[17] Increasingly, however, connections are also multi-level, involving many of the international courts and tribunals, numbering well over 100,[18] that today issue decisions affecting national authorities and citizens. There are other variations in the global picture. Some links are regional, with a particular concentration in Europe and around the European Union,[19] while others are

---

[15] A.-M. Slaughter, 'A Global Community of Courts' 44 *Harvard International Law Journal* 191 (2003).

[16] See e.g. E. A. Posner and J. C. Yoo, 'Judicial Independence in International Tribunals' 93 *California Law Review* 1 (2005) at 8, 27. See also the response by L. R. Helfer and A.-M. Slaughter, 'Why States Create International Tribunals: A Response to Professors Posner and Yoo' 93 *California Law Review* 899 (2005); and C. McCrudden, 'Common Law of Human Rights? Transnational Judicial Conversations on Constitutional Rights' 20 *Oxford Journal of Legal Studies* 499 (2000).

[17] See e.g. V. C. Jackson, *Constitutional Engagement in a Transnational Era* (Oxford University Press, 2010), particularly ch. 3.

[18] See in particular R. Mackenzie, C. Romano, Y. Shany and P. Sands, *Manual on International Courts and Tribunals*, 2nd edn (Oxford University Press, 2010). See also the useful matrix published in 2004 by the Project on International Courts and Tribunals: 'The International Judiciary in Context', at www.pict-pcti.org/publications/synoptic_chart/synop_c4.pdf. See further the most recent comprehensive study of the international court system, emphasising the extent to which the decision-making authority of the fast-growing number of permanent international courts, increased from six at the end of the Cold War to almost thirty today, alters the political balance in favour of international and other transnational law and against private or domestic public power, and in so doing encourages the development of professional legal communities (including but not restricted to judges and arbitrators) who have economic and strategic reasons as well as moral and ethical reasons for taking international and transnational law seriously: K. Alter, *The New Terrain of International Law: Courts, Politics, Rights* (Princeton University Press, 2014).

[19] See e.g. M. Claes and M. de Visser, 'Are You Networked Yet? On Dialogues in European Judicial Networks' 8 *Utrecht Law Review* 99 (2012). They distinguish networks set up by the judges themselves, such as the Conference of European Constitutional Courts, or Association of European Competition Law Judges, from those set up by EU legislation, such as the European Judicial Network, Eurojust and the European Judicial Network in Civil and Commercial Matters.

not territorially restricted.[20] Some are formal, inclusive and permanent, as with the International Association of Judges,[21] while many others are informal, selective or occasional.[22] Some are concerned with exchange of ideas, others with training.[23] Some are tied to academic activities or institutions,[24] others are exclusive to judges, while others still are part of broader professional networks including lawyers and arbitrators.[25] Some operate through personal meetings, others through virtual channels.[26] Each, however, contributes to a scenario in which judges not only know a lot more than they used to about what their international peers do and how they think, but are also more able to find and more willing to express and promote common cause, not least in giving 'sympathetic consideration'[27] to comparative judicial opinion when performing their professional role 'back home'.

---

[20] The Council of Europe's Commission on Democracy Through Law ('Venice Commission') has been a driving force in the establishment, development and support of transnational court organisations, both in Europe and beyond or transcending Europe, including: the World Conference of Constitutional Justice; the Southern African Chief Justices Forum (SACJF); the Conference of African Constitutional Jurisdictions (CJCA); the Union of Arab Constitutional Courts and Councils (UACCC); and the Association of Asian Constitutional Courts and Equivalent Institutions (AACC). Many of these bodies are organised according to a fundamental criterion other than territory, including: the Association des Cours Constitutionnelles ayant en Partage l'Usage du Français (ACCPUF); the Conference of Constitutional Control Organs of the Countries of New Democracy (CCCOCND); the Conference of Constitutional Jurisdictions of the Portuguese-Speaking Countries (CJCPLP); and the Ibero-American Conference of Constitutional Justice (CIJC). See www.venice.coe.int/WebForms/pages/?p=02_Regional.

[21] See www.iaj-uim.org/index2.html. This organisation comprises eighty-one national associations from five continents.

[22] The best known of these is perhaps the annual Global Constitutionalism Seminar of the Gruber Program for Global Justice and Women's Rights at Yale University, bringing together various eminent judges from around the globe for a four-day seminar: see www.law.yale.edu/intellectuallife/globalconstitutionalismseminar.htm.

[23] See e.g. the European Judicial Training Network, at www.ejtn.eu.

[24] As in the Global Constitutionalism Seminar at Yale, n. 22 above: see www.law.yale.edu/intellectuallife/globalconstitutionalismseminar.htm.

[25] For instance, the International Bar Association: see www.ibanet.org.

[26] The Association of the Councils of State and Supreme Administrative Jurisdictions of the European Union provides a particularly sophisticated example of a virtual network, complete with freely searchable files of around 20,000 national decisions and an 'intranet' which allows the judicial staff of member courts to enter into direct contact and pose specific questions: see Claes and de Visser, n. 19, at 110.

[27] See N. Walker, 'Beyond Boundary Disputes and Basic Grids: Mapping the Global Disorder of Normative Orders' 6 *International Journal of Constitutional Law* 373 (2008).

Turning to education and research, we observe a similar graph of exponential growth. International and comparative law curricula gradually expanded in line with the worldwide expansion of full-time university-based legal education over the second half of the twentieth century, and this accelerated in the 1980s with the surge in the number of students on exchange programmes or pursuing postgraduate legal education abroad.[28] However, only in more recent years has the 'global' idea been actively promoted, with rapid growth in the number of institutions and programmes making explicit use of the label, or otherwise showcasing their transnational offerings as a prestige indicator.

Some of this may be mere 'public relations puffing',[29] but for the most part it reflects a genuine shift in the structure and emphasis of undergraduate and postgraduate education, again initially heavily concentrated in the United States but now geographically widespread.[30] One indicator is the trend in many of the new global law schools or centres towards offering double-degree programmes or master's programmes, or even doctoral programmes[31] dedicated to international constituencies alongside more traditional exchanges. Another pointer is the development of initiatives outside established national universities: these include the growth of new transnational institutions of learning[32] and research-based legal policy advice[33] and the emergence of new territorially unanchored and broadly networked teaching or research institutions

---

[28] For a wide-ranging treatment, see the special double issue of the *German Law Journal*, vol. 10, nos. 6 and 7, July 2009: 'Following the Call of the Wild: The Promises and Perils of Transnationalizing Legal Education' (eds. N. Chiesa, A. de Luca and B. Maheandiran).

[29] W. Twining, *Globalisation and Legal Scholarship* (Nijmegen: Wolf Legal Publishers, 2011) p. 23.

[30] Prominent examples include New York University's Hauser Global Law School (www.law. nyu.edu/global/abouthauser), Harvard University's Institute for Global Law and Policy (www.iglp.law.harvard.edu), Columbia University's Center on Global Legal Transformation (http://web.law.columbia.edu/global-legal-transformation), University College London's Institute of Global Law (www.ucl.ac.uk/laws/global_law/), Queen Mary University of London's Centre for Law and Society in a Global Context (www.law.qmul.ac.uk/research/centres/clsgc/index.html) and the National University of Singapore Law Faculty, which regularly dubs itself 'Asia's Global Law School' (http://law.nus.edu.sg/). This is only the tip of a very large iceberg.

[31] See e.g. the JD/MGA (Master of Global Affairs) at the University of Toronto: www. munkschool.utoronto.ca/mag/.

[32] Most prominently in Europe, the European University Institute based since 1976 in Fiesole, Italy, with its pan-EU doctoral programme and its global postdoctoral programme: www.eui.eu/Home.aspx.

[33] See e.g. the Hague Institute for the Internationalisation of Law: www.hiil.org.

such as the Center for Transnational Legal Studies,[34] the Association of Transnational Law Schools[35] and the Law Schools Global League recently inaugurated at Tilburg University.[36]

These pedagogical developments are mirrored at the level of academic culture and disciplinary and theoretical mobilisation. This can be seen in the growth of transnational scholarly associations across the whole expanse of legal sub-disciplines – public and private, state-centred and international, doctrinal and theoretical;[37] in the recent spate of self-consciously transnational law journals across the same wide range of sub-disciplines – again sometimes with the 'global' label attached;[38] in the development of the transnational research network as a prestigious and generously sponsored context of collaborative legal research;[39] and in the emergence of academic career patterns that are more internationally mobile than in any previous generation. Patently, these developments feed off one another. Educational initiatives, associations and networks both respond to the new body of comparative, international and other transnational learning, and nurture a research culture in which post-national themes are given additional prominence. All of these developments, moreover, both benefit from and help further stimulate an environment extensively adapted to virtual forms of communication.[40]

---

[34] The Center is hosted at Georgetown University: see http://ctls.georgetown.edu.

[35] See www.associationoftransnationallawschools.blogspot.co.uk.

[36] The lecture which provided the foundation for this book was first delivered at the inauguration of the League, in June 2012: see https://blog.uvt.nl/LawSchoolsGlobalLeague/.

[37] See e.g. Le Golf, n. 9 above, at 141–2.

[38] Among those which use the 'g' word, see e.g. *Global Jurist* and *Global Constitutionalism*. Prominent among those which do not use the 'g' word, but are implicitly global in outlook, are the *International Journal of Constitutional Law* (*i-CON*) and *Transnational Legal Theory*. Many other journals display their global reach from a more situated perspective rather than, as the above do, self-consciously seeking a globally panoramic perspective. For example, many regional journals for 'Europe' or elsewhere increasingly look outwards and stress the relationship between regional and global. National journals are also increasingly global in outlook. The widely read online English-language *German Law Journal* remains remarkable for its policy of systematic devotion to the study of (one) national law and legal culture in global context – with a view both to its global influences and to its global implications. This speaks to an important trend pursued in section 2.3.1 below, namely the way in which national legal self-consciousness acts as a medium and amplifier of global legal consciousness rather than as its counter-influence.

[39] See e.g., in the European context, the highly influential and wide-ranging 7th Framework Programme for Research and Technological Development (FP7) of the European Commission: http://ec.europa.eu/research/fp7/understanding/fp7inbrief/what-is_en.html.

[40] See e.g. the case of the online *German Law Journal*, n. 38 above.

There is also a broader dynamic connecting the world of learning and the world of practice. This operates through a combination of symbolic and practical factors. Legal education remains highly dependent for funding and prestige on the prospect of a rewarding professional career. Leading law schools thrive on the endorsement of potential employers and the patronage of key legal institutions such as the judiciary. Reciprocally, leading law firms have always gained symbolic capital by recruiting from prestigious institutions of learning.[41] The cachet of the global law firm, the multinational or the global NGO is reinforced by the cachet of the global law school, and vice versa. The relationship between practice and learning, moreover, is not simply one of symbiosis – of awareness of mutual advantage. In many cases the various transnationally engaged professional and academic elites meet in the same associations or connect through the same networks. They may develop shared or overlapping agendas of applied research and a common or overlapping sense of epistemic authority. Additionally, through these connections, profiles of expertise are formed that allow some members of the transnational elite cohorts to move with relative ease between the worlds of legal or judicial practice and those of education and scholarship.[42]

Competence, reputation and economic advantage, therefore, become closely interlaced in the new spaces of transnational legal practice and reflection. And while much of the resulting transnational legal culture values and so emphasises its cosmopolitan distance from any purely domestic perspective, the sources and patterns of influence are nevertheless such as to reinforce the transnational dominance of certain national legal cultures. In particular, the expanding demand for an American, or at least an American-style legal education among those who want to work for or associate with American legal enterprises abroad, is partly about the acquisition of the relevant legal knowledge and skills and partly about rites of entrance to, and the right of membership in, a cultural elite.[43]

[41] For a critical look at these relationships in the contemporary United States context, see W. D. Henderson and R. M. Zahorsky, 'The Pedigree Problem: Are Law School Ties Choking the Profession?' *ABA Journal* (July 2012).

[42] This has always been markedly true of international law: see section 2.3 below. But it is also true of many areas of transnational private law: see e.g. R. Wai, 'Transnational Private Law and Private Ordering in a Contested Global Society' 46 *Harvard International Law Journal* 471 (2005); and Le Golf, n. 9 above.

[43] See e.g. R. A. Kagan, 'Globalization and Legal Change: The "Americanization" of European Law?' 1 *Regulation & Governance* 99 (2007); see also J. Flood, *Legal Education in the Global*

The new emphasis on the importance of a global dimension to legal education and legal practice, then, is reinforced through the mutual interests and expectations and convergent or overlapping world-views of prominent members of the professional and academic communities. In this way, the development of law's new global horizons is supported from a number of sources simultaneously and interactively.

2.3 Cultivating global law

2.3.1 The national base

It would be a mistake, however, to interpret the development of these new global connections and horizons as signalling the progressive de-nationalisation of professional and academic legal culture. On the contrary, the organisation of the legal profession, still more so that of the judiciary, remains very much a national affair. Legal education, too, continues to be organised predominantly along national lines. With some variation – primarily in common law, anglophone countries – this is reflected in the national composition of the academy, and, to a lesser extent, in research specialisation. The resilience of national organisation of the legal system should not surprise us, but neither should it cause us to doubt the depth of the globalising trend. For a growing global awareness and openness is typically endorsed and justified in professional and academic circles as a means of promoting the extension of national interests and the projection of national perspectives, even if the resulting pattern of influence between different national sites is significantly asymmetrical – as much about the 'nationalist globalisation'[44] of powerful domestic systems as it is about cross-fertilisation of ideas, methods and practices.[45] The

Context: Challenges from Globalization, Technology and Changes in Government Regulation, Report for the Legal Services Board, available at http://letr.org.uk/references/storage/NP9IP8XZ/Flood,%20legal%20education%20in%20the%20global%20context.pdf; and R. Michaels, 'Globalization and Law: Law Beyond the State' in R. Banakar and M. Travers (eds.), *An Introduction to Law and Social Theory*, 2nd edn (Oxford: Hart, 2013) pp. 289–303.

[44] L. C. Backer and B. Stancil, 'Global Law Schools on US Models: Emerging Models of Consensus-Based Internationalization or Markets-Based Americanization Models of Global Legal Education' (19 August 2011), available at http://papers.ssrn.com/sol3/papers.cfm?abstract_id=1912639.

[45] See e.g. S. Chesterman, 'The Evolution of Legal Education: Internationalization, Transnationalization, Globalization' 10 *German Law Journal* 877 (2009); H. W. Arthurs, 'Law and Learning in an Era of Globalization' 10 *German Law Journal* 629 (2009); and J. Husa, 'Turning the Curriculum Upside Down: Comparative Law as an Educational Tool for Constructing the Pluralistic Legal Mind' 10 *German Law Journal* 913 (2009).

continued embedding of the profession and the academy in a national setting, therefore, far from checking or frustrating the globalising trend, provides the main source of its strength and offers the best guarantee of its sustainability.

If we examine these dynamics in more detail we can observe that the synergy between state-based organisation and the development of a global orientation is due to a cumulation of factors. The resilient nationalism of professional and academic legal identity, the precarious anchoring and fluid situation of much transnational law and its continuing reliance on national supports, and the clear potential for national interests to be served through an openness to global influence and global business, all have a part to play.

To begin with, just as the national organisation of legal practice and legal education and the consequent national self-identification of legal professionals and teachers are historically important supports of the state-based legal order,[46] and, as such, key components of a national legal system, so they persist as its powerful legacy. The relevant modes of professional recognition and educational validation, the main career paths, the most accessible markets and the most secure forms of reputation and status all continue to be state-centred. Forms of transnational professional and educational organisation, while clearly in a phase of fertile growth, remain of supplementary importance – parasitic on the state as the primary source and default setting of professional identity. Crucially, the typical professional lawyer and judge, however far she travels along a path of transnational specialism, begins and ends her career as the licensed member of a national professional community. Legal academics too, even those who specialise in non-state-based subjects such as international law or legal theory, are still normally, if not exclusively, assessed and credited, both locally and beyond, as national types, and still normally self-assess as such.

The continuing prominence of the national legal setting is reinforced by the mobile and disembedded quality of many transnational legal rules and regimes. The growth of transnational law has certainly involved the development of various new courts and other dispute settlement forums in transnational settings, from the World Court at The Hague to the Court of Justice of the European Union in Luxembourg, and from the China International Trade Arbitration Commission in Beijing to

---

[46] See e.g. A. von Bogdandy, 'National Legal Scholarship in the European Legal Area – A Manifesto' 10 *International Journal of Constitutional Law* 614 (2012).

the Inter-American Court of Human Rights in San José, Costa Rica.[47] Yet, to recall our discussion in Chapter 1, transnational law knows no rigid 'internal borders' with national law.[48] Litigation in these arenas rarely takes place in isolation from legal dealings and hearings in national contexts, and typically involves state-based lawyers. In any event, the institutionalised forms of transnational dispute settlement are merely the tip of the iceberg. Transnational law is more likely to manifest itself as a normative stream feeding directly or indirectly into national law. International human rights law of the sort addressed by the United Nations 'core' conventions or their regional counterparts and their respective courts, international criminal law of the type that falls within the remit of the statute of the International Criminal Court, or the vast corpus of European Union law under the jurisdiction of the Court of Justice, are in fact all much more likely to be at issue in national legal proceedings or other dealings than in their dedicated transnational settings.[49] Much other transnational law, moreover, does not even provide its own adjudicatory forum and can only ever be put at issue, if at all, in a local setting. What is more, as our preliminary discussion in Chapter 1 made clear, much law that is claimed to be global by virtue of its universal warrant – a claim linguistically reinforced in everyday legal phrases like '*human* rights', '*general* principles of international law' or '*common* constitutional traditions'[50] – in fact spreads or circulates through reiteration in various local contexts, or in the universal jurisdictional reach claimed from a particular site, and may operate only or mainly on a national or cross-national basis without necessary resort to any positive source of transnational law.[51]

These various factors help to explain why openness to foreign and transnational professional markets, sources, influences and contexts of legal decision-making can enhance rather than hinder the interests and agendas of those operating in a national setting. When looking beyond the four corners of their national jurisdiction, professionals and professional trainers locate new places to do business as well as new ways of doing business, judges discover new reasons for decision and new forms of persuasive authority, and academics absorb new ideas, find new inspiration, discover new transnational 'epistemic

---

[47] See in particular Alter, n. 18 above.   [48] See Chapter 1.2.2–1.2.3 above.
[49] See e.g. K. Sikkink, *The Justice Cascade* (New York: W. W. Norton & Company, 2011).
[50] See Treaty on European Union, Art. 6(3).   [51] See Chapter 1.2.3 above.

communities'[52] and uncover new sources of educational demand. Looking beyond the state, in short, provides new markets and new resources for many key operators of the national legal systems, while at the same time contributing to the development of a cultural and practical space of trans-national law.

2.3.2   The significance of elites

The contribution of national legal actors to transnational developments becomes more salient when we consider the strength of the networks involved. The elite character of the most prominent sites and collabo-rations has a double significance. In the first place, the emergence of a stable cohort of powerful 'repeat players'[53] has generated the conditions of expertise, of trust and of mutual learning and validation necessary to forge, consolidate and deepen transnational connections. A relatively small number of global law firms and legal advocates, nationally ranked global law schools and academics, and globally networked judges, often from national apex courts, has provided the base camp for many of the practical operations of global dissemination and circulation in recent years.

In the second place, the high national standing of these elites, itself often enhanced by their global operations, undoubtedly has contributed to a pattern of emulation. Clearly, the modus operandi of successful global law firms will be copied, and the cosmopolitan mindset of the globally connected judge, though sometimes the target of organised opposition by more jurisdiction-bound colleagues,[54] also provides a climate of encouragement, endorsement and emulation for the like-minded within and beyond the national setting.[55] And in the world of the academy, many leading institutions encourage others to adopt the global brand as much by their prestigious example as by their sponsor-ship of, or openness to, active collaboration. Prominent individual

---

[52] See e.g. J. Braithwaite and P. Drahos, *Global Business Regulation* (Cambridge University Press, 2000), ch. 20, 'Contests of Actors', pp. 475–506.

[53] See the classic study of Marc Galanter: M. Galanter, 'Why the "Haves" Come Out Ahead: Speculations on the Limits of Legal Change' 9 *Law & Society Review* 95 (1974) at 97.

[54] See e.g. in the United States context, the sceptical view of many, including Supreme Court justices: N. Dorsen, 'The Relevance of Foreign Legal Materials in US Constitutional Cases: A Conversation between Justice Antonin Scalia and Justice Stephen Breyer' 3 *International Journal of Constitutional Law* 519 (2005).

[55] On the influence of transnational judicial networks, see e.g. Claes and de Visser, n. 19 above.

academics, for their part, sometimes offer themselves as explicit role models for the globally connected academic life, or may provide powerful magnets around which new transnational networks and research projects cluster.[56]

2.3.3 Embracing the global

The influence of the new elites is further enhanced by their tendency to treat the transnational horizons of legal practice and education not only as a choice to be endorsed and affirmed but as a natural and inevitable response to wider globalising trends. It is notable, for example, when reading the manifestos of the new global law schools and academies, that the introduction of a globally orientated curriculum is treated not as a form of specialisation, still less as a luxury, but as a basic imperative of a good contemporary legal education.[57] In the same way, international research networks and collaborations, even in areas traditionally treated as jurisdiction-specific, such as constitutional law, criminal law and property law, are no longer treated by funding agencies or by the many auditors of 'research excellence' and ranking agencies as exotic and exceptional, but as mainstream – even de rigueur. A similar normalisation of expectations towards greater global awareness, communication and engagement can be found in judicial training networks and in forms of professional socialisation more generally.[58]

This process of normalisation can engender a self-fulfilling prophecy. If the traditional boundaries of relevant legal knowledge are treated as obsolescent, and if, aided and abetted by information technology that can summon countless extra-jurisdictional legal materials – domestic and international, legislative and judicial, hard and soft – at the touch of a keypad, the whole of the legal world becomes everyone's available resource pool, then it becomes increasingly difficult to withstand the flood of information and increasingly artificial to erect new barriers.

---

[56] See, among many examples, the role of Joseph Weiler, among others, in the second phase of development of NYU Law School as a global law centre (www.jeanmonnetprogram. org/archive/coatofmanycolors/interview_2.html), and now, since 2013, as President of the EU-centred European University Institute; or the role of Martti Koskenniemi in the development of the Eric Castrén Institute for International Law and Human Rights at the University of Helsinki: (www.helsinki.fi/eci/).

[57] Note, for example, the tone of the contributions at the opening panel of the Harvard Law School 100th Anniversary Global Legal Education Forum on 23–25 March 2012: www. law.harvard.edu/news/spotlight/ils/global-legal-education-forum-2012.html.

[58] See e.g. Claes and de Visser, n. 19 above; and Le Golf, n. 9 above.

Access to this broader reservoir remains, of course, extremely selective on practical grounds, but to the extent that it takes place it has a 'real time' quality that underlines a sense of the convergence of national horizons in practical reflection on law and its development.

To take one example, in any previous generation even the most celebrated of cases would only be known, discussed and 'borrowed' from their national domicile 'after the fact' and, largely, in separate national discourses. Today, cases of broader interest such as American Supreme Court decisions under the Alien Tort Claims Act,[59] or South African Constitutional Court judgments on social rights,[60] or Indian Supreme Court findings on the '(un)constitutionality' of constitutional amendments,[61] or European Court of Justice holdings on the legality of United Nations resolutions,[62] or German Constitutional Court determinations on the acceptable limits of European Union treaty encroachment on national democracy,[63] have a much more immediate global significance. They have permanent domestic and foreign audiences and are subject to simultaneous cultural (and, increasingly, linguistic)[64] translation and to a process of instant dissemination and discussion in the transnational blogosphere

---

[59] See e.g. *Kiobel* v. *Royal Dutch Petroleum Co.*, 133 S Ct 1659 (2013).

[60] See e.g. *Mazibuko* v. *City of Johannesburg* (CCT 39/09) [2009] ZACC 28; 2010 (3) BCLR 239 (CC); 2010 (4) SA 1 (CC) (8 October 2009) (on the right to water).

[61] *State of Bihar* v. *Bal Mukund Sah and Others* AIR 2000 SC 1296 (14 March 2000). See also, more generally, on the transnational judicial conversation concerning the question of unconstitutional amendments: R. Dixon, 'Transnational Constitutionalism and Unconstitutional Constitutional Amendments', Public Law and Legal Theory Working Paper 349/2011 (May 2011), available at www.law.uchicago.edu/files/file/349-rd-transnational.pdf; Y. Roznai, 'Unconstitutional Constitutional Amendments – The Migration and Success of a Constitutional Idea' 61 *American Journal of Comparative Law* 657 (2013).

[62] See Joined cases C-402/05 P and C-415/05 P, *Kadi and Al Barakaat International Foundation* v. *Council and Commission*, Judgment of the Court (Grand Chamber), 3 September 2008 [2008] ECR I-6351 (*Kadi I*); and Joined cases C-584/10 P, C-593/10 P and C-595/10 P, *European Commission and Others* v. *Yassin Abdullah Kadi*, Judgment of the Court (Grand Chamber), 18 July 2013 (*Kadi II*). See also Chapter 4.4 below.

[63] See the judgment of the Federal Constitutional Court of Germany (*Bundesverfassungsgericht*) concerning the Treaty on the Functioning of the European Union (TFEU, or 'Lisbon Treaty'): *BVerfG*, joint cases 2 BvE 2/08 and 2 BvE 5/08, 30 June 2009. See also G. Beck, 'The Lisbon Judgment of the German Constitutional Court, the Primacy of EU Law and the Problem of Kompetenz-Kompetenz: A Conflict between Right and Right in which there is No Praetor' 17 *European Law Journal* 470 (2011).

[64] Typically, translation is into English. For example, the text of all German Constitutional Court decisions since 1 January 1998 is now available in official translation in English: see www.bverfg.de/en/decisions.html. However, at least one ambitious project aims to provide access to rudimentary translations, into twenty languages, of national supreme court decisions across the EU: see the Common Portal of Case Law currently being

and across various other professional and academic networks. By dint of their very contemplation as common objects they become a common reference point, a self-corroborating symbol of the existence of something tangibly 'global'; not only in law's patrimony but also, in more novel fashion, in its living development. Here the increasing velocity of trans-national movement and the resulting compression of time and space, such a key indicator of globalisation more generally,[65] have direct consequences for how we come to see the materials of legal development as forming a global set.

2.3.4 The continuum of global 'law-craft'

The idea of a continuum, or rather, of a continuum – or connected series – of continua, helps capture and account for the ways in which the development of a global horizon has involved an overcoming of old partitions and divisions both within the profession and practice of lawyering and law-making and between the various facets of the lawyer's craft considered as a whole. The forging of a global perspective, in a nutshell, implies a new continuity of location, of event, of office, of role, and of organisation, but also, and most importantly for our purposes, of jurisgenerative activity.

Continuity of location refers to the way in which domestic legal practi-tioners and teachers are also transnationally connected and in many instances internationally mobile. There is no clear division of personnel or even of occupational type mapping onto the functional division between national and transnational legal activities. Rather, as we have seen, it is often the most prominent or prestigious national practitioners and their institu-tional bases – with commercial lawyers prominent but far from exclusive members of the cast – that are to the fore transnationally. For its part, continuity of event strongly complements this sense of interflow between the national and transnational by reframing landmark domestic or trans-national legal occurrences not only as global spectacles, but as points of simultaneous reference across different systems.

Continuity of office refers to the way in which the classic domestic separation of powers and legal functions, and of their associated institu-tions, between legislative promulgation, executive application and judicial deliberation and enforcement of the law, is blurred on the transnational stage. Absent national constitutional law's stylised constructions of the

developed by the Network of the Presidents of the Supreme Courts of the EU: www.networkpresidents.eu/.

[65] See Chapter 1.1 above.

three branches, and absent 'joined up' systems of global government through which the different offices are co-articulated, these basic legal functions themselves are not so clearly identified and differentiated beyond the state. The arbitration systems and other forums of open-ended dispute resolution that are so prominent in transnational settings are as much private enforcement mechanisms or forms of applied policy-making as they are classically independent judicial functions. Equally, many of the forms of 'transnational administration' which, as we shall see, make up the object of analysis of the new Global Administrative Law,[66] and many new forms of so-called 'experimentalist' decision-making beyond the state,[67] involve forms of rule-making that are as much legislative as they are administrative. And reflecting and reinforcing these soft boundaries, among the elites who inhabit global legal circles, there is far greater transferability of position and legal function.[68]

Continuity of role stretches this point further to cover the wider range of extra-curricular occupations and tasks for which the transnational legal expert is qualified and to which she is deployed. In national systems, too, lawyers are often involved in many wider aspects of public life. They are sometimes engaged as politicians, administrators, 'neutral' institutional engineers, campaigners, watchdogs, trouble-shooters, educators, researchers, theorists or social critics, in addition to or instead of their 'official' functions as draftsmen, government lawyers, litigators, judges and doctrinal scholars. But in the transnational context, given its institutional dispersal and variety, and without the prominent official casting of the national legal system, the potential for role ubiquity and versatility is greater.[69] And finally, continuity of organisation mirrors and reinforces

---

[66] B. Kingsbury, N. Krisch and R. B. Stewart, 'The Emergence of Global Administrative Law' 68 *Law and Contemporary Problems* 15 (2005). See also Chapter 3.3.2 below.

[67] See e.g. C. Sabel and J. Zeitlin (eds.), *Experimentalist Governance in the European Union: Towards a New Architecture* (Oxford University Press, 2010). On experimentalism in the US, see e.g. M. Dorf and C. Sabel, 'A Constitution of Experimentalist Governance' 98 *Columbia Law Review* 267 (1998); C. Sabel and W. Simon, 'Minimalism and Experimentalism in American Public Law' 100 *Georgetown Law Review* 53 (2011). On experimentalism in the EU, see K. Armstrong, 'The Character of EU Law and Governance: From "Community Method" to New Modes of Governance' 64 *Current Legal Problems* 179 (2011). See also Chapter 5.2.2 below.

[68] See e.g. Le Golf, n. 9 above.

[69] This is perhaps most obviously true of the link between the role of arbiter and that of commercial practitioner. See e.g. C. Giménez Corte, '*Lex Mercatoria*: International Arbitration and Independent Guarantees: Transnational Law and How Nation States Lost the Monopoly of Legitimate Enforcement' 3 *Transnational Legal Theory* 345 (2012).

the blurring and overlapping of offices and roles. It refers to the way in which some of the key institutions and networks of transnational legal space, including judicial-academic forums and practitioner organisations, are as much sites of communication across specialist legal functions as within them, as much occasions for role extension and diversification as means of role consolidation.[70]

Global 'law-craft', therefore, speaks to a range of activities and institutions that are neither narrowly delineated nor clearly distinguished from other more localised domains of legal craftsmanship. The location, 'eventing', allocation of offices, distribution of wider roles and 'guild' organisation of global law-craft are each openly and expansively specified. They are also, as we have seen, mutually facilitating and mutually supportive. And each, as we shall see, feeds into another spectrum of activity that is much more intimately linked to global law as a doctrinal achievement, namely the continuum of jurisgenerative or law-making practice.

2.4   Global lawyers and the making of global law

Before we can appreciate how the rise of global 'law-craft' through the global lawyer and judge, and through global legal research and education, might contribute to the development of global law, we should first acquaint ourselves with the general historical pattern of involvement by those with specialist legal skill or knowledge in law creation. For it is undeniable that those who engage in the practice, theory and exposition of law have always also participated to some extent in the making of law. To think otherwise would be to mistake a highly stylised version of one particular historical phase in the production of legal authority for the general picture of legal authority across the ages.

Only in the modern constitutional state do we find, as we have just noted, a sharp division of function and separation of legal powers. More specifically, only in the modern age do we find such a clearly articulated divide between those involved in the generation and execution of law on the one hand and those involved in its declaration, interpretation, systematisation, rationalisation and dissemination on the other. Where the former activities are viewed as the proper domain of the political branches of government – the legislature for law creation and the executive for the exercise of legal powers – the latter are understood as

---

[70] See e.g. Le Golf, n. 9 above.

the proper domain of those with expertise in the law, whether judges, professional legal practitioners, teachers or others learned in legal science.[71]

Yet even within this limited historical window the division of labour is far less tidy and far more unsettled than constitutional orthodoxy typically allows. Whether, and to what extent, judges can or should avoid 'making' new law when interpreting, declaring and applying general norms in particular cases have been and, of course, remain among the most central and most contested questions of modern jurisprudence.[72] Also, to the extent that common law or customary law subsists as a source of law alongside legislation in the modern national legal system, this allows further scope for an assertive judicial role.[73] In other more general ways too, expertise is still allowed its part in the construction of law. Where modern state law is the subject of codification or restatement, this typically takes place under the direction or influence of skilled legal draftsmen.[74] In addition, the writings of eminent jurists, past or present, are often treated as authoritative or persuasive sources by the courts. And related to this, but in a less formal and explicit and more flexible and fluid pattern of influence, law professors and other expert observers and commentators of the modern state legal system are typically engaged in an ongoing process of 'doctrinal constructivism'.[75] Through the development, refinement and maintenance of general concepts and structures, these scholars assume 'real time' responsibility for keeping the normative materials of 'their' system in shape in ways that

---

[71] See, however, C. Möllers, *The Three Branches: A Comparative Model of Separation of Powers* (Oxford University Press, 2013), warning against overgeneralisation, and against reliance on 'a canonical idea of separated powers that has, in fact, never existed' (p. 8). See also ch. 1 in the same text.

[72] See e.g. S. Shapiro, 'The "Hart–Dworkin" Debate: A Short Guide for the Perplexed' in A. Ripstein (ed.), *Ronald Dworkin* (Cambridge University Press, 2007) pp. 22–55.

[73] See e.g. H. P. Glenn, *On Common Laws* (Oxford University Press, 2007) ch. 3; and T. R. S. Allen, *Constitutional Justice: A Liberal Theory of the Rule of Law* (Oxford University Press, 2003).

[74] See e.g. N. Jansen, *The Making of Legislative Authority: Non-Legislative Codifications in Historical and Comparative Perspective* (Oxford University Press, 2010) ch. 2.

[75] The common defining elements of doctrinal constructivism in the (otherwise highly variable) modern European tradition, according to Armin von Bogdandy, 'are the quest for systematicity through the development of general concepts and structures and the perception of these as internal to and operative within the legal system'. See A. von Bogdandy, 'The Past and Promise of Doctrinal Constructivism: A Strategy for Responding to the Challenges Facing Constitutional Scholarship in Europe' 7 *International Journal of Constitutional Law* 364 (2009) at 376.

both reflect and refine the views of the system's front-line judicial and legislative authorities.

If in these various ways legal scholars of the modern state-centred age have continued to exercise a not inconsiderable influence over the content and direction of the domestic law of the state, in other times and places the division of labour between political and epistemic authorities has been decidedly more blurred and the impact of the latter still more profound. Indeed, it was only with the development of the centralised state as somewhat more than a device of dynastic rule superimposed upon the status hierarchies of feudalism and other normative systems associated with the church or established custom, that such a distinction assumed its recognisable modern form. For it was not until the state began to acquire mature shape as the realisation of an abstract idea of sovereignty through a comprehensive and internally legitimated realm of public authority that the very idea of politics as an arena of debate and contestation crystallised in its ample contemporary form, together with a conception of legislation as the regular product of such a distinctively political process.[76] In earlier times, most written law was a scholarly rather than a legislative production: whether the red line of Roman Law running from the Twelve Tables through Justinian's *corpus juris civilis* to the glossators and commentators of medieval Europe and the development of local variations of the *jus commune* in Europe's early modern states; or the tradition of canon law culminating in the *Decretum Gratiani*; or codified customary law such as the Saxon Mirror;[77] or the strong textual traditions of Islamic law or Jewish law with their careful hierarchies of original sources and their intricate attribution of secondary authority to the canonised products and other documented records of later schools or scholars.[78] In all these cases the legal expert had a prominent role in the discovery, recovery, reduction, preservation, systematisation or adaptation of a law whose original authority was either deemed external to the world or otherwise rooted in an unquestioned

---

[76] See e.g. J. Waldron, *The Dignity of Legislation* (Cambridge University Press, 1999), particularly ch. 3; and K. Tuori, Ratio *and* Voluntas: *The Tension between Reason and Will in Law* (Farnham: Ashgate, 2011) ch. 7.

[77] See e.g. Jansen, n. 74 above, particularly ch. 1. See also T. Wallinga, 'The Common History of European Legal Scholarship' 4 *Erasmus Law Review* 3 (2011).

[78] See e.g. W. B. Hallaq, *The Origins and Evolution of Islamic Law* (Cambridge University Press, 2005); and S. L. Stone, 'In Pursuit of the Counter-Text: The Turn to the Jewish Legal Model in Contemporary American Legal Theory' 106 *Harvard Law Review* 813 (1992).

tradition or sense of natural order; and which, through the force of that authority, demanded to be incorporated or otherwise recognised by whatever regime claimed temporal political power and within whatever broader framework of rule and rulership it sponsored.[79]

If pre-modern law and, to a lesser extent, modern state law supply general precedents for specialist involvement in law creation, modern international law is undoubtedly a more specific precursor of global law. Only in the last decades of the nineteenth century, and in particular with the formation of the *Institut de Droit International* in 1883, did the modern idea of international law achieve disciplinary self-consciousness.[80] Where, previously, law between the public authorities of states was predicated on a mix of a thin normative reduction of realist diplomacy among sovereigns, and, more remotely, classical notions of the law of nature extended to the law of nations or *jus gentium*,[81] there now emerged, for the first time, a group of Western scholars self-described as international lawyers, dedicated to the development and systematic articulation of an autonomous framework of international rules governing the exchanges of all 'civilised' nations.[82] Here, then, we have the development for the first time of a transnational legal scholarly elite in active and continuous communication and circulation, reflective of an imperial pattern of power but also dedicated to taming the excesses of that imperial power and to 'civilising' international relations through law more generally; and importantly, involved from the outset in the development of a new branch of law and in the specification not only of its content but also of its foundational authoritative claims.[83]

---

[79] See e.g. Jansen, n. 74 above, particularly pp. 13–27. He tellingly observes that during the Middle Ages 'jurists telling ... such stories [about imperial authority] believed that the text was based on imperial authority because they felt obliged to apply it, rather than the other way around' (p. 27).

[80] See e.g. M. Koskenniemi, *The Gentle Civilizer of Nations: The Rise and Fall of International Law 1870–1960* (Cambridge University Press, 2001) ch. 1.

[81] See e.g. J. Waldron, 'Ius Gentium: A Defence of Gentili's Equation of the Law of Nations and the Law of Nature' in B. Kingsbury and B. Straumann (eds.), *The Roman Foundations of the Law of Nations. Alberico Gentili and the Justice of Empire* (Oxford University Press, 2010) pp. 283–96; J. Waldron, 'Partly Laws Common to All Mankind': *Foreign Law in American Courts* (New Haven, CT: Yale University Press, 2012) ch. 2; E. Jouannet, 'Universalism and Imperialism: The True–False Paradox of International Law?' 8 *European Journal of International Law* 379 (2007) at 379–407; and N. Walker, 'The Place of European Law' in G. de Búrca and J. H. H. Weiler (eds.), *The Worlds of European Constitutionalism* (Cambridge University Press, 2011) pp. 57–104. See also Chapter 3.2 below.

[82] Koskenniemi, n. 80 above.   [83] *Ibid.*, chs. 2–5.

Moreover, as we shall see in the next chapter, international law has been important not just as a transnational precedent but also as a platform for global law.[84] International law, significantly reconstructed and extended from its nineteenth-century baseline with the introduction of the United Nations system after the Second World War, has in some cases provided the point of departure for the development of certain global law claims, and international lawyers have in some cases given voice to such claims.[85] International law has also been a catalyst for the development of transnational law more generally,[86] the density of which is such a vital feature in the development of global law.[87] Yet we should be careful not to make too much of this. International law is undoubtedly one building block of global law, but it is by no means the only one.[88] What is more, international law, understood as a discipline with its own scholarly legacy, occupational status system, and teaching and research priorities, can also act as a check upon the development of certain global law perspectives. For modern international law, we should also recall, has been for the most part predicated upon the very maintenance of statehood as the organising principle and external boundary of jurisdiction that the claim of global law seeks to overcome.

For all these historical analogies, however, and notwithstanding the special significance of international law as precursor and platform, the contribution of global legal specialists to the making of global law is undoubtedly distinctive in its range, in its intense concentration within a specific window of time, and, arguably, in its potential impact. This distinctiveness has roots in what we have described as the continuum of the various cultural elements of global 'law-craft'. It derives in part

---

[84] See Chapter 3.2 below.

[85] For instance, the role of international lawyers in the development of Global Administrative Law: see e.g. Kingsbury, Krisch and Stewart, n. 66 above. See also the discussion in Chapter 3.3.2 below.

[86] Consider, for example, the role of international law in the making and subsequent development of the law of the European Union, *the* most developed transnational or non-state polity in the world today: see B. de Witte, 'The European Union as an International Legal Experiment' in de Búrca and Weiler (eds.), n. 81 above, pp. 19–56. Or consider the role of public international law in the contemporary development of private international law, or conflict of laws: see e.g. A. Mills, *The Confluence of Public and Private International Law: Justice, Pluralism and Subsidiarity in the International Constitutional Ordering of Private Law* (Cambridge University Press, 2009). See also Chapter 3.4.1.1 below.

[87] See Chapter 1.3 above and Chapter 3 generally.

[88] See e.g. Chapter 3 below, particularly sections 3.2 and 3.3.

from the fluid multi-level range and self-stimulating momentum of a limited and privileged cadre of lawyers, typically employed, engaged or self-directed in search of creative solutions to a wide variety of cross-jurisdictional legal problems. It is also attributable to the special opportunities supplied by the conjunction of the sheer density of the network of contemporary transnational legal sources and avenues on the one hand, and, on the other, the relative absence or mutual incoherence of global or regional public political forums and legislative institutions. The specialists of global law, often operating, as we have seen, in close-knit, elite-led association and sharply focused on their new and overlapping global horizons, become involved in 'taking law to the world'[89] through various different but mutually reinforcing modes and gradations of jurisgenerative activity.

Such jurisgenerative activity can itself be arranged along a continuum. It occurs at the level of creative practice and gradual development of 'running code',[90] from the novel contractual arrangements or forms of legal association patented by transnational commercial lawyers,[91] to the procedural rules and precedents of international arbitrators.[92] It can also take place at the level of general drafting of substantive rules or forms of institutional design, with the central involvement of lawyers and legal experts in the crafting and maintenance of an ever-expanding range of

---

[89] The chapter's title phrase is intentionally ambiguous. One interpretation suggests an accompanying attitude of civilisational superiority and of 'imperial' direction and expansion. A variation on that theme indicates idealistic ambition, even 'missionary' zeal. Or, as a more literal reading would have it, global law-craft may be more mundanely motivated and more modestly considered, reduced to the routine exercise of an increasingly familiar and widespread professional role. As noted in the Introduction to the chapter, and as subsequent discussion has illustrated, the development of global law-craft is too large and multifaceted an enterprise to be the subject of categorical moral judgment. For a thoughtful discussion of the range of attitudes involved and the deep moral dilemmas faced in the exercise of one prominent type of global 'law-craft', namely the spread of 'Rule of Law' values and practices through EU institutions and policies, see R. Kleinfeld and K. Nicolaidis, 'Can a Post-Colonial Power Export the Rule of Law? Elements of a General Framework' in G. Palombella and N. Walker (eds.), *Relocating the Rule of Law* (Oxford: Hart, 2009) pp. 139–70.

[90] See G.-P. Calliess and P. Zumbansen, *Rough Consensus and Running Code: A Theory of Transnational Private Law* (Oxford: Hart, 2010), particularly ch. 2. See also R. Wai, 'The Interlegality of Transnational Private Law' 71 *Law and Contemporary Problems* 107 (2008); and C. Cutler, *Private Power and Global Authority: Transnational Merchant Law in the Global Political Economy* (Cambridge University Press, 2003).

[91] See e.g. Calliess and Zumbansen, *ibid.*, ch. 3.

[92] See e.g. Le Golf, n. 9 above, at 134–5; and Giménez Corte, n. 69 above.

transnational industry codes,[93] corporate governance frameworks[94] and, of course, agreements within public international law or under the authority of international 'public' institutions,[95] or in drawing on foreign or international example when developing legislative and constitutional models within their own national jurisdiction.[96] Or it can operate through expansive interpretation, with judges and academic commentators construing domestic law, international law or other transnational law in the light of supposedly global standards or with a view to promoting such standards.[97] Finally, and of particular importance for present purposes, jurisgenerative activity can also take place at the more rarefied level of legal cartography, where broad claims are made about the shifting configuration of transnational legal forces. And just because of their intense mutual engagement and networking, and their privileged position in transnational regulatory circles, globally inclined academics, judges and other experts are increasingly well placed to imagine new ways of framing, naming, patterning and projecting in global terms the unwieldy multiverse of transnational law to which they and their fellow legal specialists have done so much to contribute at the levels of practice, interpretation, drafting and design. In other words, the crafting of law on the global stage by jurists and other legal specialists extends to the creative diagnosis and reclassification of the legal landscape in global terms, which lies at the heart of the very idea of global law as a self-conscious development and a reflexive process.[98]

In all of these ways and also in their dynamic combination, therefore, global lawyers and jurists are primed to play a powerfully self-reinforcing

---

[93] F. Cafaggi, 'New Foundations of Transnational Private Regulation', EUI Working Paper RSCAS 2010/53; and G. Teubner, *Constitutional Fragments: Societal Constitutionalism and Globalization* (Oxford University Press, 2012).

[94] See e.g. Calliess and Zumbansen, n. 90 above, ch. 4.

[95] See Chapter 3.3.2 below, on Global Administrative Law. On a typical model of trans-institutional norm-making (involving the World Bank, IMF and United Nations), see T. C. Halliday and B. C. Carruthers, 'The Recursivity of Law: Global Norm Making and National Lawmaking in the Globalization of Corporate Insolvency Regimes' 112 *American Journal of Sociology* 1135 (2007). On the difficult boundary between the public and the private in transnational law and the role of lawyers in negotiating these boundaries, see J. Resnik, 'Globalization(s), Privatization(s), Constitutionalization, and Statization: Icons and Experiences of Sovereignty in the 21st Century' 11 *International Journal of Constitutional Law* 162 (2013).

[96] See e.g. M. Versteeg and D. Law, 'The Evolution and Ideology of Global Constitutionalism' 99 *California Law Review* 1163 (2011).

[97] See e.g. Jackson, n. 17 above, particularly chs. 2 and 3.

[98] See further, Chapters 3–5 below.

part in the construction of the new normative space of global law. They are, indeed, both cause and effect, on the one hand contributing to the growing profile of global law with its peculiar combination of fluidly emergent doctrine and projection, and on the other hand empowered and authorised by the fact that global law, for reasons we will develop fully in due course, is in any case predisposed to exhibit that peculiar structure.[99] The various and diverse forms that the construction of global law takes, the reasons for this and the particular motivations of the actors involved, and the effects on the overall profile of global law of the interaction of its various parts, are questions we turn to in the four chapters that follow. We can now do so with a keener appreciation of the reasons why the transnational legal community is generally to the fore in this process.

---

[99] See further, Chapters 4 and 5 below.

3

Seven species of global law

3.1 Introduction: two visions of global law

In Chapter 1 we defined global law as any practical endorsement of, or commitment to, the universal or otherwise global-in-general warrant of some laws or of some dimensions of law. We noted that this was a broad definition permitting a cross-cutting range of internal distinctions. Global law so understood may or may not be sourced and institutionalised at the planetary level. It can be more or less actively endorsed and fully realised, and more or less concrete and positivised in its normative claim or orientation. It can also be either universal or merely planetary in scope or ambition, provided it meets a threshold requirement of not being confined by and to any particular sub-global territorial jurisdiction.

In the catalogue of global law set out below, each of these distinctions arises at various points, yet none provides the primary principle of classification. Instead this is supplied by a more basic form of variance that recalls one of the core dynamics of globalisation introduced in Chapter 1. That distinction lies between two conceptions and two very broad visions of global law; between two different ways of imagining how global law might shape or reshape the pattern of distribution and connection of law across the planet. One such conception reflects a focal concern to encourage a general dynamic of legal *convergence*, while the other conception reflects a focal concern to accommodate a general dynamic of legal *divergence*. Seeking to counter or overcome difference, a convergence-promoting conception treats global law as the object of collective agreement or cultivation, or as some other commonly acknowledged broad normative frame; this involves either a vertical arrangement of authoritative global rule-making or rule-application, or the global endorsement of some generic feature(s) of law. Seeking instead to manage difference, a divergence-accommodating conception employs global law as a means of tracking, harnessing and confining diversity;

this involves either a horizontal framework of co-ordination of different legal regimes or some form of legal recognition and refinement of the separate elements of a multiverse of globally extendable normative orders. In a nutshell, while convergence-promoting approaches involve one or both of the attributes of hierarchy and normative singularity, divergence-accommodating approaches are characterised by the twin themes of heterarchy and normative plurality. These summary attributes, moreover, point us to the sense in which these two conceptions are also properly to be regarded as *visions*. They are both concerned with giving legal shape to the world, with thinking about the law's relationship to the globe in architectonic terms. In imagining the world in different ways, as we shall see, they also *image* the world differently.

Shortly we will investigate in greater detail what distinguishes these convergence-promoting and divergence-accommodating conceptions and visions of global law – or what we can refer to in shorthand simply as convergent and divergent approaches – through an examination of the various different species within each general type. Before we do so, however, we should take basic note of what binds them together, because that tells us something important about the formative context of global law in general, as well as providing some preliminary pointers as to its reproductive capacity.

What convergent and divergent conceptions hold crucially in common is that both acknowledge and seek to address the increasing complexity of the post-national legal landscape – its diversity and fluidity of form, its multiplication of new forms of legally coded identity and difference, its congestion, its cross-systemic overlapping claims and focal concerns, its mechanisms of mutual recognition and interlock; and, it follows, its irreducibility to a state-sovereigntist logic of mutually exclusive jurisdictional allocation. Faced with the increasing porosity of the state-encircling inner boundaries of the legal landscape and confronted with the highly differentiated world of legal functions, forms and frontiers thereby exposed, global law in either broad conception – convergent or divergent – declines to recognise any sub-global territorial limit to its own jurisdiction. The basic scoping image of legal spatiality entertained by global law in either conception, then, is one of 'law decompartmentalised' in a double sense – both in the perceived condition of law and in the treatment of that condition; both as to the fluidly interwoven transnational legal field contemplated and as to the territorially unconfined jurisdiction deemed apt to address such a field.

Now, as the many particular examples in the main parts of the chapter will demonstrate, the causal connection between the two senses and two levels of a decompartmentalised law – between the indistinct and porous divisions of the variegated landscape of post-national law and the onset of a jurisdictionally unlimited global law, whether convergence-promoting or divergence-accommodating – is in fact intense and multi-faceted. The emergence of an expansive and elaborate menu of global legal forms *is facilitated by* the rich diversity and resulting fluidity and permissiveness of the post-national legal landscape more generally – of law unconfined by the state and spilled over into many and interfluent transnational streams. Yet, more pointedly, the various species of global law also develop and flourish *as responses to* the issues posed and problems raised by that same complexity and fluidity.

In addition, and extending the chain reaction, the various developing responses of global law serve to feed the fecundity and compound the very complexity they seek to address. As we shall elaborate in Chapter 4, this has a double-edged quality. On the one hand, just because they are responding to the same general challenge of somehow 'containing' law in a post-national landscape, the projection of each general vision – convergent and divergent – and of each particular species of global law tends to assume and to retain some measure of sympathy for much of what is projected in the other general vision and the various other species of global law. This opens up a space of intellectual permission and experimentation in which the emerging category of global law can nurture and renew itself. Yet, on the other hand, the mutual engagement of the various approaches also reflects and reinforces particular differ-ences and forms of dissonance among them. For the relationship between the different species of global law, and to some extent even within different species, while in some respects compatible, even mutu-ally supportive, can also become one of opposition and of competitive encounter. Much of the mutual stimulation of the various global law candidates, indeed, is in fact intimately bound up with their mutual tension. In this way, the self-reproduction of the new global law can be seen to be as much a product of conflict among its candidate species as of their capacity for cohabitation.

Returning to the task in hand, we can isolate seven different species of global law claim. As noted, some of these overlap with one another, some-times in a complementary way, sometimes in tension, sometimes even in opposition. Starting with the more convergent claims and proceeding to the more divergent, we can identify these seven species as *structural, formal,*

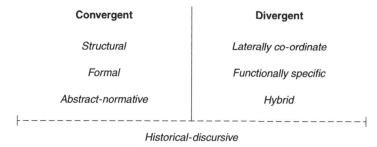

Fig. 3.1   The seven species of global law

abstract-normative, historical-discursive, laterally co-ordinate, functionally specific and *hybrid*. Let us examine each in turn.[1]

3.2   The catalogue of global law I: convergent approaches

In Chapter 2 it was pointed out that the modern tradition of international law provides an important platform for global law. The influence of international law, indeed, declares itself across all species of global law. Nevertheless, it is most roundly evident within the set of convergent approaches to global law, and most emphatically so as regards the first two species of convergent global law. These structural and formal approaches emphasise the dimension of hierarchy, albeit in quite different ways and by quite different routes. They involve an element of global direction in accordance with some kind of 'top-down' authoritative mechanism – though far from the comprehensive kind we associate with state sovereignty and its constitutional machinery. Significantly, in both cases the dominant understanding of modern international law as built upon sovereigntist premises[2] and as centred upon the voluntary undertakings and transactions of states, is stretched and modified to include a measure of general obligation to underpin and to supplement that contractual bond.[3] The third type of convergent approach – the

---

[1] This catalogue draws selectively upon my own earlier taxonomy, which was concerned with a broader range of transnational legal authority: see N. Walker, 'Beyond Boundary Disputes and Basic Grids: Mapping the Global Disorder of Normative Orders' 6 *International Journal of Constitutional Law* 373 (2008).

[2] See Chapter 1.2.3 and Chapter 2.3 above.

[3] The voluntarist approach to international law finds famous expression in the *Lotus* decision of the Permanent Court of International Justice, the court holding that '[i]nternational law governs relations between independent States. The rules of law binding upon States therefore emanate from their own free will as expressed in

abstract-normative approach – entails instead some kind of common normative scheme which frames, directs or conditions the global legal landscape as a whole, in all its diversity. Here international law is a less constant background influence, though still very important in some variants.

3.2.1 Structural approaches

Structural versions of global law supply a vision of globally encompassing normative direction as generated and expressed through legally underpinned institutional architecture, the sole or widest forms of which are situated at the planetary level. The global, or globally aspirational, quality of the relevant law here is apparent, first, in its planetary comprehensiveness of coverage and, secondly, in a claim to normative gravity that is adequate to that planetary ambition. For not only does global law thus conceived purport to embrace all states as its subject and objects, but it does so by reference to a normative design that stands apart from, and where necessary purports to prevail over, local normative forms and actors. The emphasis is upon planetary-level peak institutions with strong legislative or executive capacity as the key instruments of their ambition.

Global law's candidature under this head is one of considerable vintage, with Kant's 1795 blueprint for *Perpetual Peace*[4] a significant historical landmark and, indeed, a renewed point of reference in recent years.[5] Today, of course, the main focus of understanding and projection of global law in structural terms is the particular design set out in the UN Charter and developed in its gradually extended post-Second World

conventions or by usages generally accepted as expressing principles of law.' *SS Lotus* (Fr. v. Turk.), 1927 PCIJ Series A, No. 10 (7 Sept.), at 18. For a typical account of the voluntarist background, see A. V. Lowe, *International Law* (Oxford University Press, 2007). Contemporary international law knows many revisionist accounts of the history of its discipline, but all continue to acknowledge the importance of the voluntarist strain as a bedrock of the modern approach: see e.g. E. Jouannet, *The Liberal-Welfarist Law of Nations: A History of International Law* (Cambridge University Press, 2012); S. C. Neff, *Justice Among Nations: A History of International Law* (Harvard University Press, 2014) esp. part III; and J. H. H. Weiler, 'The Geology of International Law – Governance, Democracy and Legitimacy' 64 *German Yearbook of International Law* 547 (2004).

[4] I. Kant, 'Perpetual Peace: A Philosophical Essay' in L. W. Beck, R. E. Anchor and E. L. Fackenheim (eds.), *On History*, orig. edn 1795 (New York: Macmillan, 1963) pp. 85–135.

[5] See e.g. F. R. Tesón, *A Philosophy of International Law* (Boulder, CO: Westview Press, 1998); and P. Capps, 'The Kantian Project in Modern International Legal Theory' 12 *European Journal of International Law* 1003 (2001).

War reconstruction of international law and international relations.[6] The UN system is quite unprecedented in its scale of achievement, though in some respects it builds upon the example of the inter-war League of Nations, which itself broke new ground in its attempts to institutionalise transnational governance.[7] The basic requirements to maintain international peace and security and respect human rights supply the core operative norms of the UN system, but its sphere of influence ranges much wider than these key commitments. Through its Security Council, General Assembly and Secretary-General, and also through its Economic and Social Council and many other specialised institutions alongside its raft of rights-monitoring bodies, including UNESCO, the World Bank and the World Health Organization, the UN framework possesses and exercises a depth and scope of normative authority unprecedented in any self-styled planetary legal regime.

The prominence of the UN is not only a matter of its gradually extended institutional depth and breadth, but also rests upon wider cultural and geopolitical factors. Given the symbolic power of its well-maintained creation myth as a global initiative risen phoenix-like from the ashes of two World Wars;[8] given its heightened international profile and new opportunity context in the face of the proliferation of 'new wars'[9] that do not follow an inter-state pattern, and the more generally altered global security context post-1989 following the end of Cold War bipolarity; given the familiarity of its architecture – assembly, council, large-scale administrative agencies, etc. – from the national template of government; and given also its highly visible self-projection as a superordinate system of global regulation, the position of the UN system at the head of any inventory of legal globalisation is unsurprising. It is undoubtedly perceived by many as *the* plausible prototype of global law,[10] and as the baseline and catalyst for its further development, just

---

[6] For overviews, see e.g. P. Kennedy, *The Parliament of Man: The Past, Present and Future of the United Nations* (New York: Vintage, 2007); and M. Mazower, *Governing the World: The History of an Idea, 1815 to the Present* (New York: Penguin, 2013) part II. In a more explicitly legal and, indeed, constitutional vein, see B. Fassbender, *The United Nations Charter and the Constitution of the International Community* (Leiden: Martinus Nijhoff, 2009).

[7] See e.g. Mazower, n. 6 above, ch. 5.   [8] *Ibid.*, ch. 7.

[9] M. Kaldor, *New and Old Wars: Organised Violence in a Global Era*, 3rd edn (Cambridge: Polity Press, 2012).

[10] See e.g. Fassbender, n. 6 above; C. Tomuschat, 'Obligations Arising for States Without or Against their Will' 241 *Recueil des Cours* 195 (1993); and J. Habermas, 'Does the

as it is widely viewed as the point of departure for any possible development of a global government.[11]

In many ways, however, the global projection of the UN's structural capacity, even within the still narrow parameters of its substantive remit, remains a provisional achievement. As an aspiration, it remains ambivalent and conflicted, lacking consistent specification or commitment. Both the limitations and the irresolution of the UN's global role have much to do with its Janus-faced position in the modern history of international law. The stubborn imprint of the very state-centred, voluntaristic understanding of international law that the development of the United Nations has sought to challenge is etched in the organisation's own foundation, and is preserved and nurtured as an alternative aspect of its forward-looking dynamic. Bluntly, the United Nations, for all the imagery of a global compact, was in initial fact the creature of a few Great Power states bound in wartime alliance and bound to commit to maintain that alliance.[12] And in its subsequent unfolding it bears some of the marks of these more basic conditions of origin.

These contending impulses and unresolved tensions are manifest not only in the fragility of the national alliances and the variability of the national commitments upon which the UN's political capital depends, but also, and of more immediate relevance, in many key legal design features. Its overall legal framework is imperfectly realised in both key aspects of its claim to global rule: in terms of its normative gravity or bindingness as well as in terms of the outer reaches of its authority. The extent to which the different outputs of the UN's various organs have binding effect is variable and controversial.[13] Its judicial arm, the International Court of Justice, does not possess compulsory jurisdiction over state parties absent their agreement.[14] More generally, the UN is, in theory, an organisation based upon club membership. This implies two limits. First, and more fundamentally, the club is restricted to states alone, and so the traditional

---

Constitutionalisation of International Law Still Have a Chance?', ch. 8 in J. Habermas, *The Divided West* (Cambridge: Polity Press, 2006).

[11] See e.g. T. G. Weiss and R. Thakur, *Global Governance and the UN: An Unfinished Journey* (Bloomington, IN: Indiana University Press, 2010).

[12] See e.g. Mazower, n. 6 above, ch. 7.

[13] See e.g. M. D. Öberg, 'The Legal Effects of Resolutions of the UN Security Council and General Assembly in the Jurisprudence of the ICJ' 16 *European Journal of International Law* 879 (2005).

[14] Statute of the International Court of Justice, Art. 36; as of 22 November 2013, seventy states have made declarations recognising the jurisdiction of the ICJ as compulsory.

demarcation of international law as exclusively inter-*national* persists. This remains an important species barrier, even if the development of the UN and of a denser framework of international law more generally has engaged a whole new class of non-state actors,[15] and despite its growth both reflecting and having further stimulated the recognition of the individual as an additional – or even the ultimate – subject of the international legal system.[16] Secondly, club membership is by definition a question of application and acceptance – and so a voluntary matter on both sides – rather than one of automatic jurisdiction.

Yet we should not overstate these limitations, or neglect the ways in which the gradual embedding of the United Nations as an institutional centre has rendered them less relevant. In practice the benefits of membership, and the benefits of state recognition more generally (with which UN membership is closely bound up),[17] and the corresponding disadvantages and perils of non-membership and non-recognition, mean that participation in the UN system is effectively universal and compulsory. The UN Charter, in other words, has become a 'world order' treaty for all existing or aspiring state parties.[18] And reinforcing its quasi-compulsory jurisdiction, the UN also issues a form of higher law and presents itself as an organ of paramount authority. This is a matter both of normative design and, at least in some measure, of effective practice. The combination of the supremacy clause in Article 103 of the Charter[19] and the system of enforcement of the collective security framework under

---

[15] Including international organisations, NGOs, corporations and 'peoples': see e.g. Lowe, n. 3 above, pp. 14–18.

[16] With particular regard to its human rights agenda. See section 3.2.3.1 below.

[17] Even though it is generally accepted by international lawyers today that the declaratory rather than the constitutive theory of state recognition is correct, membership of international organisations such as the European Union and, most of all, the United Nations, has become so politically important that the act of recognition by these organisations is more significant than ever. According to Lowe, n. 3 above, for example: 'The decision of the General Assembly, acting on the recommendation of the Security Council, on the admission of the entity as a Member State of the United Nations is in practice the definitive seal on the Statehood of the new State' (p. 163); and ch. 4 generally. On the contemporary relevance of UN recognition to the Palestine question, see J. H. H. Weiler, 'Differentiated Statehood? "Pre-States"? Palestine@the UN' 24 *European Journal of International Law* 1 (2013).

[18] See e.g. E. de Wet, 'The Constitutionalisation of Public International Law' in M. Rosenfeld and A. Sajó (eds.), *The Oxford Handbook of Comparative Constitutional Law* (Oxford University Press, 2012) p. 1224.

[19] Article 103 reads: 'In the event of a conflict between the obligations of the Members of the United Nations under the present Charter and their obligations under any other international agreement, their obligations under the present Charter shall prevail.'

Chapter VII – increasingly activated in the post-Cold War years when the Security Council veto is no longer routinely exercised against institutional initiatives dedicated to the maintenance or restoration of international peace – means that the textually affirmed superiority of its norms to other rules of international law is underscored by significant coercive capacity.[20] More so than any other current transnational system of authority, more so than any other candidate species of global law, and more so than any predecessor global structural model, the United Nations system links law to a claimed monopoly of the means of legitimate violence in a manner that stands both as a powerful (if fitful) reminder of conventional understandings of the paradigm of state-centred legal authority and as a direct challenge to the dominance of that paradigm.

3.2.2 Formal approaches

The variety of understandings of law that lay emphasis upon legal form, sometimes called legal formalism,[21] tend to focus upon what makes law a distinctive type of social practice. The theme of distinctiveness is developed in two related ways. It may concern what is peculiar to the basic form, method and achievement of legal technique, in particular, a practice of close adherence to fixed rules and procedures and a commitment to rationally determinate reasoning in the application of law; or it may refer to the specificity of the legal form more generally, and so to the ways in which law and legal institutions, systems and decision-making methodologies can be identified apart from other social and political institutions, systems and decision-making methodologies, and may be seen to operate independently of them. Both distinguishing aspects – inner form and outer form – are implicated in various, largely implicit,[22] moves and

---

[20] See e.g. Ş. Kardaş, 'Examining the Role of the UN Security Council in Post-Cold War Interventions: The Case for Authorized Humanitarian Intervention' 3 *USAK Yearbook of International Politics and Law* 55 (2010); and E. de Wet, *The Chapter VII Powers of the United Nations Security Council* (Oxford : Hart, 2004).

[21] Legal formalism is an idea widely considered significant but of quite diverse meaning. It is an important category in legal philosophy, but also in legal history and sociology. See e.g. D. Kennedy, 'Legal Formalism' in N. J. Smelser and P. B. Baltes (eds.), *Encyclopedia of the Social and Behavioral Sciences*, vol. XIII (New York: Elsevier, 2001) pp. 8634–8; and B. Leiter, 'Legal Formalism and Legal Realism: What is the Issue?' 16 *Legal Theory* 111 (2010).

[22] The formal approach to global law merits the descriptor 'implicit' for two reasons. First, unlike the other species of global law, the 'g' word is seldom explicitly used in its connection, although the formal approach is sometimes used in connection with the

tendencies towards the construction of global law as a formal achievement. For what this type of position involves is an assertion or an
aspiration that certain rules of general warrant and lexical priority,
and an associated system or attitude of legal thought, somehow order,
condition and contain the totality of international law, and perhaps
of transnational law more generally, in so doing demonstrating the
distinctiveness of the legal way of conducting international relations.[23]

The global credentials of this type of approach rest upon a combination of factors. Like the structural approach, the formal approach in its
global variant ventures beyond the limits of explicit state consent as the
standard justification of international law to make somewhat thicker
claims. But in this case these thicker claims are tied to an ambitiously
self-standing conception of the form of legal order and its mode of
realisation. The basic idea here is of international law developed such
that it is a self-organising, self-extending and self-limiting affair.
Formalism so understood is dependent upon the elevated status, the
exhaustive reach and integrative quality of a certain fundamental set of
norms, and, if more or less explicitly, upon the association of these
norms with a deeper seam of ethical justification associated with a
certain type of rule-following and rule-respecting attitude.[24]

The idea of global law as a self-norming achievement, employing as it
does a perspective that views law as a 'pure' normative construction,
owes an intellectual and cultural debt to the work of Hans Kelsen and to
an influential lineage of twentieth-century international legal jurists
inspired by his approach.[25] In particular, the idea of the formal hierarchy
of a global system of rules – one which in its most reductive formulation

internationalisation or globalisation of constitutional law: a discourse that is associated
with more explicitly global claims. See e.g. A. L. Paulus, 'The International Legal System
as a Constitution' in J. L. Dunoff and J. P. Trachtman (eds.), *Ruling the World?
Constitutionalism, International Law, and Global Governance* (Cambridge University
Press, 2009) pp. 69–112. See also section 3.3.1 below. Secondly, the emphasis on refining
the formal characteristics of international law is rarely linked to a clear programme of
extending its influence. Rather, the stress tends to be technical, and often linked to the
defence of the integrity of international law, rather than its expansion.

[23] For overviews, see e.g. Paulus, n. 22 above; de Wet, n. 18 above; and J. Klabbers, A. Peters
and G. Ulfstein, *The Constitutionalization of International Law* (Oxford University
Press, 2009), in particular ch. 1, Klabbers, 'Setting the Scene' pp. 11–19.

[24] See e.g. Paulus, n. 22 above. See also, more generally, Z. Bankowski, 'Don't Think About
It? Legalism and Legality' 15 *Rechtstheorie Beiheft* 45 (1993).

[25] See e.g. J. von Bernstorff, *The Public International Law Theory of Hans Kelsen* (Cambridge
University Press, 2012); and A. O' Donoghue, 'Alfred Verdross and the Contemporary
Constitutionalization Debate' 32 *Oxford Journal of Legal Studies* 799 (2012).

countenances the notion that *all* law is predicated on a monist or singular sense of global legal order[26] – is a projection *of* law and legal authority that is generated *within* law itself. Global law so conceived, therefore, is conceptually quite separate from any institutionally generated structural hierarchy for norm generation, application and enforcement, such as the special global political framework of the UN. In empirical terms, however, the connections between structural and formal ideas of global law are close, if not necessarily harmonious, with structural developments stimulating the development of the formal approach both through the encouragement they offer and through the challenge they pose.

On the one hand, the development of the UN system has certainly offered much support for a formally expansive notion of global law. It has provided a broad platform of substantive jurisgenerative capacity and regulatory output which, in its scope of ambition, matches and helps to justify the refinement of international law as an integrated system of higher global law. The growth of the UN and the increased prominence of international law has undoubtedly also increased the cultural standing and self-confidence of the active and expanding community of international lawyers situated in and across the universities, state departments, private consultancy and litigation, and in the new institutions of international law themselves. While one manifestation of this new prominence has been a significant growth in critical scholarship in international law,[27] another product – often, indeed, one of the targets of the new critical scholarship, has been the cultivation of a fertile interface between practice, doctrine and scholarship, and so also between normative output and its ambitious systematisation.[28]

---

[26] See in particular Kelsen's 1926 Hague Lecture on the systemic relationship between domestic law and public international law: H. Kelsen, 'Les rapports de système entre le droit interne et le droit international public' 14 *Recueil des Cours* 231 (1926) at 320–31.

[27] See e.g. A. Carty, 'Critical International Law: Recent Trends in the Theory of International Law' 2 *European Journal of International Law* 66 (1991); S. Marks (ed.), *International Law on the Left: Re-examining Marxist Legacies* (Cambridge University Press, 2008); E. MacDonald, *International Law and Ethics After the Critical Challenge: Framing the Legal within the Post-foundational* (Leiden: Martinus Nijhoff, 2011); B. Bowring, 'What is Radical in Radical International Law?' in J. Klabbers (ed.), *Finnish Yearbook of International Law, Vol. XXII, 2011* (Oxford: Hart, 2013); and J.-M. Barreto, *Human Rights from a Third World Perspective: Critique, History and International Law* (Cambridge Scholars Press, 2013).

[28] See e.g. M. Koskenniemi, *The Gentle Civilizer of Nations: The Rise and Fall of International Law 1870–1960* (Cambridge University Press, 2001).

On the other hand, however, some part of the recent effort to reinforce the unity of form of international law, including a prominent report by the International Law Commission[29] – a subsidiary organ of the General Assembly – has been in defensive reaction against and response to the very same arc of expansion. For the modern growth of a UN-centred body of international law is also reflected in an exponential increase in functional specialisation, and this has ignited fears of 'fragmentation'.[30] If international law spawns too many special regimes, it may become more difficult for the centre to hold; hence the need to invest more heavily in doctrines and structures that will reassert the formal and general against the substantive and particular.

A leading exhibit in the case for a formally hierarchical species of global law is that of *jus cogens* obligations. These are peremptory norms recognised by the international community of states as a whole. Not only is no specific derogation allowed from any such norm, but the general formulation of the norm is also impervious to modification except 'by a subsequent norm of general international law having the same character'.[31] *Jus cogens* norms are a category of indefinite and progressive extension. They include the prohibition of aggression, genocide, piracy, slavery and torture, and, less certainly, the prohibition of apartheid, the right to self-determination and permanent sovereignty over natural resources. Like general rules of customary international law, *jus cogens* norms depend both upon general state practice and upon broad acceptance of the norm's status as legally binding, otherwise known as *opinio juris*. Unlike general rules of customary international law, however, persistent objection on the part of any individual state does not allow that particular state to avoid the obligation in question.

---

[29] *Fragmentation of International Law: Difficulties Arising from the Diversification and Expansion of International Law*, Report of the Study Group of the International Law Commission, finalised by Martti Koskenniemi: 13 April 2006, UN Doc. A/CN.4/L.682 pp. 1–256; and 18 July 2006, UN Doc. A/CN.4/L.702 pp. 1–25.

[30] See e.g. M. Koskenniemi, 'The Fate of Public International Law: Between Technique and Politics' 70 *Modern Law Review* 1 (2007); A. Lindroos, 'Addressing Norm Conflicts in a Fragmented Legal System: The Doctrine of *Lex Specialis*' 74 *Nordic Journal of International Law* 27 (2005); A. Lindroos and M. Mehling, 'Dispelling the Chimera of "Self-Contained Regimes": International Law and the WTO' 16 *European Journal of International Law* 857 (2006); B. Simma and D. Pulkowski, 'Of Planets and the Universe: Self-contained Regimes in International Law' 17 *European Journal of International Law* 483 (2006); and A. Fischer-Lescano and G. Teubner, 'Regime Collisions: The Vain Search for Legal Unity in the Fragmentation of Global Law' 25 *Michigan Journal of International Law* 999 (2004).

[31] Vienna Convention on the Law of Treaties, 1969, Art. 53.

The idea of *jus cogens*, although of nineteenth-century vintage, has, like the emerging structural strand of global law, achieved a far greater currency in the post-Second World War age. Responding to the various pressures of the normative expansion of international law noted above, *jus cogens* has been the subject of ever more intense debate and growing support in the community of international law scholarship. It was given textual recognition in Article 53 of the 1969 Vienna Convention on the Law of Treaties.[32] It has figured in the reasoning and pronouncements of many of the key international courts of the past century, from the pre-war Permanent Court of International Justice to the Nuremberg War Crimes Tribunal, and from the post-war International Court of Justice to the new International Criminal Court. Its force has gradually extended from the invalidation of inter-state treaties in violation of its norms to the control of all other norms of international law, in particular customary international law and the decisions of international organisations.[33]

In addition, *jus cogens* inhabits a wider legal landscape increasingly adjusted to its promise of the primacy of a general systemic frame, and so to the exhaustive and non-negotiable reach and application of certain global rules. In particular, the parallel growth of obligations *erga omnes* for matters of sufficient collective significance to be deemed to be owed to the international community as a whole rather than merely *inter partes*, complements *jus cogens* in its expansive ambition. The general principles of international law, and the body of customary international law more generally, provide other if less specific support for the idea of international law as an encompassing and self-standing global legal order rather than a mere bundle of agreements.[34] And finally, the more systematic development within contemporary international law of

---

[32] Article 53 reads in full: 'A treaty is void if, at the time of its conclusion, it conflicts with a peremptory norm of general international law. For the purposes of the present Convention, a peremptory norm of general international law is a norm accepted and recognized by the international community of States as a whole as a norm from which no derogation is permitted and which can be modified only by a subsequent norm of general international law having the same character.'

[33] See e.g. de Wet, n. 18 above, pp. 1214–15; Lowe, n. 3 above, pp. 58–60; and R. Nieto-Navia, 'International Peremptory Norms (*Jus Cogens*) and International Humanitarian Law' in L. C. Vohrah et al. (eds.), *Man's Inhumanity to Man: Essays on International Law in Honour of Antonio Cassese* (The Hague: Kluwer Law International, 2003) pp. 595–640. See also H. Ruiz Fabri, 'Enhancing the Rhetoric of *Jus Cogens*' 23 *European Journal of International Law* 1049 (2012).

[34] See the Statute of the International Court of Justice, Art. 38. See also e.g. de Wet, n. 18 above, pp.1215–18; and Lowe, n. 3 above, ch. 2.

secondary rules for the recognition, ranking and amendment of primary international law, and regarding the attribution and consequences of (state) responsibility, further reinforces the sense of a self-norming body of law detached from its national sources, and so claiming a global rather than a merely inter-*national* jurisdiction.[35]

Yet this is far from the whole story of the relationship between formalism and the development of global law. Just as the structural approach is Janus-faced in its outlook on account of its origins in international law – tending to look back to a more voluntaristic and so more restrictive understanding as well as forward to a more expansive horizon – a similar tension arises with formalism. On the one hand, as we have seen, the preoccupation with law's special form can lead to an ambitious model of integration of the global domain. The emphasis on autonomy and self-norming reflects and feeds a *mentalité* in which law, and its professional guardians, occupy not just a distinctive position but a privileged one. Global law, on this view, can be seen as the perfection of a project where not only do the particular virtues associated with a narrowly rule-bound form of law win out, but where other, and distinctly non-formal, values and commitments held by the very moral and epistemic 'community'[36] of international lawyers who affirm these formal virtues are also folded into the enterprise, in particular those associated with the expansion of customary international law and *jus cogens*. Self-norming, from this perspective, becomes as much about permission as limitation, a form of self-reference which is as conducive to professional self-authorisation as it is to disciplinary self-restraint.

On the other hand, and in some measure in reaction to this expansive approach, there is an alternative version of formalism which argues 'backwards' towards a more pared-down version of international law. Here, formalism as fidelity to rules is first and foremost about adherence to certain elementary procedures of law-ascertainment. It concerns, in particular, the identification of certain clearly verifiable, closed-ended and externally located sources of law, predominantly treaties and other international legal acts.[37] On this view, the distinctive contribution of the

---

[35] See e.g. A. Nollkaemper, 'The Power of Secondary Rules to Connect the International and National Legal Orders' in T. Broude and Y. Shany (eds.), *Multi-sourced Equivalent Norms in International Law* (Oxford: Hart, 2011) pp. 45–67.

[36] See e.g. A. Peters, 'Membership in the Global Constitutional Community' in Klabbers, Peters and Ulfstein, n. 23 above, pp. 153–262.

[37] See in particular J. d'Aspremont, *Formalism and the Sources of International Law: A Theory of the Ascertainment of Legal Rules* (Oxford University Press, 2011).

rule-following method lies in its making law a reliable instrument to give effect to source-based authority. That is to say, here the autonomy of law is in the service of a broader sense of *heteronomy*. It speaks to the capacity for faithful transmission and articulation of an external authority rather than, as with the globally expansive model, the extension and fuller realisation of law's own authority.

Of course, these different strains retain much in common. In both cases there is a preoccupation with rules and their obedience, and with the integrity of an idea of the 'international' as a single arena of legal order. In both cases, there is a resistance to law's fragmentary impulses, and to the ways in which the material diversity of the transnational legal domain frustrates any idea of methodological coherence. However, these common dispositions should not blind us to the ways in which these two formalisms differ, and so to the contentiously ambitious quality of the more global strain.

We are now in a position to summarise what the structural and formal species of the convergent approach have in common. Each works with a pyramidal vision of global arrangements; and each also with a sense of a singular legal order for a global community operating at the apex of the *pyramid*. In the structural case, the higher legal order is institutionally specific and institutionally enabled, centred on the paramount authority and political capacity of the UN. In the formal case, the higher legal order is instead conceived in more abstract terms, as a way of ranking and framing international law as a whole. In terms of the various criteria we have developed for the assessment of global law, we observe further similarities. Both structural and formal variants of the convergent approach are reasonably well grounded in practice, relatively concrete, and typically focused on global generality rather than strict universality. As regards grounding, they speak to institutional developments and doctrines that have already gained traction in the legal world, even if in matters such as doctrinal innovation associated with the system of collective security in Chapter VII of the Charter, or in the development of *jus cogens* and customary international law, their development remains an often contentious work in progress,[38] and even if the close relationship between scholarship, membership of elite legal communities and networks, and *opinio juris* entails that there is much scope for normative boot-strapping as a means of reinforcing existing practice. In this regard, indeed, it is no coincidence that the structural and formal

---

[38] See Chapter 4 below.

approaches are central to the conscious constructivism associated with the emergence of the discourse of global and international *constitutional* law, a theme to which we return below.[39] As regards concreteness, the structural and formal approaches alike speak to identifiable rules and principles of law rather than to amorphous features of law in general. And, finally, as regards generality, in both cases the concern is primarily with the pervasiveness of global coverage and with the emergence of a global community of law, albeit with states still the key object of reference, rather than with an unqualified sense of universal normativity.

3.2.3 Abstract-normative approaches

The category of abstract-normative claims is less easily pigeon-holed. It is much broader and more diverse than either structural or formal approaches, encompassing a wider range of sub-types of global law under our various defining criteria. It is an approach to global law that seeks to identify certain rules or other properties of law that are generic in nature – that speak to the ways in which we may conceive of law as a singular category rather than as a diversity of legal orders. Global law as an abstract-normative claim, therefore, embraces all invocations of certain core ideals, basic principles or broad normative templates or orientations, as means to guide, constrain or otherwise condition more local and specific elaborations of legal order. It is a category that, unlike the formal and structural approaches, does not seek to provide a higher level of authority whose legal rules or acts outrank and so take priority over lower-level rules in the case of conflict, but neither does it claim to provide its own comprehensive global order. Rather, it seeks to address, inform and influence the broad content or conditions of application of the variety of legal orders situated across the globe.

Abstract-normative versions of global law, therefore, are necessarily abstract inasmuch as they must operate at a level that is detached from the detail of any particular jurisdiction. They excavate the doctrinal topsoil of law in search of a more profound normative register. Yet abstract-normative approaches nevertheless remain, in different ways, closely associated with the rules of positive law. At one end of the spectrum, indeed, abstract-normative approaches help supply what we might call an architecture of 'layered positivity', with the global layer itself deemed to possess the form and status of a positive law, however

[39] See section 3.3.1 below.

generally pitched, that is superimposed upon more concrete local forms of positive law.[40] However, elsewhere on the spectrum we find many other abstract-normative approaches that cannot be understood, or at least cannot easily be understood, in such positive terms. They operate at a level of normative generalisation, or moral idealisation, and typically some combination of the two, that resists characterisation as discrete positive law. Yet their architectural perspective remains one that acknowledges, embraces and informs positive law – one we might describe as 'framed positivity'. Such approaches, therefore, retain normative significance. They offer themselves as framing devices which, although themselves not positive law, nevertheless supply a second-order framework and lens through which various rules or bodies of positive law may be viewed, interpreted and refined.[41]

3.2.3.1 Layered positivity: the case of human rights

The discourse of human rights supplies the most obvious and appropriate candidate for broadly encompassing claims of legality at the global level involving a pattern of 'layered positivity'. Yet it is a candidature that is also both externally challenged and internally conflicted. The mix of prominence and underlying contentiousness is due to a combination of factors.

In the first place, in the contemporary age there is significant overlap and a clear symbiosis between the dominant legal and politico-ethical registers of human rights, but also an element of tension in the relationship between them. On the one hand, there stands the formidable and self-reinforcing post-war legal framework of rights proclamation and protection initially promoted by the United Nations Charter and by the subsequent Universal Declaration of Human Rights of 1948. Here, indeed, we observe a broader synergy between the structural achievement of international law in opening up a global horizon and the particular abstract-normative vision of human rights law.[42] The new

---

[40] One writer has described this process as one of 'dual positivization', with specific reference to the way in which human rights standards within national law are reflected and reinforced in international treaties. See G. L. Neuman, 'Human Rights and Constitutional Rights: Harmony and Dissonance' 55 *Stanford Law Review* 1863 (2003) at 1864.

[41] Even in this limiting case, therefore, the 'double normativity' we identified as a general characteristic of global law is preserved. See further Chapter 1.2.3 above and Chapter 5.2.4 below.

[42] See section 3.2.1 above.

institutionally enabled and legally coded human rights regime ranges from the planetary level of the nine 'core' international treaties,[43] their various monitoring and decision-making bodies and the specialised UN bodies such as the Human Rights Council and the system of Special Rapporteurs, through the regional level and its various continental human rights instruments and courts, to the national level and the rapid post-war spread of constitutional entrenchment and review of human rights.[44]

On the other hand, the language of human rights also has a clear and wide resonance in contemporary ethical discourse. In part, this connects to the deeper and long-standing political culture of Western modernity more generally. Reaching an early peak in the path-breaking constitutional settlements of the late eighteenth century, an unprecedented Enlightenment emphasis upon persons, individually and collectively, as authors of their own world and as its key centres of morality, dovetailed with a gradual movement from a natural rights tradition with strong religious foundations to the promulgation of Bills of Rights as catalogues of positive entitlement.[45] In part, however, the *international* prominence of the rights agenda also connects to the particular circumstances of 1945; to the Holocaust and to other examples, also peculiarly modern, of the brutality of states empowered by a sense of uncensored collective authorship and by the sophistication of new technologies of violence and oppression.[46] In this regard, the post-war international human rights regime is as much about dealing with the new pathologies of modernity – with 'creating fire walls against barbarism'[47] – as it is with the long maturing of its civilising side.

---

[43] The 'core' human rights instruments are listed on the website of the Office of the High Commissioner for Human Rights: www.ohchr.org/EN/ProfessionalInterest/Pages/CoreInstruments.aspx.

[44] P. Alston and R. Goodman, *International Human Rights* (Oxford University Press, 2012) chs. 8–12. See also A. Stone Sweet, 'A Cosmopolitan Legal Order: Constitutional Pluralism and Rights Adjudication in Europe' 1 *Global Constitutionalism* 53 (2012).

[45] See e.g. J. Waldron, 'Introduction. Natural Rights in the 17th, 18th and 19th Centuries' in J. Waldron (ed.), *'Nonsense upon Stilts': Bentham, Burke and Marx on the Rights of Man* (London: Routledge, 2009) pp. 1–25; A. Pagden, *The Enlightenment: And Why it Still Matters* (Oxford University Press, 2013).

[46] See e.g. E. J. Hobsbawm, *Age of Extremes: The Short Twentieth Century, 1914–1991* (London: Michael Joseph, 1994).

[47] M. Ignatieff, *Human Rights as Politics and Idolatry* (Princeton University Press, 2003) p. 5. See also M. A. Glendon, *A World Made New: Eleanor Roosevelt and the Universal Declaration of Human Rights* (New York: Random House, 2001).

There is evidently some strain between these two parts of the story of the journey of human rights to their contemporary prominence, with one stressing the centuries-long gestation of ethical consensus, only loosely and unevenly coupled with secular legal development, and the other downplaying the importance of this moral background and instead prioritising the seismic political events of the mid- and late twentieth century as supplying the immediate geopolitical momentum and a direct legal-institutional catalyst.[48] But they can also be understood as in some measure mutually supportive.[49] Each can be seen as contributing to a deep-seated cultural tendency, often requiring reassertion against powerful counter-tendencies, to promote and defend the individual as a rights-bearer – a tendency that has both fed the development of the multi-level global legal regime, and is further reinforced by the spread of that regime.[50]

A second factor contributing to the human rights agenda being both of central significance to legal globalisation and a matter of deep and continuing political controversy has to do with the borderless ambition of that agenda. As one aspect of its association with the culture of political modernity, the language of human rights – legal and moral – is presumptively universal, and so global, in its personal scope. Its claims are based upon the entitlement of *all* humans – the new self-authorising subjects of the modern world – to be treated as equals in respect of certain fundamental features of their autonomy and well-being, and to be so just in virtue of their common humanity. It follows that human rights law and its accompanying moral discourse, with their foundations at the very centre of the reconstituted post-war international order, have supplied a key impetus for the development *within* international law and

---

[48] Samuel Moyn dates the origins of the international human rights movement even later, namely in the 1970s: see S. Moyn, *The Last Utopia: Human Rights in History* (Cambridge, MA: Harvard University Press, 2010).

[49] See e.g. P. Alston, 'Does the Past Matter? On the Origins of Human Rights' 126 *Harvard Law Review* 2043 (2013), in which he is critical of both the discontinuity thesis of Moyn and others (at 2066) and the linear progressive thesis of such as Jenny Martinez (at 2063): see J. Martinez, *The Slave Trade and the Origins of International Human Rights Law* (Oxford University Press, 2012). He argues persuasively (at 2078) that 'the interpretations offered by Martinez and Moyn are unhelpful mirror images of one another. Martinez exaggerates the continuities involved in two centuries of history, while Moyn exaggerates the discontinuities.'

[50] On the continuing vital role of states as incubators of the legal protection of human rights, even in the post-1945 era, see e.g. A. Vincent, *The Politics of Human Rights* (Oxford University Press, 2010). Vincent describes citizen rights as 'mentors' of international human rights.

among international lawyers of an approach that no longer treats states as the ultimate international legal subjects, as in the long-standing conventional understanding of the modern discipline, but which increasingly looks instead to individuals.[51]

Yet the high transnational profile of the law and moral rhetoric of human rights, and its key role in the justification of the extended horizons of modern international law, are also a source of much disagreement and the cause of much scepticism. The post-war human rights project has been much criticised on account of its supposed Western bias and for its pivotal role in sustaining the hegemony of the Global North within international law more generally. Its proclaimed universalism is viewed in many circles as a cover for the generalisation of a particular Eurocentric tradition favouring individual over community, entitlement over obligation, and a conception of the good life that privileges the negative freedom of person and property from public power over the positive freedom to share and enjoy resources on a more equitable basis.[52]

Where this does not result in the general disavowal of the human rights approach,[53] it instead gives rise to internal critique, and to a third key feature of contemporary human rights discourse: namely, an emphasis upon the flexible remit of human rights. For if human rights are in principle concerned with equal entitlement to whatever catalogue of goods is considered basic to our common humanity, then the indeterminacy and contestability of that catalogue means that the language of human rights contains an in-built tendency to expansion. In fact, the very idea of 'second' generation (social) and 'third' generation (collective) rights as a supplement to the Western tradition of 'first' generation negative rights emphasised in the initial phase of the internationalisation of rights (and the very fact that the language of rights 'generations' has become dated!) suggests a progressive dynamic in which different categories of rights, championed by different interests

---

[51] For an influential early statement of the post-war paradigm shift, see e.g. H. Lauterpacht, *International Law and Human Rights* (New York: Praeger, 1950); see also M. Koskenniemi, 'Lauterpacht: The Victorian Tradition in International Law' 2 *European Journal of International Law* 215 (1997).

[52] See e.g. U. Baxi, *The Future of Human Rights*, 2nd edn (Oxford University Press, 2006); W. Twining, *General Jurisprudence: Understanding Law from a Global Perspective* (Cambridge University Press, 2009) ch. 9; J. R. Bauer and D. A. Bell (eds.), *The East Asian Challenge to Human Rights* (Cambridge University Press, 1999) p. 23; and A. Sen, 'Elements of a Theory of Human Rights' 32 *Philosophy and Public Affairs* 315 (2004).

[53] See e.g. Baxi, n. 52 above.

and compatible with different overall frameworks of political morality, are self-consciously linked. Ever since the Vienna Declaration adopted at the World Conference on Human Rights in Vienna in 1993, indeed, the character of human rights not only as universal, but also as 'indivisible, interdependent and interrelated' has been routinely stressed in the discourse of transnational human rights.[54] The narrative of subject-matter open-endedness, therefore, by highlighting the transformative possibilities of human rights discourse, stands as an important conse-quence and reinforcing cause of an equally open-ended inclusiveness of rights-holding populations. In this way ideas of 'global' personal jurisdiction and 'global' comprehensiveness of scope – or material jurisdiction – serve to reinforce each other.[55]

If we consider these factors in the round – the incomplete comple-mentarity of the legal and moral languages of human rights, presumptive universality of application and open-endedness of subject matter, then the expansionist dynamic within the human rights agenda becomes evident. Yet how this expansionism manifests itself today in terms of a self-conscious discourse of human rights *qua* global law is quite diverse, and far from uncontentious, reflecting the underlying tension between different narratives of origin discussed above.

One approach returns to the post-war Universal Declaration as the key point of departure. It focuses on its far-reaching foundational commitment, and tends to be simultaneously critical and aspirational.[56] It tells a story of partial and uneven success, of the ebb and flow of political support and institutional commitment to human rights protec-tion over the lifetime of the Declaration. It emphasises the importance of the Declaration as an earnest of continuing vigilance in the face of mass human rights abuses and as a point of departure for engagement with new areas of human rights and with the voices of new human rights claimants, but also as a reminder of shortfall in both of these enterprises. Tellingly illustrative of the strategies of positivisation that the human

[54] See e.g. C. Norchi, 'Human Rights: A Global Common Interest' in J. E. Krasno (ed.), *The United Nations: Confronting the Challenges of a Global Society* (Boulder, CO: Lynne Rienner, 2004) p. 87.
[55] See e.g. N. Walker, 'Universalism and Particularism in Human Rights' in C. Holder and D. Reidy (eds.), *Human Rights: The Hard Questions* (Cambridge University Press, 2013) pp. 39–58.
[56] J. von Bernstorff, 'The Changing Fortunes of the Universal Declaration of Human Rights: Genesis and Symbolic Dimensions of the Turn to Rights in International Law' 19 *European Journal of International Law* 903 (2008).

rights agenda attracts, the Declaration, in this approach, also provides the focal point of an ongoing constructivist effort of self-norming, with many of its supporters seeking to elevate its founding status from rhetorical to doctrinal – from mere exhortation to an established part of customary international law.[57]

Another increasingly influential strand involves a somewhat different, in some ways opposing emphasis. Rather than continuing to treat the Declaration moment as axiomatic while cautioning against the exaggerated claims and premature triumphalism of post-1945 human rights rhetoric, this other approach returns to the deeper historical roots to tell a more continuous tale, but one that has also achieved transformative momentum in the contemporary era. It stresses how these deeper roots supplied a key resource in nurturing recent growth, and exposes what might be seen as the false modesty of global human rights in failing to give full acknowledgment to this development. In particular, it highlights what it takes to be an under-acknowledged dimension of the legal import and impact of the general turn to rights, stressing the extent to which a 'global model'[58] of human rights has already infiltrated judicial and wider juristic consciousness and altered the basic coding of many of the world's national and transnational legal systems.

The nub of this argument is that the way in which human rights discourse has unfolded over time has involved a complex trade-off between depth and breadth. The dominant philosophy of fundamental rights already well established at the point of emergence of the post-war system, as we have noted, insisted upon the limited range and special importance of rights, and upon their imposition of primarily negative obligations upon states. That dominant approach in both international and constitutional law also tended to view the currency of rights as restricted to relations between individuals and governments, and to consider rights to be possessed of such normative force that they might only be outweighed under exceptional and narrowly delimited

---

[57] See e.g. J. P. Humphrey, 'The Universal Declaration of Human Rights: Its History, Impact and Juridical Character' in B. G. Ramcharan (ed.), *Human Rights: Thirty Years After the Universal Declaration* (The Hague: Martinus Nijhoff, 1979) pp. 2l, 37; L. Sohn, 'The Human Rights Law of the Charter' 12 *Texas International Law Journal* 129 (1977) at 133; M. S. McDougal, H. Lasswell and I. Chen, *Human Rights and World Public Order: The Basic Policies of an International Law of Human Dignity* (New Haven, CT: Yale University Press, 1980) pp. 273–4, 325–7; A. D'Amato, *International Law: Process and Prospect* (Dobbs Ferry, NY: Transnational Publishers, 1986) pp. 123–47.

[58] See in particular K. Möller, *The Global Model of Constitutional Rights* (Oxford University Press, 2012).

circumstances. Today, an argument can be made that each of these conditions no longer holds, and that the background receptiveness of the basic legal grammar of the modern age to rights has facilitated their significant reshaping. Rights, as we have seen, have an increasingly broad scope, now no longer committed to a restricted core of freedom-protecting interests but just as concerned with social well-being, and partly because of this they are more likely to impose positive obligations upon states. In addition, in this new broader scheme of rights and responsibilities, private parties have increasingly joined states as those with a duty to respect the rights of others under the horizontal effect doctrine. The cumulative effect of all of these trends is to deprive rights of their distinctive evangelical tone and special normative force vis-à-vis other types of law. Instead, rights become a pervasive feature of law, their relations *inter se* dependent upon burgeoning doctrines of balancing and proportionality rather than a mechanical expression of priority.[59] On this view, rights are gradually becoming a key global index of legally recognised relations, a broad plateau rather than a narrow peak.

3.2.3.2 Framed positivity

Those claims of global law falling under the banner of 'framed positivity' perform an organising and influencing function at an even more abstract level of normativity than that conveyed by the various rights-based global frameworks. Unlike rights, these cannot easily be reduced to a discrete set of general precepts of positive law. These non-positive framing devices are nevertheless an important part of our inquiry into the distinctiveness of global law for two reasons. First, the legal scholar-analyst, such an important figure in the development of global law in general, is particularly to the fore in their construction; and secondly, the constructions themselves involve some of the most explicit and fully rounded considerations of what is distinctively 'global' about the new approach.

One prominent example of this kind of 'framed positivity' is found in the work of Rafael Domingo. In its careful treatment of the genealogy of contemporary arrangements, moreover, his perspective augments our

[59] *Ibid.*, chs. 5–7. Möller draws critically on the philosophical work of Robert Alexy, a significant background influence for much contemporary advocacy of proportionality and balancing: see in particular R. Alexy, *A Theory of Constitutional Rights* (Oxford University Press, 2002); see also A. Stone Sweet and J. Matthews, 'Proportionality, Balancing and Global Constitutionalism' 47 *Columbia Journal of Transnational Law* 72 (2008–9).

understanding of the history of thinking about law in global perspective
and about what might be distinctive about the contemporary phase.
What Domingo explicitly labels 'the new global law'[60] resembles many
of the new human rights-centred approaches in treating, not the state,
but the individual in her full range of social ties and relations, as the
ultimate subject of the new legal order. His approach also claims to share
with modern international law more generally certain key background
principles considered essential to any and all forms of law, namely
justice, reasonableness and coercion. According to Domingo, however,
where global law as a gradually emergent category clearly distinguishes
itself from the modern tradition of international law is in its endorsement of the further umbrella principles of universality, solidarity,
subsidiarity and horizontality. These global principles are counterposed
to what Domingo styles as the more narrowly internationalist principles
of totality, individuality, centralism and verticality.[61]

In developing his vision Domingo reminds us that the idea of global
legal community which underpins his approach has a long pedigree. Just
as significantly, however, he calls our attention to the highly idealistic
quality of much of this heritage of thought. The notion of mankind
joined in harmonious order beyond particular communities of interest
or attachment was a vision shared by world-views as diverse as Stoic
cosmopolitanism, the Christian ideal of a world united by charity,
various more or less religiously grounded conceptions of natural law,
and the Kantian project of world peace. However, these visions possessed
a literally utopian quality – in 'no place' fully realised yet tending to draw
inspiration from very particular places and centres of knowledge and
belief and their very limited imagination of the global compass of
civilisations. In sum, as anticipated in our opening discussion of global
law's key terms, earlier forms of global law tended, at least rhetorically, to
rely upon 'top-down' metaphysical forms of universalism rather than
projects with any commitment to or prospect of global-in-general
coverage.[62]

In practice, the earlier understandings of transnational law that did
succeed in gaining traction as positive law tended to be of a quite different order. They were more modest in character, responding as they did

[60] R. Domingo, *The New Global Law* (Cambridge University Press, 2010). See also
R. Domingo, 'Gaius, Vattel, and the New Global Law Paradigm' 22 *European Journal
of International Law* 627 (2011).
[61] Domingo, *The New Global Law*, n. 60 above, pp. 157–8.   [62] See Chapter 1.2.3.2 above.

to key practical imperatives of their age. The *jus gentium*, with its roots in the need to regulate the affairs of non-citizens to whom the *jus civile* could not apply, met the requirements of Rome's territorial empire. Modern state-centred international law originated in, and has long continued to reflect, the balance of interests of the dominant European powers, each with their overseas empires. Yet the more expansive understanding of global law, which for earlier pre-modern and modern writers was no more than an exalted aspiration, has, according to Domingo, become the new practical imperative of the age of global interdependence. For him, the new law of global association to which he subscribes, with its novel catalogue of umbrella principles, is as much a child of its time as its more limited predecessors. It supplies the appropriate – and in his view now clearly emergent – response to the pathologies of vulnerable interdependence witnessed in successive World Wars and throughout the Cold War, 9/11 and countless other globally ramified insecurities of the contemporary age.[63]

This last point indicates an important sense in which Domingo's approach is characteristic of the new global law more generally. For all that his vision is highly abstract in specification and panoramic in scope, by insisting that global law's time is ripe because of objective developments in global political circumstances it nevertheless makes a claim that goes beyond pure ambition. It seeks – to recall another of our key terms – to make a 'practical' contribution to the understanding of global law *as it is*, in however emergent and under-realised a form, rather than simply how it might and should become. And so it adds to the sense of global law as an active project in law-making, and of its commentators as participants in that active project. It might be objected that, just on account of his efforts to treat global law as a live influence on doctrine rather than a matter of normative speculation, Domingo is drawn to make implausibly optimistic assumptions about the suitability of ambient conditions and the degree of relevant normative momentum. Yet that does not take away from the seriousness with which he treats his own involvement as an engaged rather than a detached exercise.

If Domingo stresses the distinctiveness and the transformative effect of the circumstances of contemporary global legal development, another influential recent approach that shares much of his vision of horizontal global coherence, and much of his commitment to the development of a historical narrative able to present global law in a practical light, instead

---

[63] Domingo, *The New Global Law*, n. 60 above, ch. 4.

stresses continuity over the longer stretch of political modernity. According to the so-called 'cosmopolitan constitutionalism' of Mattias Kumm, our modernist past, far from being an outmoded frame of reference, remains key to the future.[64] The philosophical kernel of public law – the law governing matters of general public concern and regulating those institutions charged with representing the public interest – is claimed not to have altered since the advent of constitutionalism through the medium of the maturing state system of late eighteenth-century Europe and America. Crucially, however, what, for Kumm, is constitutionally basic, and basically unaltered, is not a matter of visible institutional architecture, but the underlying normative principles and the template of social relations that nurtures these normative principles. More specifically, akin to the rights-centred approach considered above, these normative principles flow out of a modern vision of political society as a collective self-construct rather than, as in the pre-modern world, the reflection of or response to an independently given order of things. In this understanding of how the social world is enacted, persons are no longer in thrall to a sense of fixed and pre-given order and status. They are instead now both self-conceived and other-conceiving as free and equal individuals, acting together to develop and implement their own conception of the common interest or public good. It is in recognition and support of this self-corroborating dynamic of generalised equal freedom, says Kumm, that we generate a set of universal commitments to principles such as legality, subsidiarity, adequate participation and accountability, public reason and rights-protection.[65]

Against this larger canvas, he argues, the shape and detail of the state-centred system of the modern age assumes a more modest significance than is often appreciated within legal thought. It is exposed as but one historically contingent blueprint for giving general effect to the framing principles, rather than an exclusive, dominant or even optimal regulatory scheme. Instead, under conditions of intensifying globalisation, the sense – already present but understated within the framework of formally identical but mutually exclusive sovereignties – that quite different constitutional arrangements can and should share a common cosmopolitan ethic, becomes more

---

[64] See e.g. M. Kumm, 'The Cosmopolitan Turn in Constitutionalism: On the Relationship between Constitutionalism in and beyond the State' in Dunoff and Trachtman, *Ruling the World?*, n. 22 above, pp. 258–325. For a similar cosmopolitan perspective, see Stone Sweet, n. 43 above.

[65] Kumm, n. 64 above, at pp. 289–305.

palpable. Different polities must be attuned to the fact that they share, and indeed overlap, the same global space, and so must subscribe to the same basic public standards both as common terms of co-existence and as threshold conditions of internal political morality. They all, in other words, have equal cause and obligation to commit to Kumm's basic universal principles, with the state now but one of various interdependent players on a wider stage. As free and equal persons operating under certain constraints of interest, information, geography and affinity, we continue to respect particular contexts of decision-making and public-interest formation, and the principles of subsidiarity, participation and accountability in particular recognise this. However, as free and equal persons we are also categorically committed to acknowledgment of the freedom and equality of all others, and so to the universalisability of our political condition and of the rights associated with that condition. In this way, we can reconcile our attachment to particular polities and sites of authority with a belief in a common normative framework whose baseline guarantees of freedom and equality inform the terms of our various particular manifestations of public authority.

In the final analysis, then, for Kumm, the division of the world into particular polities and particular systems of positive law remains inevitable. Yet the particular form such division takes is not so. Rather, the institutional architecture is sensitive to shifts in the underlying circuits of social and economic power. Yet the strong universalist pole of the resiliently modernist constitutional commitment implies that the particular pedigree of any constitutional edifice – including any democratic deficiencies of that pedigree – is less important than subscription to those very ideals and principles of freedom and equality that both underpin democratic pedigree and would provide its 'natural' rights-coded complement.[66]

At an even more general level of abstraction we encounter within this sub-category of 'framed positivity' a final series of thinkers for whom global law is, so to speak, a matter of depth rather than elevation. In terms of the visual imaging of global law, the appropriate metaphor for

---

[66] *Ibid.* See also M. Kumm, 'The Best of Times and the Worst of Times: Between Constitutional Triumphalism and Nostalgia' in P. Dobner and M. Loughlin (eds.), *The Twilight of Constitutionalism?* (Oxford University Press, 2010) pp. 201–19. A somewhat similar though more schematic and arguably more state-centric attempt to link domestic and international law within an integrated cosmopolitan vision is set out in a post-humously published work of Ronald Dworkin: see R. Dworkin, 'A New Philosophy for International Law' 41 *Philosophy and Public Affairs* 2 (2013).

this latter breed of abstract-normative global law is that of the *vessel* – embracing and containing from below – as opposed to the *umbrella* of human rights or general cosmopolitan principle, providing key protection and direction from above.[67] Rather than through rarefied pre-positive or proto-positive principles or axioms, global law in this perspective instead operates upon specific laws and legal order, in the phrase of Kaarlo Tuori, as a form of rudimentary 'deep structure'.[68] The idea here is of a kind of general legal grid that underlies and allows us to identify common themes between different legal orders, and thereby understand the basis for familiarity, and indeed mobility, between these orders. Klaus Günther, for example, has mooted 'a universal code of legality'[69] that transcends jurisdictional borders. The code comprises a basic set of co-ordinates, or building blocks, which can be developed and arranged differently in different legal orders. In Günther's scheme, these include the very idea of legal subjectivity and the broad categories in terms of which relations between legal subjects are constructed – rights, duties, permissions, obligations and the like. The code also embraces key distinctions such as strict liability versus fault-based liability, and voluntary versus involuntary obligations, as well as more operationally focused but still general concepts and principles such as those guiding the burden of proof, requiring a fair hearing and neutral adjudication, and demanding predictability of liability and sanction.

The very idea of the Rule of Law supplies another candidate for global law *qua* deep structure. Indeed, literally understood, the Rule of Law supplies *the* most basic plane on which a conception of law as a global accomplishment is capable of development. It does so on account of its double claim, first, as to the fundamental authority of law (the law 'Rules'),[70] and, secondly, about the general and singular quality of 'the law' thus authoritatively conceived (the rule of 'Law'). Yet, notwithstanding the pervasive spread of Rule of Law thinking and its rhetorical centrality to many contemporary projects of planned legal

---

[67] See Fig. 4.1, 'Seven images representing conceptions of global law', in Chapter 4.1 below.

[68] K. Tuori, Ratio *and* Voluntas: *The Tension between Reason and Will in Law* (Farnham: Ashgate, 2011) p. 313. Tuori sometimes uses the term 'deep culture' to convey the same meaning: see e.g. pp. 40–4.

[69] K. Günther, 'Legal Pluralism or Uniform Concept of Law? Globalisation as a Problem of Legal Theory' 5 *NoFo – Journal of Extreme Legal Positivism* 5 (2008).

[70] See e.g. J. Waldron, 'Is the Rule of Law an Essentially Contested Concept (in Florida)?' 21 *Law and Philosophy* 137 (2002).

'export',[71] reservations about the various emphases that this thinking displays challenge its candidature as a viable species of global law. The Rule of Law ideal, in one of its most familiar and readily circulated expressions, may be seen as too 'thin' and permissive or, in another, as too skewed in favour of one particular kind of political ethic to be equipped to perform a global role. A first strand stresses the role of law as a fundamental ordering device, a basic measure of social and political conduct. And while the Rule of Law so conceived is often claimed to supply certain general benefits in terms of certainty, predictability and security, the familiar counter-argument holds that this tends both to overstate the regularity of the legal form and to exaggerate the capacity of such formal means to guard against substantively undesirable ends. A second strand, often found in combination with the first, emphasises the Rule of Law as the converse of the arbitrary 'rule of man', and this often translates into an important but narrow focus on reining in government; important in its identification of a key battleground of law's engagement with the political realm, but narrow both in its concentration on the institution of the state rather than corporate and other private spheres of influence and in its negative emphasis upon state power as something that law should primarily be concerned to limit and contain rather than to enable and release.[72]

There is a less common but more rounded understanding of the Rule of Law implicit in a number of recent conceptions of global law. These focus on the development of a particular ethical attitude associated with legality. That attitude emphasises balance and equilibrium, embracing and reconciling the very diversity of legal forms and variety of legal functions that feeds the criticism of the more conventional understandings of the Rule of Law as unduly narrow. The stress is upon a duality that repeats across a number of different registers of legal attention. One basis for this can be found in Jürgen Habermas's influential thesis about

---

[71] For critical treatment of the export of the Rule of Law as a Western-dominated form of political and commercial practice, see S. Humphreys, *Theatre of the Rule of Law: Transnational Legal Intervention in Theory and Practice* (Cambridge University Press, 2012); and R. Kleinfeld and K. Nicolaidis, 'Can a Post-Colonial Power Export the Rule of Law? Elements of a General Framework' in G. Palombella and N. Walker (eds.), *Relocating the Rule of Law* (Oxford: Hart, 2009) pp. 139–69. On the centrality and versatile applications of Rule of Law discourse within the human rights and security portfolios of the United Nations, see www.un.org/en/ruleoflaw/.

[72] See e.g. B. Z. Tamanaha, *On the Rule of Law: History, Politics, Theory* (Cambridge University Press, 2005).

the symbiosis of public and private autonomy.[73] On this view, a vibrant, democratically responsive public sphere supplies the political culture in which individual rights are more likely to be fostered and protected, just as the protection of individual rights secures the basis for a healthy democratic politics.

Other versions of the duality thesis place less stress on the productive relationship of public and private domains under the Rule of Law and more on the enduring necessity of their co-existence. Gianluigi Palombella, for example, argues that the constitutional distinction between rights and legislation, understood in terms akin to Habermas as providing for the protection of private entitlement and the deliberated articulation of the public interest respectively, maps onto the deeper historical distinction between *jurisdictio* and *gubernaculum*.[74] The former involves the establishment of general legal boundaries of acceptable conduct, while the latter refers to the positive action of government command. *Jurisdictio* alerts us to the role of the state or other political authority as umpire, establishing and policing the institutions of private law. *Gubernaculum* focuses on the state or other political authority as an interested agent of the collective will. In turn, these constitutional and institutional distinctions map onto a wider philosophical distinction between the Right and the Good – the former a universal yardstick of just entitlement and responsibility and the latter a particular expression of the common welfare. Other terms can be added to this set of oppositional pairs – Justice and Sovereignty, *ratio* and *voluntas* etc. – but the basic insight is that while positive law in all of its variants is deeply implicated on both sides of the divide, the Rule of Law conceived of as an integrative achievement is about acknowledging and maintaining an equilibrium that allows each desideratum to prosper, and permits all the virtues of law to be placed in balance.

We shall have more to say about these various abstract-normative approaches – layering as well as framing, umbrella as well as vessel – in later chapters. For now, it is worth making two brief points about them as a set. First, it is remarkable how such diverse approaches succeed in

---

[73] See e.g. J. Habermas, 'Constitutional Democracy: A Paradoxical Union of Contradictory Principles?' 29 *Political Theory* 766 (2001).

[74] See e.g. G. Palombella, *È possibile una legalità globale?* (Bologna: Il Mulino, 2012); and G. Palombella, 'The Rule of Law and its Core' in Palombella and Walker, n. 71 above, pp. 17–42.

converging upon a global horizon. Whether the institutional backdrop is international human rights or the modern state tradition in constitutional law, and whether the philosophical backdrop is Kantian cosmopolitanism, Christian ethics and natural law, or Habermasian discourse theory, these very different materials prove to be equally adaptable, sometimes explicitly but always implicitly, to an idea of an unbounded global jurisdiction. Certainly, the sense that there is more to Law than the aggregation of laws, and that there is something in the deeper layering of positive legality or in the pre-positive framing of positive legality that is also and already quintessentially legal, has always been present as a current of legal thought. Yet this kind of universalistic approach typically remained both an idealised vision and one that was associated with a bounded sense of law's community – whether limited to empire, or to Christendom, or to the 'civilised' nations.[75] Only in contemporary conditions, with the compression of time and space we associate with globalisation[76] and the concomitant stretching of law's known horizon, does this kind of universalistic approach come to be associated with the idea and the incipient practice of a global-in-general warrant.

Secondly, in pursuing their various lines of argument, the abstract-normative approaches also have in common with each other, and, indeed, with the formal approaches we discussed earlier, an emphasis on the significance of law's own historical resources. The institutional reference or philosophical inspiration may markedly differ, as may the form and content of global coverage, but in each approach the new law claims to run deeper than a mere reaction to new circumstances. Rather than discontinue older lines of legal thought, the new approaches purport to develop them. The focus may be on the entirety of the modern age, as in Kumm's insistence on the continuity of cosmopolitan thought across the long epoch of modernity. Or it may claim even more venerable roots, as in Günther's claim for the classical pedigree of law's universal code, or Tuori's assertion that 'deep structure' is part of the *longue durée* of law, supplying a common geological core for successive surface cultures.[77]

Often too, in these narratives of historical depth, there is an emphasis on specific legal disciplinary discourses as carriers of a particular way of legal thinking and acting. By a disciplinary discourse we mean a

---

[75] See Domingo, *The New Global Law*, n. 60 above, chs. 1–3.

[76] See e.g. A. Giddens, *The Consequences of Modernity* (Stanford University Press, 1990); and see Chapter 1.2.3 above.

[77] See Günther, n. 69 above; and Tuori, n. 68 above, ch. 1.

categorisation of legal doctrine and practice in terms of its amenability to a specific type of understanding and treatment – whether on account of its particular subject matter, function, institutional context, style of reasoning or (usually) some combination of these – thereby constituting a distinct branch of law's practical reason. Legal disciplinary discourses, typically shaped in the interaction of learning and use, thus offer a flexible continuity. On the one hand, they possess a resilience which permits the conscious linkage of different historical phases of legal development. On the other, they supply a point of reference for the reflexive adaptation of certain currents of legal thought to new circumstances. We see this, for example, in the close attention paid in the new literature on global law to the versatile past of the idea of *jus gentium*,[78] and also to renewed excavations of the theme of *jus commune* or common law,[79] and of *jus publicum* or public law,[80] all of which have figured in different ways in the elaboration of various umbrella and vessel versions of the abstract-normative approach.[81] Through these and other disciplinary vehicles to be considered below, the new global law in its more explicitly scholarly variants pays homage to a complex history of learning and doctrinal development.

3.3   The catalogue of global law II: historical-discursive approaches

Historical-discursive approaches take the task of re-engagement with extant legal disciplines a stage further. They involve the explicit adaptation of older templates of state law to the global domain, in particular in

---

[78] J. Waldron, 'Foreign Law and the Modern *Ius Gentium*' 119 *Harvard Law Review* 129 (2005); and J. Waldron, *'Partly Laws Common to All Mankind': Foreign Law in American Courts* (New Haven, CT: Yale University Press, 2012) chs. 3–5.

[79] H. P. Glenn, *On Common Laws* (Oxford University Press, 2007).

[80] See e.g. A. von Bogdandy and J. Bast (eds.), *Principles of European Constitutional Law*, rev. edn (Oxford: Hart, 2010); M. Loughlin, *Foundations of Public Law* (Oxford University Press, 2010).

[81] This is perhaps most obviously true of the human rights umbrella, the many sponsors of which invoke a wide range of disciplinary sources. But it can also be found, for example, in the work of Kumm, who draws explicitly on the public law tradition (see e.g. M. Kumm, 'How does European Union Law Fit into the World of Public Law? *Costa*, *Kadi* and Three Models of Public Law' in J. Neyer and A. Wiener (eds.), *Political Theory of the European Union* (Oxford University Press, 2011) pp. 111–38), or in the deep and wide-ranging archaeological excavations of Tuori (n. 68 above) and Günther (n. 69 above).

the form of Global Administrative Law[82] or global constitutionalism,[83] or, to take an example of double adaptation of an older discourse, the constitutionalisation of international law.[84] Here, therefore, the disciplinary scheme offers something more than a transmission belt through which to channel the resources for developing a new platform of global law, as in the examples given above. Rather, suitably remodelled, the disciplinary scheme itself supplies the new platform.

These historical-discursive approaches are offered as a distinct subset of global law. The key image here is not of a pyramid, or an umbrella, or a vessel, but of a *thread* running through the course of legal history and weaving itself into the broader transnational pattern of contemporary law. Yet it would be a mistake to understand the historical-discursive approaches in discrete terms. It is their historical depth that sets them apart, but in their emergent global manifestation they overlap to a considerable extent with the various other species types. In so doing, they are restricted neither to attempts to check and overcome difference through mechanisms of normative convergence nor to the mere tracking and managing of divergence. Instead, they supply protean labels, sufficiently open-ended to embrace a wide range of positions along the spectrum of species types. Depending on what is adopted, and how it is adapted, these approaches may be more or less hierarchical and more or less imposing of a singular approach. This helps account both for the extent of their appeal to some, and for the ambivalence or scepticism with which they are received by others. Indeed, in their versatility, and in the range of reactions they produce, this set of approaches provides the paradigm case of the new global law's complex relationship to the themes of convergence and divergence. After our discussion of 'framed positivity' under the abstract-normative approach, it also offers a further and uniquely vivid study in miniature of the role of the wider scholarly community in influencing and receiving ideas of global law.

3.3.1   Global constitutionalism and the constitutionalisation of international law

Global constitutionalism and its satellite, the constitutionalisation of international law, boast a particularly wide range of applications, and it

---

[82] See, for example, the signature article by B. Kingsbury, N. Krisch and R. B. Stewart, 'The Emergence of Global Administrative Law' 68 *Law and Contemporary Problems* 15 (2005).

[83] See, for example, the journal *Global Constitutionalism*, first published in 2012.

[84] De Wet, n. 18 above.

is with these that we begin. Three cross-cutting distinctions frame the field of global constitutionalism – all of them deeply embedded in the history of constitutional thought – and provide the key to its capacity to provide such diverse images of global law, and to its availability as a common currency of debate between quite different positions. A fourth and equally venerable distinction, as we shall see, introduces a fault-line that accounts for a deeper scepticism about the project of global constitutionalism as a whole, and which helps explain the attraction of the alternative approach of Global Administrative Law.

3.3.1.1   The antinomies of global constitutionalism

A first distinction contrasts the idea of a single, more or less integrated transnational constitutional order with that of a proliferation of such orders, and so maps precisely onto one of the two general criteria setting convergent approaches apart from divergent approaches to global law. Global constitutionalism's ability to countenance either singularity or plurality can be traced to the semantic roots of the constitutional concept, and, indeed, to its most basic formal implications. The idea of a constitution implies a particular 'constituted' entity to which it is attached, whether the human body or the equally individuated 'body politic'. This constituted entity is both a discrete object, self-contained and so clearly detached from other objects external to it, and one that possesses an internal integrity or holistic quality. Although the constitution thus conceived has classical roots,[85] in the history of the modern age it is the state that has come to supply the key locus and provide the mature form of the constitutional polity.[86] Indeed, so intimate is the connection between constitution and state, and so pronounced their pattern of mutual shaping, that in the early modern period the notion of a constitution typically corresponded directly to the concrete empirical 'fact' of the state. It denoted that which is already 'constituted' – the overall political and governmental system in place – and only later did

---

[85] That said, continuity, both of language and of meaning, is complex and contentious. See e.g. C. H. McIlwain, *Constitutionalism, Ancient and Modern*, 3rd edn (Cornell University Press, 1966); G. Sartori, 'Constitutionalism: A Preliminary Discussion' 56 *American Political Science Review* 853 (1962); G. Maddox, 'A Note on the Meaning of "Constitution"' 76 *American Political Science Review* 805 (1982) (with Sartori's 'comment': G. Sartori, 'Comment on Maddox' 78 *American Political Science Review* 497 (1984)). See also C. Thornhill, *A Sociology of Constitutions: Constitutions and State Legitimacy in Historical-Sociological Perspective* (Cambridge University Press, 2011).

[86] See e.g. D. Grimm, 'Types of Constitution' in Rosenfeld and Sajó, n. 18 above, pp. 98–132.

the constitution acquire the more abstracted meaning of a framework of laws or a canonical document 'constitutive' of the state.[87] It follows from this close bond that the constitutional landscape has in the modern age been dominated by the multiplicity of such discrete state constitutional orders and locales, in principle mutually respecting and so mutually exclusive in their claims to sovereign authority.[88] And in response to the emergence of a denser pattern of transnational legal ordering, much of what passes as the new global constitutionalism involves adapting this older perspective in more or less radical ways to new phenomena. As we shall see, either it focuses on the various new discrete transnational political forms that are claimed to be recognisable in 'constitutional' terms, or, in accordance with the very same holistic model of constitutional being, it concentrates on the global level itself as a single instance of expansive constitutional order. On account of the preoccupation of much constitutional thought with questions of polity individuation, therefore, the menu of global constitutionalism may refer either to the many or to the one.

A second distinction is closely related to the first. It concerns the contrast between particularity and universality of perspective. On the one hand, in its polity-specific focus constitutional thought announces the distinctiveness of each separate constitutional entity in terms of historical origins and trajectory, institutional profile, political culture and community of attachment. The growing emphasis on democratic constitutionalism over the modern age serves to underline that distinctiveness.[89] If the constitution is founded upon the expression of popular sovereignty, or at least homologated in these terms, and if the institutional provisions of that constitution facilitate the democratic flourishing of its constituent community, then each constitution will both announce a distinctive pedigree and help nurture a distinctive political culture. On the other hand, the very premise and promise of popular sovereignty is also a universal one. The claim to the basic right of collective self-government is predicated upon notions of equality of

---

[87] See e.g. D. Grimm, 'The Achievement of Constitutionalism and its Prospects in a Changed World' in Dobner and Loughlin, n. 66 above, pp. 3–22, at 5–6.

[88] See e.g. Grimm, *ibid.*; N. Walker, 'Beyond the Holistic Constitution?' in Dobner and Loughlin, n. 66 above, pp. 291–308; and M. Loughlin, *The Idea of Public Law* (Oxford University Press, 2003) ch. 5.

[89] See e.g. Grimm, n. 87 above; Habermas, n. 73 above; and J. Cohen, *Globalization and Sovereignty: Rethinking Legality, Legitimacy, and Constitutionalism* (Cambridge University Press, 2012).

voice and autonomy of choice that are in principle available to everyone, and so the modern constitutional tradition is also about aspirations held in common across different collectivities and drawing upon the same stock of institutional tools and methods for their realisation.[90]

While different approaches may well emphasise one perspective over the other, their common philosophical underpinning suggests a more intimate practical connection. Indeed, powerful rhetorical reference both to the particular nation and people and to rights-holding and popular sovereignty as universal entitlements or aspirations can be found in the antecedents and texts of many modern documentary constitutions, including the eighteenth-century French and American classics. This bears powerful witness to the inextricability of particular and universal considerations in the historical cultivation of the idea of the constitutional polity.[91] The close yet sometimes conflicted relationship between particular and universal, as we shall see, continues to attend understandings and projections of post-national constitutionalism.

A third major constitutional distinction traces a line we have already encountered between *gubernaculum* and *jurisdictio*.[92] It is constitutional law, as the self-styled highest category of public law, which has supplied the specialist medium of state law through which the twin ideas of governing capacity and of the general limitation upon public power – so important to the Rule of Law in general – have been co-sponsored and reconciled. Yet it is also true that influential streams of constitutional thought have emphasised one of these two approaches above the other. For some, constitutionalism directs us first and foremost to the source of constituent power and the terms of its effective translation into legal authority.[93] For many others, constitutionalism is tantamount to the

---

[90] See e.g. N. Walker, 'Constitutionalism and the Incompleteness of Democracy: An Iterative Relationship' 39 *Rechtsfilosofie & Rechtstheorie* 206 (2010); and J. Waldron, 'Can There Be a Democratic Jurisprudence?' 58 *Emory Law Journal* 688 (2009).

[91] See e.g. D. Armitage, *The Declaration of Independence: A Global History* (Harvard University Press, 2009); B. Yack, 'Nationalism, Popular Sovereignty, and the Liberal Democratic State' in T. V. Paul, J. Ikenberry and J. A. Hall (eds.), *The Nation-State in Question* (Princeton University Press, 2003) pp. 29–50; and L. Jaume, 'Constituent Power in France: The Revolution and its Consequences' in M. Loughlin and N. Walker (eds.), *The Paradox of Constitutionalism: Constituent Power and Constitutional Form* (Oxford University Press, 2007) pp. 67–86.

[92] See Palombella, 'The Rule of Law and its Core', n. 74 above; see also Grimm, n. 86 above.

[93] See e.g. A. Kalyvas, 'Popular Sovereignty, Democracy and the Constituent Power' 12 *Constellations* 223 (2005); see also Loughlin and Walker, n. 91 above.

idea of legally limited government.[94] Again, both notions, and the tension between them, are present in discussions of global constitutionalism, sometimes in conjunction with a focus on polity or system individuation – local or global – but sometimes instead as general tendencies that cut across all polities.

If we assemble our first three distinguishing frames – singularity and plurality, universality and particularity, capacity and constraint – we can identify a number of more or less convergent strands of global constitutionalism. To begin with, towards the convergent end of the spectrum, we find versions of global constitutionalism that stress singularity of normative order, architectural integrity and the existence of some kind of global constitutional system, however rudimentary. The emphasis here may be on global governmental capacity, or more modestly, on a framework of global constraints, or it may be upon an integrated system of capacities and constraints. Alongside the singular approach, we find, secondly, a stream of global constitutional thought in which consideration is given to the development of common constitutional principles or mechanisms bearing upon governing capacity or constraint, but in a manner that is general or universal, and so polity-indifferent. Towards the divergent end of the spectrum, thirdly and finally, the emphasis will instead be on sector-specific forms of constitutionalisation and what is distinctive and different about their particular constitutive dynamics and regulatory regimes. Let us now examine these various positions in a little more depth.

3.3.1.2 Global constitutionalism as singularity

Those who see global constitutionalism as a *singular* framework tend also to insist upon the continuing centrality of international law, and, indeed, to subscribe to the more specialist language of the constitutionalisation of international law. They include some positions we have already encountered under the structural approach.[95] What is emphasised here is the adaptability to the global domain of the very pyramidal structure of state-centred constitutional law, centred around the governing capacity of the institutions of the United Nations.[96] In addition, the notion of an 'international community' often figures prominently in this

---

[94] See e.g. Sartori, 'Constitutionalism: A Preliminary Discussion', n. 85 above.
[95] See section 3.2.1 above.
[96] See in particular Fassbender, n. 6 above; G. Ulfstein, 'Institutions and Competences' in Klabbers, Peters and Ulfstein, n. 23 above; and de Wet, n. 18 above, p. 1224.

kind of analysis. The San Francisco conference which drafted the UN Charter is viewed as a kind of constitutional convention, providing the occasion for the assertion of 'We the Peoples of the United Nations' as an equivalent to – or at least some kind of approximation to – a global constituent power.[97] The Charter's stress on peace, security and basic rights, backed up by the increasingly utilised enforcement powers of the Security Council, also supplies the UN with at least a minimal version of the kind of capacity to articulate and enforce collective commitments that we associate with the more developed political form and 'constituted power' of the state.

A more elaborate and expansive version of the singular approach to global constitutionalism places less emphasis on the functional capacity of the United Nations and more on its supply of a 'connecting factor'[98] within a more broadly inclusive constitutional framework of international law. The focus here is less narrow, the authoritative premise less hierarchical, the analogy drawn between the constitutional properties of the UN and those of the sovereign state much more remote. Instead, on account of its core ordering function, its general membership, its articulation of at least a rudimentary 'constitutional' framework of the separation of powers, and its encouragement of a human rights discourse which operates transversally across so many different legal subject areas (including the basic standards contained in those *jus cogens* and *erga omnes* obligations we have already encountered under the formal hierarchical model)[99] the UN supplies the binding element within a wider and flatter framework of international legal community embracing the states and other international organisations.[100]

Yet not all accounts of the supposedly constitutional properties of the planet considered as a single order or system are inclined to give priority to the United Nations, whether at the apex of a hierarchy or at the centre of a network. Jeremy Waldron, for example, argues that respect for the Rule of Law at the global level depends on our conceiving of states less as authors and ruling subjects of the international legal order, as they are

---

[97] See e.g. B. Fassbender, '"We the People of the United Nations": Constituent Power and Constitutional Form in International Law' in Loughlin and Walker, n. 91 above, pp. 269–90.

[98] De Wet, n. 18 above, p. 1224.   [99] See section 3.2.2 above.

[100] See e.g. Peters, n. 36 above; Paulus, n. 22 above; and C. Walter, 'International Law in a Process of Constitutionalization' in J. E. Nijman and A. Nollkaemper (eds.), *New Perspectives on the Divide Between National and International Law* (Oxford University Press, 2007) pp. 191–210.

understood to be under the traditional state sovereigntist model, and more as officials of a multipolar system of world governance.[101] On this view, which – in an increasingly familiar move[102] – identifies individuals rather than states as ultimate beneficiaries of the global legal system, and which envisages national governments as responsible both for safeguarding individual rights and for the pursuit of numerous collective interests under the loosely co-ordinated global treaty framework, states are identified as subject *to*, rather than subjects *of*, the Rule of Law. That is to say, they are primarily agents in the pursuit and safeguarding of the Rule of Law, and so constrained by the terms of their agency, rather than recipients of its protection. And what makes this shift in perspective fundamentally constitutional in nature is that the structure of legal relations it identifies requires us to think of the world order as a highly decentralised constitutional state writ large. In the global constitutional order *qua* state, states stand alongside international institutions in an intermediate role between the people(s) and the global system as a whole, occupying a position akin to that of government agencies at the national level.

Other models of a decentralised system pay more attention to key regional organisations as building blocks of global constitutional order. Alec Stone Sweet, for instance, has spoken of the emergence of a 'cosmopolitan order' of rights adjudication, one centred upon, but by no means exclusive to, Europe.[103] He emphasises how, today, neither the national nor the transnational realm describes an institutional (still less cultural) unity of rights protection. The European level of rights adjudication now involves the Court of Justice servicing the European Union, including its recently minted Charter of Fundamental Rights,[104] and its twenty-eight member states. It also involves the European Court of Human Rights servicing the Council of Europe's European Convention on Human Rights, and its forty-seven member states, which include all of the member states of the European Union and will soon be extended

---

[101] J. Waldron, 'Are Sovereigns Entitled to the Benefit of the International Rule of Law?' 22 *European Journal of International Law* 315 (2011). See also, in the same edition, the replies to Waldron: A. Somek, 'A Bureaucratic Turn?'; T. Poole, 'Sovereign Indignities: International Law as Public Law'; D. Dyzenhaus, 'Positivism and the Pesky Sovereign'; and S. Besson, 'Sovereignty, International Law and Democracy'.

[102] Especially in the context of human rights. See section 3.2.3.1 above.

[103] Stone Sweet, n. 44 above.

[104] For the full text of the Charter, see *Official Journal of the European Communities*, 26 October 2012 (OJ C 326/12) pp. 391–407.

to cover the European Union itself.[105] In addition to these main pillars, there is a plethora of other international tribunals whose jurisdiction includes Europe or pays attention to the European jurisprudence.[106] So too, at the national level, we typically find a diversity of rights-recognising jurisdictions. The various forums – constitutional courts, administrative courts, ordinary appellate courts, functionally specialist courts – do not converge at a single state-sovereign apex. In such a doubly decentred authority system, no-one has the last word (as opposed to the *latest* word) either at or between different levels, and common jurisprudential cause is as likely to be found with courts outside the national jurisdiction as within. System heterarchy, but also system identity and the very capacity for self-reproduction, is a function both of multi-levelness and of plurality within levels, which features reinforce each other in a continuous play of consensus-building and competition between courts. Dialogue between judicial bodies, and the search for common ground, or, at least, the appeal to common public reason in defence of continued difference, is, on this analysis, not necessarily the echo of a deep moral universalism, or the fruit of a growing sense of family resemblance. It is also, and more immediately, a structural inevitability born of the incomplete but interdependent authority of the multiple judicial sites.

3.3.1.3 Global constitutionalism as commonality

For these writers, therefore, the still tentative emergence of a global constitutional order is more about constraining than cultivating trans-national public power. That is to say, the focus of attention is more on *jurisdictio* and less on *gubernaculum*. And there is an indistinct line between approaches at the margins of the singular approach, such as Waldron's decentralised global governance or Stone Sweet's rights-centred cosmopolitan order, which posit a single loosely assembled yet encompassing global constitutional system, and those perspectives that instead see *common* constitutional themes recur across a variety of local or otherwise specialist systems. Such perspectives stress the universal relevance and the general spread of constitutional ideas and mechanisms

---

[105] See Art. 59(2) ECHR; and Art. 6(2) Treaty on European Union, as amended by the Treaty of Lisbon. See also T. Lock, 'EU Accession to the ECHR: Implications for Judicial Review in Strasbourg' 35 *European Law Review* 777 (2010).

[106] For example, the Inter-American Court of Human Rights often cites the jurisprudence of the European Court of Human Rights.

across and between polities, and in so doing downplay the distinguishing features of these polities.

The focus of this second 'system-indifferent' outlook on global constitutionalism may nevertheless still be very much on the international or supranational domain, as is the case with those positions that emphasise the global spread of 'sectoral constitutionalisation'.[107] Their point of departure is the structural similarity and cross-cloning of the hybrid 'treaty-constitutions'[108] of special international organisations or regimes, such as the International Labour Organization or the World Trade Organization, or the uniquely well-developed case of the European Union. These are each framing instruments for the legal domains in question. They are constitution-like not just in terms of providing an institutional and norm-generating apparatus and claiming an original juridical authority, but also, and increasingly, in endorsing or encouraging a broader form of *erga omnes* applicability in terms of the allocation of rights and responsibilities among the individuals affected by the regimes.[109]

However, given the long intertwinement of states and constitutions in the modern age, it is unsurprising that the focus of many positions that stress the general relevance and common global spread of constitutional ideas across still distinctive polities remains instead on states. Global constitutional thought, indeed, is more pronounced than any of the other emergent species of global law in its continuing in some versions to privilege states as the key unit of production. This vision of global constitutional universalism – or what we might call the *internationalisation of constitutional law* as opposed to the *constitutionalisation of international law* – concentrates on thick circuits of cross-state connection between national constitutional courts and their judges, and also between constitutional drafters and national legislators.[110] Sociologically, these connections owe much to the kind of evolving professional transnationalism discussed in the previous chapter,[111] while, normatively, they depend on a sense of there being a bank, or

---

[107] See e.g. Peters, n. 36 above, pp. 201–3.   [108] *Ibid.*, p. 203.   [109] *Ibid.*, pp. 212–15.

[110] See e.g. V. C. Jackson, *Constitutional Engagement in a Transnational Era* (Oxford University Press, 2010); W.-C. Chang and J.-R. Yeh, 'Internationalization of Constitutional Law' in Rosenfeld and Sajó, n. 18, pp. 1165–84; C. Bell, 'What We Talk About When We Talk About International Constitutional Law' 5 *Transnational Legal Theory* 241 (2014).

[111] See Chapter 2.2 above.

perhaps a warehouse,[112] of general or generalisable legal ideas[113] as the subject matter of exchanges and transfers between national judges and other key legal actors. To be sure, international and transnational texts, courts and other institutions may still provide important encouragement and corroboration of such universalising efforts.[114] And, as we shall see, relations between national and transnational courts provide a relatively rich resource for reflection on the terms and limits of development of common or universal normative horizons from 'plural' sources under the laterally integrative species of global law.[115] However, the main players and movers remain national ones, contemplating and finding – or denying and resisting – common cause on matters as diverse as fundamental rights, the federal distribution of authority, the horizontal separation of powers, and doctrines of balancing and proportionality.[116]

This state-centred strain of universal or global-in-general constitutionalism is also remarkable for the range and extent of its simultaneous engagement of scholarly and law-making communities. The global migration of constitutional ideas is a theme that has become mainstreamed not only within broader academic discussion of constitutional development in various national contexts but also within the jurisprudence of national courts and the practice of national legislators.[117] What is more, there is a high level of mutual engagement among all relevant parties; between academic, practitioner and law-making constituencies both within and across different national and even transnational sites.[118] And so the kind of intimate cross-fertilisation between scholarship, doctrine and practice that we are accustomed to within the specialist and relatively tight-knit world of international law, including those

---

[112] See G. Frankenberg, 'Constitutional Transfer: The IKEA Theory Revisited' 8 *International Journal of Constitutional Law* 563 (2010).

[113] See Waldron, *'Partly Laws Common to All Mankind'*, n. 78 above. See more generally, section 3.2.3.2 above.

[114] A point already made in relation to human rights law: see section 3.2.3.1 above. See also K. Sikkink, *The Justice Cascade* (New York: W. W. Norton & Company, 2011).

[115] See section 3.4.1 below.

[116] See Jackson, n. 110 above; Frankenberg, n. 112 above; and Waldron, 'Foreign Law and the Modern *Ius Gentium*', n. 78 above. See also L. Weinrib, 'The Postwar Paradigm and American Exceptionalism' in S. Choudhry (ed.), *The Migration of Constitutional Ideas* (Cambridge University Press, 2007) pp. 84–112.

[117] See generally, Choudhry, n. 116 above; Waldron, 'Foreign Law and the Modern *Ius Gentium*', n. 78 above; Jackson, n. 110 above; and M. Versteeg and D. Law, 'The Evolution and Ideology of Global Constitutionalism' 99 *California Law Review* 1163 (2011).

[118] See e.g. Weinrib, n. 116 above; and Frankenberg, n. 112 above.

structural and formal aspects of international law that have provided the catalyst for the development of newly constitutionalised forms of international law and of global law more generally, has also begun to develop within and across the much more dispersed world of state-centred international constitutional law.

The impetus for this thick engagement, moreover, has come as much from the domain of practice as from the domain of theory. It has flowed not only from the steady accumulation of transnational professional and academic exchange and organisation and the accompanying mutual opening and cross-fertilisation of doctrine, but also from high-profile cases and controversies in globally influential jurisdictions, in particular the United States.[119] Indeed, more directly than in many areas of global law, in the case of the internationalisation of constitutional law – and, as we shall shortly explain, across global constitutionalism more generally – strong affirmation and deep scepticism go hand in hand. They provide a framework of mutual stimulation and mutual reinforcement – a discursive arena of active side-taking in which the idea of global law is simultaneously made more visible and audible, but also more openly contentious.[120]

3.3.1.4   Global constitutionalism as plurality

If, thirdly and finally, we turn to these forms of global constitutionalism situated towards the divergent end of the spectrum, we observe how they too emphasise the multiplicity of polities and the *plurality* of operating systems in the new global order. Unlike those in search of common or universal constitutional themes and traits, however, they stress the particularity and distinctiveness of each unit. The focus here is on the increasing differentiation of various social fields and functions as they extend transnationally, and how each field possesses its own logic of development and regulatory needs.

Gunther Teubner, a leading exponent of the theory of 'societal constitutionalism', and, more generally, of systems theory, has developed

---

[119] See e.g. *Lawrence* v. *Texas* 539 US 558 (2003); and *Roper* v. *Simmons* 543 US 551 (2005). See the discussion in the *International Journal of Constitutional Law* (i-CON) between Justice Scalia and Justice Breyer: N. Dorsen, 'The Relevance of Foreign Legal Materials in US Constitutional Cases: A Conversation between Justice Antonin Scalia and Justice Stephen Breyer' 3 *International Journal of Constitutional Law* 519 (2005). See also Walker, n. 1 above.

[120] See further Chapter 4 below.

the most refined version of this approach.[121] Despite his use of constitutional language, Teubner is at pains to distinguish his position from the
conventional wisdom of political constitutionalism. The idea of the
constitution as a 'foundational'[122] documentary initiative through which
pre-political collective potential, or constituent power, is transformed into
full-blown legal and political community is one that his systems-theoretical
approach finds highly underspecified and misleading even at the level of the
state. And it becomes all the more inadequate in the highly fragmented
transnational sphere where the 'general ubiquity'[123] of internal state
competence and capacity knows no parallel. The collective subjects of
transnational regimes are more specialist, their remit more restricted. The
idea of a cosmopolitan 'people' or 'public' forming the basis of an encompassing normatively ordered political society, therefore, holds little
relevance – even as founding myth still less as an empirical substrate. It is
not only the case that 'public policy' sectors familiar from the integrated
state polity divide into many transnational regimes – as already indicated in
our reference to sectoral constitutionalisation and hybrid treaty-
constitutions. More than that, different societal sub-systems which include
but also extend beyond the conventional purview of state-centred public
policy into traditionally 'private' domains, for example in the organisation
of the economy, or of education or sport, or of the arts or the sciences, or of
the communications sector, operate according to quite different codes and
currencies – money in the economy, power in politics, knowledge in
education and science. These different sub-systems and sub-system codes,
moreover, view and employ the normative influence and incentives of law
in quite distinct and more or less central ways.[124]

    Yet Teubner would maintain that the idea of transnational *constitu-
tionalism*, quite differently conceived from the statist original, remains
somehow important as a way of accounting for this highly differentiated
societal formation and for understanding the legitimacy requirements of
the new global configuration. Drawing on some of the deeper insights of
systems theory,[125] Teubner chooses not to discard the idea of constituent
power. Rather, he reinterprets it as '*a communicative potential*, a type of

[121] See in particular G. Teubner, *Constitutional Fragments: Societal Constitutionalism and
Globalization* (Oxford University Press, 2012).
[122] See N. Krisch, *Beyond Constitutionalism: The Pluralist Structure of Postnational Law*
(Oxford University Press, 2010) p. 47.
[123] Teubner, n. 121 above, p. 132.   [124] *Ibid.*, ch. 4.
[125] See e.g. N. Luhmann, *Law as a Social System*, trans. K. Ziegert (Oxford University Press,
2004).

social energy'[126] – a way of characterising the collective "'constitutional subject" [as] not simply a semantic artifact ... but rather a pulsating process at the interface of consciousness and communication'.[127] Teubner, in short, treats societal constitutionalism as a capsule term for the fluid forms and myriad routes of systemic autopoiesis – of sectoral *self*-constitution. And in doing so he distinguishes between the widely replicated and increasingly intensified function of sectoral differentiation and specialisation, which he sees as a key feature of the *general* dynamic of transnational society, and the *particular* self-generating process followed and form taken, which varies significantly not only from the original statist paradigm but also between different global subsectors. The many 'capillary constitutions'[128] of transnational society, to which more or less formal legal texts – from framework treaties to industry codes – contribute to a variable extent, supply in their very different contexts both a symbolic mark of collective self-understanding and self-projection and an operating code or social technology for the framing of collective action.

In a key set of observations, Teubner argues that in their discrete specialisation and functional concentration, the sub-spheres of transnational society escape our received modern, state-centred distinction between a generically public and a generically private sphere. They cannot, therefore, be assessed and evaluated in accordance with conventional standards of a holistic public interest and public good. Rather, we should understand and judge their constitutional adequacy in terms of their success in achieving a balance between the autonomy and self-limitation of the various different functional sectors *inter se* in a highly fragmented global order – with autonomy as a deep freedom and equality-respecting modern ideal retained and inherited from the statist tradition.[129] On this view, the central 'constitutive' puzzle faced by the stakeholders of relatively autonomous global subsectors and their various audiences concerns how to balance the freedom of those most centrally concerned with and affected by a practice to govern that practice against the need to limit the expansion of that practice into other spheres and so curb its tendency to encroach on the autonomy of other sectors of social practice and *their* key stakeholders. For all that it

---

[126] Teubner, n. 121 above, p. 62 (emphasis in original).   [127] *Ibid.*, p. 63.

[128] *Ibid.*, p. 83.

[129] See e.g. G. Teubner, 'Constitutionalising Polycontextuality' 20 *Social and Legal Studies* 209 (2011).

has a transnationally specific shape and feel, however, this is a puzzle that Teubner believes can still nevertheless be rendered in constitutionally recognisable terms. For, arguably, as a matter of political morality, it is the equivalent under a globally differentiated order of the constitutive design puzzle of the high modern order: namely, how to safeguard the 'internal sovereignty' of 'the people' while ensuring that their 'external sovereignty' does not compromise the internal sovereignty of others.[130]

3.3.1.5 The Janus faces of contemporary constitutionalism

Crucially, the scope for self-styled constitutionalists to work across the three key distinctions that we have indicated – singularity and plurality, universality and particularity, capacity and constraint – supplies the latitude that allows a radical 'divider' like Teubner to share a common lexicon with all manner of institutional centralists and normative universalists, just as it permits all sorts of state-centred theorists and practitioners to speak the same language as those for whom the state is a less empirically significant or normatively elevated player. Yet a fourth and final basic cut within constitutional thought explains why for many it remains fundamentally inappropriate to the global domain, and perhaps to the transnational domain more generally.[131] That distinction lies between constitution as establishment – as an always already 'constituted' and crystallised state of political being – and constitution as blueprint – as 'a thing *antecedent* to government'[132] and a 'constitutive' project for a political society. In turn, this feeds into a larger set of oppositions in constitutional thought – retrospective and prospective, factual and normative, consolidatory and innovative, unwritten and written, even ancient and modern.[133]

Yet in practice the relationship between these two dimensions in the modern constitutional age has been one of symbiosis as much as conflict. For within the national constitutional tradition the capacity and legitimacy to undertake a constitutional commitment presupposes and

---

[130] *Ibid.* See also Krisch, n. 122 above, espousing very similar views about the need to 'balance inclusiveness and particularity' (p. 101) in autonomous sectors, while eschewing the language of constitutionalism.

[131] See e.g. M. Loughlin, 'What is Constitutionalisation?' in Dobner and Loughlin, n. 66 above, pp. 47–72; and R. Wahl, 'In Defence of "Constitution"' in Dobner and Loughlin, n. 66 above, pp. 220–44. See also Grimm, nn. 86 and 87 above.

[132] T. Paine, *Rights of Man*, orig. edn 1791 (London: Wordsworth Editions, 1996) p. 36 (emphasis in original).

[133] See e.g. M. Loughlin, 'Constitutional Theory: A 25th Anniversary Essay' 25 *Oxford Journal of Legal Studies* 183 (2005).

requires some kind of prior settlement or understanding, a platform of established common cause. The constitutional perspective, in other words, is inevitably Janus-faced. In order to look forward, it must first claim to be able to look back, to anchor itself in an already somehow embedded, or at least socially imagined, sense of political community. 'We the people' must presuppose their prior existence in order to act as such.[134] Yet it is precisely that prior sense of political community, many would argue, that is missing from, or at most only vestigially or incipiently present within transnational society, and which cannot be conjured up simply through invoking the constitutional label or even by simulating the constitution-making process.[135]

And so, it is objected from this sceptical point of view, constitutionalism is poorly suited to the transnational or global stage. Its achievement may be criticised as anaemic, as one that lacks socio-cultural underpinning, and therefore with little basis on which to derive authority directly from transnational sources and in persistent danger of overselling and overreaching itself. It may, for example, rely heavily upon the indirect legitimacy of state consent and a bottom-up delegated mandate, as in many of the visions of global constitutionalism as a singular achievement.[136] That sense of state consent as central is also at the heart of the persistent objection to the international constitutional lawyer's enthusiastic endorsement of the state-to-state migration of constitutional ideas and concepts. For if the source of authority remains the state, then the key test, so to speak, is at the point of immigration rather than emigration, and international constitutionalism *qua* global constitutionalism is reduced to as much or as little as any individual state constitutional order wants to make of it.[137]

More generally global constitutionalism, as we have already intimated, may avoid the hard questions that derive from its lack of socio-cultural

---

[134] H. Lindahl, 'Sovereignty and Symbolization' 28 *Rechtstheorie* 347 (1997).

[135] See e.g. Loughlin, n. 131 above; Grimm, nn. 86 and 87 above; A. Somek, *The Cosmopolitan Constitution* (Oxford University Press, 2014); G. W. Anderson, 'Beyond "Constitutionalism Beyond the State"' 39 *Journal of Law and Society* 359 (2012); and E. Christodoulidis, 'A Default Constitutionalism? A Disquieting Note on Europe's Many Constitutions' in K. Tuori and S. Sankari (eds.), *The Many Constitutions of Europe* (Farnham: Ashgate, 2010) pp. 31–48. Much of the scepticism about the ultimately abortive EU constitutional process in 2003–5 concerned precisely whether following the rules and canons of constitution-making could make up for the absence of a prior sense of continental political community: see e.g. N. Walker, 'The EU's Unresolved Constitution' in Rosenfeld and Sajó, n. 18 above, pp. 1185–1208.

[136] See e.g. Fassbender, nn. 6 and 97 above.

[137] See e.g. comments by Justice Scalia in n. 119 above.

underpinnings by a skewed or selective approach to the various other oppositions we have discussed. Like the opposition between establishment and projection, our first three oppositions – the one and the many, particular and universal, capacity and constraint – tend to be balanced and reconciled within the state constitutional tradition. Within global constitutionalism, however, there is a tendency to choose or accentuate one over the other. We see this, for example, in the unmoored universalism of some of the singular global constitutional models or system-indifferent models, presented as unauthored networks of 'good' practice; or in the tendency in some other singular models to look only or mainly at constitutional constraints and gloss over the issue of capacity, with its closer connections to power and its constituents; or in the difficulty societal constitutionalism has – quite the opposite to that of unmoored universalism – in moving beyond its particular anchor and taking some account of constitutionalism's universal heritage.

Such scepticism as these approaches call forth, as we have seen, questions the basic fit between constitutionalism and the global context. At best, constitutionalism becomes a less central way of making sense of the legal landscape, its insight in explaining and its value in lending authority to the emerging global configuration a partial one. At worst, however, scepticism threatens to shade into wholesale negativism. On this view, the application of constitutionalism within a global horizon is simply a category mistake – a concept whose modern meaning was forged in the state and which is out of place anywhere other than the state.[138]

3.3.2   Global Administrative Law

If global constitutional law's refusal to be pigeon-holed within either convergent or divergent conceptions of global law is due to its sheer open-endedness of reference, the same cannot be said of a second key 'non-aligned' historical-discursive initiative. Global Administrative Law (GAL) began as a research project at New York University Law School in the early years of the present century. It provides probably *the* most conspicuous contemporary instance of a concerted effort at scholarly recasting of legal problems and participation in the search for new

---

[138] See e.g. A. Moravcsik, 'Europe Without Illusions: A Category Error' 112 *Prospect Magazine* 22 (2005). And see, more generally, the state-based critique of global law developed in Chapter 6.2 et seq. below.

institutional and doctrinal solutions in global terms. Highly successful as an academic movement, it has developed into a field of research with a presence in every continent and embracing a wide range of topics of inquiry.[139] Nevertheless, its basic object of reference reveals a standing concern with the regulation of a particular kind of activity – global administration. And in so doing GAL, in contrast to global constitutionalism, embraces a very specific – if increasingly crowded – perspective upon global law, one situated towards the complex middle of the convergent/divergent spectrum.

The focus of GAL is on the proliferation of certain sites of transnational regulation and decision-making that were until recently 'little-noticed'.[140] These sites exercise authority of the kind traditionally associated with the public authority of the state, but do so in circumstances where states either play no part in the generation of norms, or where the link with the original authority of the state has been radically attenuated or lost. The new regulatory forms range widely across the poorly charted 'administrative' space between the world of international 'legislation' and its primary treaty rights and obligations on the one hand, and 'judicial' bodies solely concerned with dispute resolution on the other. They include the globally extended administrative and regulatory activities of UN bodies such as the World Health Organization and the Financial Action Task Force; informal transnational financial networks such as the Basle Committee of heads of central banks; bottom-up co-ordinated administration between national regulators with overlapping objectives in matters such as nuclear safety and biodiversity conservation; hybrid public/private transnational

---

[139] The literature is huge. For the seminal text, see Kingsbury, Krisch and Stewart, n. 82 above. See also S. Cassese, 'Administrative Law without the State? The Challenge of Global Regulation' 37 *New York University Journal of International Law and Politics* 663 (2005); S. Cassese, B. Carotti, L. Casini, E. Cavalieri and E. MacDonald (eds.), *Global Administrative Law: The Casebook*, 3rd edn (New York: IRPA-IILJ, 2012). For an overview of publications, activities and networks, see the project website www.iilj. org/gal/ under the Institute for International Law and Justice at New York University Law School. For similar transnational visions of public law that emphasise regional or cosmopolitan standards, see e.g. A. von Bogdandy, P. Dann and M. Goldmann, 'Developing the Publicness of Public International Law: Towards a Legal Framework for Global Governance Activities' 9 *German Law Journal* 1375 (2008); von Bogdandy and Bast, n. 80 above; and D. Dyzenhaus (ed.), *The Unity of Public Law* (Oxford: Hart, 2004). See also, on 'publicness' in law more generally, Waldron, n. 90 above; N. Walker, 'On the Necessarily Public Quality of Law' in C. Michelon, G. Clunie, C. McCorkindale and H. Psarras (eds.), *The Public in Law: Representations of the Political in Legal Discourse* (London: Ashgate, 2012) pp. 3–31; and Loughlin, n. 80 above.

[140] Kingsbury, Krisch and Stewart, n. 82 above, at 15.

representative bodies such as the Internet Corporation for Assigned Names and Numbers (ICANN); and purely privately initiated but broadly publicly endorsed bodies such as the International Organization for Standardization (ISO), concerned with product harmonisation, or international sport's World Anti-Doping Agency.[141]

In the development of this orientation, GAL's emphasis tends to be on 'throughput' or process, and 'output' or substantive outcomes, over 'input' and pedigree.[142] In this regard, its similarities to societal constitutionalism are instructive, but the differences are just as telling. They serve to highlight the vulnerability of the global constitutionalist approach in general to the kind of scepticism about its post-national pedigree discussed above, and reveal why GAL stands as a clear alternative. On the one hand, the GAL approach, like that of societal constitutionalism, strongly questions whether the state-based formula for identifying constituent power and translating it into constitutional form is fit for reproduction at the transnational level, and is sceptical about the democratic credentials of any such attempt to conceive of public power beyond the state in constitutional terms.[143] On the other hand, unlike societal constitutionalism, GAL does not attempt to persevere with the analogy between the state-based formula and the generative conditions and source-specific legitimacy of specialist transnational sectors or systems. From the perspective of GAL, any such analogy is false and misleading. Absent the cultural and political conditions of state-based input legitimacy, it is not only inappropriate but may be libelled as a *misappropriation* of a cognitive and symbolic resource to rely upon the language so intimately associated with that background: hence the eschewal of constitutional discourse by many proponents of GAL.[144]

Where GAL does seek a significant degree of continuity with the state tradition is instead with the post-constituent or 'downstream' rules of public law. It is proposed that the manifold sites of transnational administrative justice operating in the absence of – or, at least, much attenuated

[141] *Ibid.*, at 20–3.
[142] See e.g. D. Dyzenhaus, 'Accountability and the Concept of (Global) Administrative Law' *Acta Juridica* 3 (2009).
[143] See e.g. N. Krisch, 'Global Administrative Law and the Constitutional Ambition' in Dobner and Loughlin, n. 66 above, pp. 245–66. See also E. MacDonald, 'The "Emergence" of Global Administrative Law?', 4th Global Administrative Law Seminar, Viterbo, 13–14 June 2008. The full text is available at www.iilj.org/gal/documents/MacDonald.pdf.
[144] See e.g. Krisch, n. 143 above.

from – state constitutional roots, should be framed and guided by general principles familiar from national administrative law: namely procedural due process, transparency, legality, rationality, reason-giving and proportionality, together with respect for the Rule of Law and basic protection of human rights.[145] What is more, there are some signs that this borrowing from the state tradition is gradually becoming internalised in the transnational domain. Over time, it is claimed by one prominent GAL scholar, these normative ideals, each concerned not with the generation of power but with the tasks of 'channelling, managing, shaping and constraining political power'[146] during or 'after the fact' of its emergence in the countless crevices of transnational authority, are tending to circulate more widely and more readily. Gradually, 'as the layers of common normative practice thicken, they come to be argued for and adopted through a mixture of comparative study and a sense that they are (or are becoming) obligatory'.[147]

Why is Global Administrative Law aptly portrayed as occupying an indistinct middle ground between convergent and divergent conceptions of global law? This can be demonstrated by recalling the various oppositions in terms of which we sought to classify the diverse forms of global constitutional law. Where global constitutionalism can conceive of 'system' either in singular or in plural terms, GAL can only see plurality and diversity. Where global constitutional law is concerned both with *gubernaculum* and with *jurisdictio* – with capacity as well as constraint – GAL is primarily concerned with the legal regulation and containment of power. Yet if these two factors suggest a divergence-accommodating approach, with regard to the other key distinction – universal versus particular – GAL stands resolutely on the universal side of the divide. GAL's image of the unfolding transnational legal world may be one of a diverse manifold – a manifold, moreover, whose constitutive conditions and 'constitutional' pedigree lie beyond GAL's ambit – but its response is far from one of acquiescence. Rather, an entire catalogue of post-constituent rules of national public law is ambitiously recast as a manifesto of globally convergent legal standards of transnational administration. GAL may assume neither the global hierarchy of the structural

---

[145] See B. Kingsbury, 'The Concept of "Law" in Global Administrative Law' 20 *European Journal of International Law* 23 (2009); and B. Kingsbury, 'International Law as Interpublic Law' in II. R. Richardson and M. S. Williams (eds.), *NOMOS XLIX: Moral Universalism and Pluralism* (New York University Press, 2009) pp. 167–204.
[146] Kingsbury, 'The Concept of "Law"', n. 145 above, at 32.   [147] *Ibid.*, at 30.

or formal approaches nor the encompassing normative singularity of the abstract-normative approaches, both of which themes are also taken up by the more convergent strains of global constitutionalism. But it does seek to answer its contemplation of the variety of transnational legal capacity by endorsing a common set of procedures for holding such divergent power to account. In claiming this middle ground it adopts a posture that is both modest and assertive: modest in its rejection of the constitutional route, yet, in ways that will emerge as characteristic of much global law, assertive in its ambition to make normative order out of the disorder of fast-evolving transnational institutional trends.[148]

3.4   The catalogue of global law III: divergent approaches

3.4.1   Laterally co-ordinate approaches

Unlike the historical-discursive models just considered, laterally co-ordinate approaches proceed unambiguously from a divergence-accommodating perspective. Concerned to provide a means of reconciling difference and resolving disputes between diverse but overlapping and interdependent legal regimes, they depart, quite unequivocally, from the premises of plurality and heterarchy rather than unity and hierarchy. The defining image of global law here is of a *chain* whose many links connect the disparate parts of our legal world.

The laterally co-ordinate species includes new iterations of the legal discipline we know as the conflict of laws, or as private international law. This is a legal field which some of its proponents claim to be in the process of evolution beyond a state-centred model of conflict management. On this view, it is adapting to fit a global environment in which we must acknowledge and treat a greater number of boundary problems between an expanding number of non-state legal orders equipped with their own courts or other dispute resolution mechanisms, including the UN and its various associated treaty bodies, the EU and other regional systems of economic and political integration, the WTO and other specialist regimes of public international law, as well as a great variety of private or hybrid forms of ordering.[149] In a closely related development, the laterally co-ordinate category of global law also extends to new

---

[148] See Chapter 5.2.2 below.
[149] The literature here is already huge, and rapidly expanding. See e.g. H. Muir Watt, 'Private International Law Beyond the Schism' 2 *Transnational Legal Theory* 347 (2011); C. Scott, F. Cafaggi and L. Senden, 'The Conceptual and Constitutional

mediating ideas such as 'interface norms'[150] and 'contrapunctual law'[151] – to take two key concepts from the self-consciously post-national strain of legal pluralism.[152] These new pluralist models are distinguished by their efforts to reach some kind of harmony or accommodation through a structure of norms or attitudes of conditional mutual recognition between non-hierarchically aligned legal orders. Let us now explore these sub-categories in greater depth.

3.4.1.1   The conflict of laws

If we begin with the conflict of laws, again we find a historical-discursive dynamic at work in the emergence of a global legal horizon. However, unlike the explicit revivalism of the new *jus gentium*,[153] or the studied transformation and rebranding involved in adding the prefix 'global' to constitutional or administrative law, the adjustment required of the field of conflict of laws to meet new global conditions and to address the growth of non-state legal orders is approached in more gradual and less discontinuous terms. At the centre of the new global perspective the original animating idea of the conflict of laws remains intact: namely, a concern with the choice of the applicable legal system to determine a

Challenge of Transnational Private Regulation' 38 *Journal of Law and Society* 1 (2011); J. Bonhoff and A. Meuwese, 'The Meta-regulation of Transnational Private Regulation' 38 *Journal of Law and Society* 138 (2011); P. Zumbansen, 'Transnational Legal Pluralism' 1 *Transnational Legal Theory* 141 (2010); A. Mills, *The Confluence of Public and Private International Law: Justice, Pluralism and Subsidiarity in the International Constitutional Ordering of Private Law* (Cambridge University Press, 2009); R. Wai, 'Transnational Liftoff and Juridical Touchdown: The Regulatory Function of Private International Law in an Era of Globalization' 40 *Columbia Journal of Transnational Law* 209 (2002); T. Büthe and W. Mattli, *New Global Rulers: The Privatization of Regulation in the World Economy* (Princeton University Press, 2011); P. Schiff Berman, *Global Legal Pluralism: A Jurisprudence of Law Beyond Borders* (Cambridge University Press, 2012); and K. Knop, R. Michaels and A. Riles, 'From Multiculturalism to Technique: Feminism, Culture, and the Conflict of Laws Style' 64 *Stanford Law Review* 589 (2012). See also the significant body of work by Christian Joerges, especially in the EU context. For discussion, see the special issue of *Transnational Legal Theory* (vol. 2, no. 2, 2011); and in particular C. Joerges, P. F. Kjaer and T. Ralli, 'A New Type of Conflicts Law as Constitutional Form in the Postnational Constellation' 2 *Transnational Legal Theory* 153 (2011).
[150] Krisch, n. 122 above.
[151] M. Maduro, 'Contrapunctual Law: Europe's Constitutional Pluralism in Action' in N. Walker (ed.), *Sovereignty in Transition: Essays in European Law* (Oxford: Hart, 2003) pp. 501–37.
[152] See, for example, a recent collection on pluralism by Matej Avbelj and Jan Komárek: M. Avbelj and J. Komárek (eds.), *Constitutional Pluralism in the European Union and Beyond* (Oxford: Hart, 2012); and Schiff Berman, n. 149 above.
[153] See e.g. Waldron, *'Partly Laws Common to All Mankind'*, n. 78 above.

dispute involving the legal claims of private parties, or with the appropriate jurisdiction to hear such a dispute, where different legal orders possess overlapping and competing claims to competence.

Reinforcing this sense of continuity, the newly emergent approach is often presented as a reassertion of an older if lately somewhat neglected conception of the place of the conflict of laws in the legal cosmos. According to this influential view, the conflict of laws was first conceived of as part and parcel of a universal legal framework. It was contained within and emerged from a notion of *jus gentium*, originally understood in imperial terms as an other-regarding outgrowth of Roman law and of a Roman-law-centred view of the world, but gradually extended to embrace a more cosmopolitan vision – as more generally concerned with the principles relating to the overall distribution of regulatory authority between different legal orders.[154] That is to say, a system-transcending conception of the conflict of laws is deemed to have been already factored into a pre-modern vision of an integrated global law, even if, as was typically the case, such a vision tended towards both idealism and a limited spatial and cultural vision of globality.[155]

And while, under the influence of writers such as Savigny and Mancini, the idea of a common set of international secondary rules for determining choice of laws and jurisdiction survived well into the nineteenth century,[156] it gradually lost ground to a more multivocal approach. As the modern state-centred international order became fully established in the twentieth century, the conflict of laws, even at the level of theoretical representation, came more to resemble a parochial form of boundary-maintenance separately sponsored by each domestic legal order according to its own standards of fairness and propriety. Under the newly emergent global approach, however, the tide has arguably begun to turn again. For the notion has recently gained ground of the conflict of laws as a common enterprise of 'global governance'[157] through the 'meta-regulation'[158] of the increasingly

---

[154] See e.g. A. Mills, 'The Private History of International Law' 55 *International and Comparative Law Quarterly* 1 (2006). See also Mills, n. 149 above, ch. 2; and A. Mills, 'Variable Geometry, Peer Governance, and the Public International Perspective on Private International Law' in D. Fernandez Arroyo and H. Muir Watt (eds.), *Private International Law as Global Governance* (Oxford University Press, forthcoming, 2014) ch. 13.

[155] See e.g. Domingo, *The New Global Law*, n. 60 above, chs. 1–4; see also section 3.2.3.2 above.

[156] Mills, n. 149 above, p. 66.   [157] Muir Watt, n. 149 above.

[158] Bonhoff and Meuwese, n. 149 above.

dense and intricate relations between different regulatory regimes, rather than as a locally controlled vehicle for the resolution of occasional inter-systemic puzzles.

And alongside this suggestion of a structural shift to a more cosmo-politan standpoint, the substantive scope of the emerging law of con-flicts may also be evolving – and, again, in so doing, perhaps recalling something of an earlier perspective. For in the face of the emergent global conflicts environment there is a growing sense of the pertinence of a shared 'public' interest in choice of law rules involving transna-tional regimes even in matters affecting traditionally 'private' forms of economic activity. This implies the softening of another division endorsed and enforced by the modern state system between what is properly a matter of sovereign attention and what is not. It suggests that the 'schism'[159] treating the regulation of cross-border markets and economic activity as separate and immune from properly inter*national* politics and law, and which helped produce such an emphatic modern distinction between private international law with its 'thin' inter-systemic accommodations on the one hand, and public international law with its trans-systemic normative standards on the other, has begun to be challenged by a more integrated understanding of private and public domains redolent of an earlier less state-centred age.

The actual case made by the sponsors of the movement towards a more global understanding of the conflict of laws, however, remains tentative. It focuses as much on the palpable presence of the problem as on its possible solutions – as concerned with the demands posed by an increasingly differentiated legal environment as with the detailed artic-ulation of new ways of thinking about the conflict of laws as a tool for managing that environment. Yet private international lawyers who subscribe to the new global paradigm can point to certain incipient tendencies in support of their perspective. They can, for instance, indicate the continuing and intensifying work of the Hague Conference on Private International Law as the main source of the progressive unification of the conflict of laws.[160] Founded in 1893, it is a body that that has long operated through creating and assisting in the implementation of multilateral conventions on the harmonisation of choice of law rules. And in recent years it has augmented this ever-increasing formal output with various 'soft law' instruments that invite

[159] Muir Watt, n. 149 above.   [160] Mills, n. 149 above, pp. 215–16.

states and other global parties to adopt as good practice its non-binding recommendations.[161]

Another indicator of the evolution of the conflict of laws towards a more global methodology is the example of federal states such as the United States, Australia and Canada, and, more pertinently, the quasi-federal structure of the European Union.[162] Each provides an instructive illustration of how the autonomy of territorial legal sub-systems within a dispersed polity can be reconciled through a central authority that insists upon a common set of rules on the choice of law and the allocation of jurisdiction. Clearly, there may be limits to the extent to which there exists the legal competence, still less the political capacity, to translate this kind of central authority to the global level. However, the European Union in particular remains a suggestive precedent. Despite lacking much of the institutional apparatus and political legitimacy of a state, it possesses a highly developed regulatory capability in the area of the mutual enforcement of civil and criminal judgments and ensuring the compatibility of rules of conflict of laws and jurisdiction.[163] In fact, the very strength of its conflicts jurisdiction, as, indeed, of its broader framework of mutual recognition of national standards in the circulation of goods and services in the internal market, is a clear reflection of the 'in-between' status of the EU polity. Just because, even at its mature but increasingly politically contentious half-century,[164] it lacks the ambition or the capability of the state to achieve legal uniformity or harmonisation throughout its territory across the wide expanse of public policy, the EU's ability to use law to ensure credible and efficient common commitment to its core market-making project instead depends heavily upon the security of a 'second best' legal agenda of mutual toleration of difference.[165]

---

[161] See e.g. Special Commission on Choice of Law in International Contracts, 'Draft Hague Principles as approved by the November 2012 Special Commission Meeting on Choice of Law in International Contracts and Recommendations for the Commentary', Hague Conference on Private International Law, 12–16 November 2012, available at www.hcch.net/upload/wop/contracts2012principles_e.pdf. See also S. C. Symeonides, 'The Hague Principles on Choice of Law for International Contracts: Some Preliminary Comments' 61 *American Journal of Comparative Law* 873 (2013).

[162] Mills, n. 149 above, ch. 4.

[163] Art. 81(2), Consolidated Version of the Treaty on the Functioning of the European Union, 2008 OJ C 115/47 (hereinafter, 'TFEU').

[164] See e.g. F. de Witte and M. Dawson, 'Constitutional Balance in the EU after the Euro-Crisis' 76 *Modern Law Review* 817 (2013).

[165] See e.g. M. Berglund, *Cross-border Enforcement of Claims in the EU: History, Present Time and Future* (Alphen aan den Rijn: Kluwer Law International, 2009); C. Janssens,

So the European Union provides a kind of litmus test of the capacity of any transnational legal complex, and by extension the overall global complex, to use a conflicts-based approach to contain and manage difference. But the EU also informs our understanding of the wider global picture in other more direct ways. For as well as providing a microcosm of the problems, challenges and possible solutions of a global conflict of laws, it also represents a key middle-level player in the wider global dynamic. Internally, there are many points of conflict between the EU's substantive jurisdiction and various national jurisdictions. These contentions may concern the fundamental limits of the transfer of state sovereignty to the EU in matters such as basic rights protection,[166] internal security policy[167] and fiscal autonomy,[168] as highlighted in a continuing series of highly profiled cases before the Court of Justice and Europe's most prominent constitutional courts.[169] Or, just as significantly, they may refer to more general clashes of competence between the EU's core common market-making agenda and various national projects concerned to preserve particular standards of social protection.[170] As has been argued, the combination of a standing tension

The Principle of Mutual Recognition in EU Law (Oxford University Press, 2013); J. Pelkmans, 'Mutual Recognition: Economic and Regulatory Logic in Goods and Services' in T. Eger and H.-B. Schaefer (eds.), Research Handbook on the Economics of EU Law (Cheltenham: Edward Elgar, 2012) pp. 113–45.

[166] See recently, e.g., Case C-617/10 Åklagaren v. Hans Åkerberg Fransson, Judgment of the Court (Grand Chamber), 26 February 2013 (on the applicability of the EU Charter of Fundamental Rights to measures implementing Swedish criminal law); and N. Lavranos, 'The ECJ's Judgments in Melloni and Åkerberg Fransson: Une Ménage à Trois Difficulté' 4 European Law Reporter 133 (2013).

[167] See recently, e.g., Case C-399/11 Melloni v. Ministerio Fiscal, Judgment of the Court (Grand Chamber), 26 February 2013 (on the legality of the European Arrest Warrant in light of the Spanish constitutional rights framework); and Lavranos, n. 166 above.

[168] See recently, e.g., the judgment of the Federal Constitutional Court of Germany (Bundesverfassungsgericht) on the legality of the European Stability Mechanism in light of German constitutional protection of core sovereign powers: BVerfG 2 BvR 1390/12, 12 September 2012. See also K. Schneider, 'Yes, But … One More Thing: Karlsruhe's Ruling on the European Stability Mechanism' 14 German Law Journal 53 (2013).

[169] See e.g. Avbelj and Komárek, n. 152 above; and G. Itzcovich, 'Legal Order, Legal Pluralism, Fundamental Principles. Europe and its Law in Three Concepts' 18 European Law Journal 358 (2012).

[170] See e.g. the Court of Justice's controversial case law on the extent to which collective action by trade unions can be used to resist social dumping within the EU: C-341/05 Laval un Partneri [2007] ECR I-11767; C-438/05 The International Transport Workers' Federation and the Finnish Seamen's Union [2007] ECR I-10779; C-346/06 Rüffert [2008] ECR I-1989. See also e.g. R. Zahn, 'The Viking and Laval Cases in the Context of European Enlargement' 3 Web Journal of

between substantive legal policy priorities at the two levels – state and EU – and the close and unavoidable interdependence of their respective 'partial' jurisdictions leads to the proliferation of 'diagonal'[171] conflicts. These go beyond a simple opposition of national and transnational political will. Instead, in such scenarios different interest constellations that cut across national and transnational levels – producers and consumers, employers and employees, professionals and clients – approach the contentious interface of national and European law from divergent perspectives and pursuing different readings of the appropriate terms of the overall fit.[172] Externally, too, we can see key points of conflict in the EU's relations with other transnational legal orders reaching beyond the continent, most notably the UN[173] and the WTO.[174] But here the EU supplies just one vein of contestation, albeit a prominent one, in a wider lattice of cross-cutting jurisdictions. The broader proliferation of transnational rule-making bodies exercising both public and private forms of authority and the greater density of transnational law brings with it a much wider range of functional specialisation and an accompanying canalisation of legal doctrine and argument. Trade law, human rights law,

---

Current Legal Issues (2008), http://dspace4dev.stir.ac.uk/bitstream/1893/6003/1/ WebJCLI.pdf.

[171] C. Joerges, 'The Idea of a Three-Dimensional Conflicts Law as Constitutional Form' in C. Joerges and E.-U. Petersmann (eds.), *Constitutionalism, Multilevel Trade Governance and International Economic Law* (Oxford: Hart, 2011) p. 413; C. Joerges, 'The Impact of European Integration on Private Law: Reductionist Perceptions, True Conflicts and a New Constitutional Perspective' 3 *European Law Journal* 378 (1997); B. Currie, 'Notes on Methods and Objectives in the Conflict of Law' in B. Currie (ed.), *Selected Essays on the Conflict of Laws* (Durham, NC: Duke University Press) p. 1773; and H. Muir Watt, 'Choice of Law in Integrated and Interconnected Markets: A Matter of Political Economy' 9 *Columbia Journal of European Law* 383 (2003).

[172] See e.g. Joerges, Kjaer and Ralli, n. 149 above. See also P. F. Kjaer, 'The Political Foundations of Conflicts Law' 12 *Transnational Legal Theory* 227 (2011).

[173] See in particular Joined cases C-402/05 P and C-415/05 P, *Kadi and Al Barakaat International Foundation* v. *Council and Commission*, Judgment of the Court (Grand Chamber), 3 September 2008, [2008] ECR I-6351 (*Kadi I*); and Joined cases C-584/10 P, C-593/10 P and C-595/10 P, *European Commission and Others* v. *Yassin Abdullah Kadi*, Judgment of the Court (Grand Chamber), 18 July 2013 (*Kadi II*). See also J. Kokott and C. Sobotta, 'The *Kadi* Case – Constitutional Core Values and International Law – Finding the Balance?' 23 *European Journal of International Law* 1015 (2012); for discussion, see Chapter 4.4 below.

[174] See e.g. Case C-35/96 *Hermés International* v. *FHT Marketing Choice BV* [1998] ECR I-3603. See also F. Snyder, 'The Gatekeepers: The European Courts and WTO Law' 40 *Common Market Law Review* 313 (2003).

environmental law, criminal law, security law, humanitarian law: these, as we have already noted in our discussion of societal constitutionalism, tend to develop as quite distinct legal discourses in particular institutional settings and each with their own policy priorities.[175]

Acute questions arise over the appropriate grounds and the authoritative forum for reconciling these priorities. On the one hand, courts of broad jurisdiction such as national constitutional courts and the International Court of Justice are increasingly required to weigh the competing demands of principles and priorities drawn from different functional areas. Should, for example, the law of human rights rather than the law of armed conflict govern the assessment of the legality of the threat of nuclear arms?[176] Or what should be the balance between the law of self-determination, security law and humanitarian law in judging the legality of the wall built by Israel around parts of the occupied Palestinian Territory?[177] On the other hand, specialist tribunals may be minded to give priority to one particular functional normative framework over others, but often do so in the shadow of the possibility of other specialist jurisdictions entering the fray and adopting a different perspective. In the well-known case of the Mox Plant nuclear facility at Sellafield, United Kingdom, for instance, not only was the crucial question of the danger posed to the environment by radioactive emissions amenable to treatment in accordance with different normative codes, but, in addition, reflecting that diversity, that question could be raised in quite different adjudicatory or other decisional settings. These ranged from the UNCLOS Arbitral Tribunal on the law of the sea, and the OSPAR Convention Tribunal concerned with protecting the marine environment, to the European Court of Justice with its broader environmental remit and its dedication to retaining exclusive jurisdiction over all matters engaging EU law.[178]

---

[175] See section 3.3.2 above.

[176] International Court of Justice (ICJ), *Legality of the Threat or Use of Nuclear Weapons*, Advisory Opinion of 8 July 1996, ICJ Reports 1996, p. 226.

[177] ICJ, *Legal Consequences of the Construction of a Wall in the Occupied Palestinian Territory*, Advisory Opinion of 9 July 2004, ICJ Reports 2004, p. 136.

[178] Case C-459/03 *Commission v. Ireland* ('*MOX Plant case*') [2006] ECR I-4635; and UNCLOS Arbitral Tribunal, Order No. 6 of 6 June 2008, Termination of Proceedings, available at www.pca-cpa.org/upload/files/MOX%20Plant%20Order%20No.%206.pdf. For discussion, see R. Churchill and J. Scott, 'The Mox Plant Litigation: The First Half-Life' 53 *International and Comparative Law Quarterly* 643 (2004); N. Lavranos, 'The Epilogue in the Mox Plant Dispute: An End without Findings' 18 *European Energy and Environmental Law Review* 180 (2009); and Koskenniemi, n. 30 above, at 7-9.

This broader global framework of 'regime collision'[179] underlines the limitations of any framework of conflict of laws predicated upon the state as the exclusive or dominant source of law. Instead, we see a kind of *double deformalisation* at work. In the first place, the focus is no longer exclusively or mainly upon state parties as the classic subject of formal agreements or other general rules of international law. In the second place, the contexts in which choice of law questions arise are as likely to be horizontally as vertically shaped. The paradigm conflicts case is no longer the appropriate formal second-order rule to determine the choice of first-order law between state legal orders which are symmetrical and largely mutually exclusive in their comprehensive territorial competence. Increasingly, what is instead at issue is the relevant terms of trade and mix of first-order authority between regimes with quite different but often significantly overlapping substantive jurisdictions.

3.4.1.2   The new legal pluralism

The recent reinvestment in the broader language of legal pluralism may be seen as a response to this double deformalisation. Often at quite distant remove from either the classical sources or more recent adaptations of the conflict of laws, the new legal pluralism provides a more customised attempt to supply laterally co-ordinate answers to the problems of regime fragmentation and collision.[180]

The relevant sense of legal pluralism at work in the new global perspective is also quite distinct from earlier uses of that same conceptual vocabulary. It differs both from the traditional invocation of language of legal pluralism in the context of imperial relations between coloniser and colonised and their respective legal systems, and from its later application to multiple legal orders co-existing within the one 'national time-space'.[181] Rather, the new strain of legal pluralism refers to the terms of exchange between different legal systems in the absence of any mutually acknowledged hierarchy, or indeed of any generally authoritative *tertium quid* to deal with conflicts. Instead, the new approach stresses the uneven, unpredictable and contingent quality of

---

[179] Fischer-Lescano and Teubner, n. 30 above.

[180] See e.g. Schiff Berman, n. 149 above; and M. Delmas-Marty, *Ordering Pluralism: A Conceptual Framework for Understanding the Transnational Legal World*, trans. N. Norberg (Oxford: Hart, 2009).

[181] B. de Sousa Santos, *Toward a New Legal Common Sense Law, Globalization, and Emancipation*, 2nd edn (Cambridge University Press, 2004) p. 92. See also R. Michaels, 'Global Legal Pluralism' 5 *Annual Review of Law and Social Science* 243 (2009).

interactions between heterarchical legal orders, and the need to find agreement and to generate and establish authority *in situ*. Such general principles as can be fashioned, such bridging mechanism as may be devised, or such common orientations as may be discerned in the new pluralism tend to emerge organically – and sometimes only bilaterally – from the interaction between legal orders. They tend also to be subject to ongoing revision, and to be couched in such broad, fluid and under-determined terms that they require additional refinement or negotiation in order to resolve any concrete dispute.

Sometimes this strain of pluralism goes under the name of 'constitutional pluralism',[182] while at other times the qualifying adjective is absent.[183] The addition of the 'constitutional' modifier may suggest something about the elevated standing of the institutional parties to the pluralistic relationship, as is typically the case in the frequent use of the constitutional label to describe legal relations between national courts and legal systems and the court and central institutions of the EU;[184] or it may imply the derivation of the pluralist maxim or orientation from a broader tradition of constitutional thought in intra-state and other settings.[185] However, these are mere tendencies, and there is, in fact, no clear and undisputed line of principle between constitutional and other unqualified forms of legal pluralism in the matter of lateral co-ordination between legal orders.[186]

In so far as we are able to identify different strains of new global pluralist thought, it is instead in terms of a gradation between 'thin' and 'thick', between highly contingent and ad hoc forms of accommodation on the one hand and relatively stable and generalised rules or guidelines on the other. At the 'thin' end of the spectrum we find so-called 'radical

---

[182] See e.g. N. Walker, 'The Idea of Constitutional Pluralism' 65 *Modern Law Review* 315 (2002); N. Roughan, *Authorities: Conflicts, Cooperation, and Transnational Legal Theory* (Oxford University Press, 2013).

[183] See e.g. Krisch, n. 122 above; and Schiff Berman, n. 149 above.

[184] See e.g. N. Walker, 'Constitutionalism and Pluralism in Global Context' in Avbelj and Komárek, n. 152 above, p. 18.

[185] See e.g. Kumm, n. 64 above.

[186] Nico Krisch, for example, distances himself from constitutional language in the development of a pluralist approach, but only after having defined constitutionalism in strong state-centric 'foundational' terms. He proceeds to develop a test of the 'public autonomy' of those political forms that inhabit his institutional landscape which would meet the less exacting standard of constitutionalism of many other analysts: see Krisch, n. 122 above, pp. 89–103. See also G. Shaffer, 'A Transnational Take on Krisch's Pluralist Structure of Postnational Law' 23 *European Journal of International Law* 565 (2012).

pluralism'.[187] According to this approach, the relationship between different orders neither stems from nor contributes to a general set of pluralist norms but is merely a product of relations of power and strategic considerations. Such a relationship should perhaps not be considered in legal terms at all, but merely as the outcome of a broader competition of resource, influence and self-interest.[188] Or, to draw again from the well-developed example of relations between the EU and its member states, the radical conception of pluralism may be one for which a legal dimension exists only in the form of those bridging mechanisms such as an inter-systemic preliminary reference jurisdiction, a context-specific principle of subsidiarity, or a division of authority between legislative institutions, that are actively chosen by the parties to the relationship and which remain within their ultimate 'contractual' gift.[189]

It is not only the legal quality, but also the very global credentials of radical pluralism that are fragile. If law is either irrelevant in this perspective, or simply a miscellaneous toolbox to be drawn on as the parties demand and the context allows, then the sense of there being any global warrant and justification for this approach becomes elusive. To the extent that it can be retrieved, this can only be done by taking a step back and pointing to the global nature of the legal *predicament* as seen through the lens of radical pluralism. Whereas we have observed that some forms of the abstract-normative approach operate through 'framed positivity',[190] the global contribution of radical pluralism is more as a kind of 'framed non-positivity'. That is to say, it does not provide a perspective that informs, delimits or harmonises the meaning of differ-ent positive laws in circumstances of a global multiplicity of legal orders, as is the case with 'framed positivity'. Instead, it points to the basic incommensurability of these order-specific positive laws and the unavailability of any solvent other than either the mutual negotiation

---

[187] N. MacCormick, 'Beyond the Sovereign State' 56 *Modern Law Review* 1 (1993); see also N. MacCormick, 'Risking Constitutional Collision in Europe?' 18 *Oxford Journal of Legal Studies* 517 (1998), at 528–32, in which he moves away from an unqualified radical pluralism to 'pluralism under international law'. See also N. Krisch 'Who's Afraid of Radical Pluralism? Legal Order and Political Stability in the Postnational Space' 24 *Ratio Juris* 386 (2011); and N. Walker, 'Reconciling MacCormick: Constitutional Pluralism and the Unity of Practical Reason' 24 *Ratio Juris* 369 (2011).

[188] See e.g. J. H. H. Weiler, *The Constitution of Europe* (Cambridge University Press, 1999) p. 320, discussing the relevance of the logic of mutually assured destruction in explain-ing the strategic behaviour of both national and supranational courts in the EU context.

[189] See e.g. Walker, n. 182 above; and Schiff Berman, n. 149 above.

[190] See section 3.2.3.2 above.

and embrace of an additional connecting positive law or a mutual recognition that any sense of a 'law in common' may on occasion 'run out' and require to be replaced by other forms of ordering and alternative modes of co-existence.

It is as we begin to take our distance from this radical pole of the pluralist spectrum that we encounter types such as Nico Krisch's 'interface norms'.[191] The idea here is to develop very general principles or methodologies of mutual toleration and responsiveness between different orders that are locked in a recursive relationship of interdependence. Emphasis is placed on courts developing arm's-length forms of inter-systemic accommodation, ranging from a requirement to 'take into account' the norms of the other order, through various forms of conditional recognition of the other norm, to a general commitment to find a lowest common denominator or 'incompletely theorised agreement'[192] between legal orders. The key to this approach, and what sets it apart from the more radical or 'realist' forms of radical pluralism, is to find general value in the very idea of inter-systemic accommodation. In particular, it is to appreciate what such accommodation might imply for the general balance of transnational power and the checking of unilateral jurisdictional excess, for the encouragement of tie-breaking or dialogue, or for the equal recognition of different and diverse constituencies and their corresponding legal regimes.

Krisch is not unaware of how the relationship between different legal regimes may alter and deepen as it becomes more embedded.[193] But this more evolutionary perspective lies at the heart of Miguel Maduro's somewhat 'thicker' idea of contrapunctual law.[194] In this approach, which yet again draws heavily on the densely interpenetrated example of EU law and the national law of its member states, the focus is upon the gradual harmonisation of the different elements as a distinct legal melody. Particular reference is paid to the need for mutual adjustment in ultimate search of a justificatory framework that is generalisable across all inter-systemic components without destroying the autonomous integrity of the parts. As with Krisch, there is no a priori normative framework to guide relations, but unlike Krisch there is close attention to the prospect, arising out of an initial propensity to give and take, of an

---

[191] Krisch, n. 122 above, pp. 285–96.
[192] C. R. Sunstein, 'Incompletely Theorized Agreements' 108 *Harvard Law Review* 1773 (1995).
[193] Krisch, n. 122 above, pp. 294–6.   [194] Maduro, n. 151 above.

inter-systemic partial convergence of horizons that extends beyond mere mutual tolerance and accommodation.

At the 'thickest' end of the spectrum, finally, we find versions of so-called constitutional pluralism which in their contemplation of general relational norms begin to shade into the kind of general application of cosmopolitan principles that we have already encountered under the abstract-normative approach, and indeed under global constitutionalism more generally.[195] Those who see a role for general pre-positive or thinly positivist principles of participation, accountability, subsidiarity and legality,[196] or for a general formula balancing voice, rights and efficiency of substantive outcomes,[197] are pluralist inasmuch as they recognise that relations between legal orders are a vital part of the glue of a highly diversified global legal constellation. But they are also universalist to the extent that they claim the same general principles to be applicable to inter-systemic relations as to infra-systemic relations. For them, the conflict of particular laws and legal orders is viewed as just one more context and one more challenge for the articulation of a general higher Law rather than as a distinct space for the development of a special relational legal ethics. Yet again, therefore, we see how diversely accommodating individual species of global law can be, and how, in consequence, the margin between one species of global law and another, and between convergent and divergent conceptions more generally, can become blurred and indistinct.[198]

3.4.2   Functionally specific approaches

Many of the functionally specific projects of transnational law that have emerged in recent years, and to which the laterally integrative approaches are a response, have themselves also developed a more or less explicit global warrant. This, as we shall see, only serves to reinforce an image of the legal world as one of presumptively unreconciled parts, and so as tending towards divergence.

The central image of global law here is of a segmented structure. Unlike the laterally integrative models, the concern of the functionally

---

[195] See sections 3.2.3 and 3.3 above.   [196] Kumm, n. 64 above.
[197] See D. Halberstam, 'Constitutional Heterarchy: The Centrality of Conflict in the European Union and the United States' in Dunoff and Trachtman, n. 22 above, pp. 326–55.
[198] See further Chapter 4.2 below.

specific projects is with the internal ordering of the different global sections, or *segments*, rather than with the chain that links them and the legal tissue – however thinly stretched – that connects them. Such projects clearly overlap and connect with some of the decentralised understandings of global or international constitutional law[199] as well as with Global Administrative Law's focus on the diversity of transnational governance. Unlike these historical-discursive approaches, however, much functionally specific global legal practice and its associated scholarship does not seek to emphasise the general applicability of various long-standing constitutional or administrative law themes, principles or conceptual language to the internal working of each area in question. Instead the focus tends to be upon the specific goals and outputs of the relevant sector or upon its particular institutional methodologies. Indeed, a common tendency of such approaches, as is the case within the many highly specialised streams of contemporary law more generally, is to treat law in instrumental terms, as a means to particular policy ends or as a mere vehicle of this or that institutional design.[200]

The emergence of this species, therefore, is neither a cue for exploring what is general and pervasive about law – as is most starkly evident of the abstract-normative approach to global law – nor an occasion to contemplate law as the governing factor in a system of institutional hierarchy or normative co-ordination – as in the structural or formal approaches. Instead, it provides a basis for highlighting what is distinctive and diverse and also what is consequential and derivative about the legal form of different policy sectors. In short, in much sector-specific global legal policy development, law itself is relegated to the status of the dependent – or at least heavily interdependent – variable; legal form follows and serves policy function rather than providing a robust independent factor in framing and generating functional development.

---

[199] These range from the decentralised international constitutionalism of Anne Peters in Klabbers, Peters and Ulfstein, n. 23 above, to the systems theoretical position of Gunther Teubner, most recently in his *Constitutional Fragments*, n. 121 above. See also Walker, n. 184 above, pp. 17–38. And see generally section 3.2.3 above.

[200] On the secular turned towards the instrumental treatment of law, see B. Z. Tamanaha, *Law as a Means to an End: Threat to the Rule of Law* (Cambridge University Press, 2006). See also N. Walker, 'Out of Place and Out of Time: Law's Fading Co-ordinates' 14 *Edinburgh Law Review* 13 (2010).

Functionally specific global legal projects, often called regimes,[201] can be found in areas as diverse as climate change, the preservation of cultural goods, nuclear proliferation and criminal law, to name but a very few. In line with the sense of law as supplying the dependent variable, the language and analytical frame of other disciplines, most notably the economic language of 'global public goods',[202] tends to be

[201] The language of regimes is widely used within the study of transnationalism and global-isation, cutting across legal theory, international relations, international political economy and international sociology; its absence of a disciplinary-specific meaning in law, indeed, mirrors the general tendency to understand law as the dependent or interdependent variable in this area of research. See e.g. Fischer-Lescano and Teubner, n. 30 above; M. A. Young (ed.), *Regime Interaction in International Law: Facing Fragmentation* (Cambridge University Press, 2012); S. Jasanoff (ed.), *States of Knowledge: The Co-production of Science and Social Order* (London: Routledge, 2004); S. Sassen, *Territory, Authority, Rights: From Medieval to Global Assemblages* (Princeton University Press, 2006); A. Hasenclever, P. Mayer and V. Rittberger, *Theories of International Regimes* (Cambridge University Press, 1997); M. J. Petersen, 'International Regimes as Concept', *e-International Relations*, 21 December 2012, www.e-ir.info/2012/12/21/international-regimes-as-concept/; K. Alter and S. Meunier, 'The Politics of International Regime Complexity: Symposium' 7 *Perspectives on Politics* 13 (2009); R. O. Keohane and D. G. Victor, 'The Regime Complex for Climate Change' 9 *Perspectives on Politics* 7 (2011); J. D. Colgan, R. O. Keohane and T. Van de Graaf, 'Punctuated Equilibrium in the Energy Regime Complex' 7 *Review of International Organizations* 117 (2012); and L. R. Helfer, 'Regime Shifting: The TRIPS Agreement and New Dynamics of International Intellectual Property Lawmaking' 29 *Yale Journal of International Law* 1 (2004).

[202] See in particular 'Symposium on Global Public Goods' 23(3) *European Journal of International Law* (2012), which derived from a joint research forum of the American and European Societies of International Law; F. Cafaggi and D. D. Carron, 'Global Public Good amidst a Plurality of Legal Orders: A Symposium' 23 *European Journal of International Law* 643 (2012). See also articles on particular global regimes and their associated public goods: P. C. Mavroidis, 'Free Lunches? WTO as Public Good, and the WTO's View of Public Goods' 23 *European Journal of International Law* 731 (2012); F. Francioni, 'Public and Private in the International Protection of Global Cultural Goods' 23 *European Journal of International Law* 719 (2012); and E. Morgera, 'Bilateralism at the Service of Community Interests? Non-judicial Enforcement of Global Public Goods in the Context of Global Environmental Law' 23 *European Journal of International Law* 743 (2012). On the origins of global public goods research, see e.g. the foundational United Nations Development Programme (UNDP) projects on global public goods, in I. Kaul, I. Grunberg and M. A. Stern (eds.), *Global Public Goods: International Cooperation in the 21st Century* (Oxford University Press, 1999); and in I. Kaul, P. Concicao, K. Le Goulven and R. U. Mendoza (eds.), *Providing Global Public Goods: Managing Globalization* (Oxford University Press, 2003). See also the work of economists such as S. Barrett, *Why Cooperate? The Incentive to Supply Global Public Goods* (Oxford University Press, 2007); T. Sandler, *Global Collective Action* (Cambridge University Press, 2004); and W. D. Nordhaus, 'Paul Samuelson and Global Public Goods' in M. Szenberg, L. Ramrattan and A. A. Gottesman (eds.), *Samuelsonian Economics and the Twenty-First Century* (Oxford University Press, 2006) pp. 88–98.

relied upon to account for the emergence of such projects and to explain both the benefits and difficulties associated with them.[203]

In the classical economic sense, public goods are socially assured or generated goods characterised, first and foremost, by non-excludability of access to their enjoyment – just as public 'bads' may be said to suffer from non-excludability of vulnerability to harm[204] – and, secondly, by non-rivalry of consumption.[205] The conditions of non-excludability and non-rivalrousness are in fact rarely fully in place, with street lighting and flood control systems among the few examples of 'pure' public goods. But even in their typically partial and imperfect form, where some exclusion or differential levels of access are possible, or where the common resource pool may be subject to depletion beyond a certain level of exploitation,[206] public goods create a distinct structure of incentives. They are goods from which all may benefit. But they are also goods to the provision or production of which any particular private party may lack the incentive to contribute, or which, at least in some circumstances, any party may degrade by excessive use. That is so on account of the free-riding temptations and over-consumption opportunities supplied by the very fact of non-excludability. It is this structure of incentives and costs that explains the need for compulsory public provision, and for the invocation of the state and its government as the vehicle of such provision.

Yet in an increasingly porous and interdependent world many of the most significant public goods – or 'bads' – are liable to become non-excludable or only partially excludable across territories and societies that extend beyond national or even regional borders. With regard to

[203] On the close connections between functional specialisation, transnationalism and interdisciplinarity in legal research, see P. Zumbansen, 'Governance: An Interdisciplinary Perspective' in D. Levi-Faur (ed.), The Oxford Handbook on Governance (Oxford University Press, 2012) pp. 83–96.

[204] F. Cafaggi, 'Transnational Private Regulation and the Production of Global Public Goods and Private "Bads"' 23 European Journal of International Law 695 (2012). See also e.g. I. Loader and N. Walker, Civilising Security (Cambridge University Press, 2007) chs. 6 and 9.

[205] See e.g. M. Olsen, The Logic of Collective Action (Cambridge, MA: Harvard University Press, 1971).

[206] In the classical literature, 'common pool resources' is a term reserved for those goods that are non-excludable, but unlike 'pure' public goods, also subtractable (rather than non-rivalrous): see e.g. E. Ostrom, Governing the Commons: The Evolution of Institutions for Collective Action (Cambridge University Press, 1990). In practice, however, as already noted, the distinguishing features of public goods tend to be matters of degree rather than categorical.

dangers such as global warming, nuclear war or global 'terror', the globe itself begins to approximate to a single, indivisible community of risk in the face of the common 'externalities' associated with various forms of transnational economic, political or military activity. In other areas such as trade law, internet law and sports law, where there are also specialist global legal regimes or complexes,[207] the deep mobilising concern may be less – or at least less immediately – on account of the scale of any unavoidable common predicament. Rather, it may be due more to the tendentially territorially unbounded or expansive quality, or potential, of the underlying practice, and so to the possibilities of non-rivalrous and, therefore, positive sum benefits associated with common provision and regulation, and the corresponding iniquities associated with free riding, arbitrary exclusion or differential access or exploitation.[208] In crude terms, the securing of the public good in these latter cases may be more a question of active construction rather than reactive preservation, of co-operative achievement rather than defensive consolidation. In all cases, however, there is some sense of the relevant environment itself as globally extensive and globally connected, and so of global law as a reflection of an emergent global society.

Precisely on account of their in-principle non-excludability, the existence of such public goods – wherever they lie on the action–reaction spectrum – invites some kind of global regulatory response, and in some measure supplies the motivational basis for such a response. This helps to explain why so many functionally specific transnational legal projects begin to be conceived of in such open-ended planetary-wide terms. Yet the other part of the explanation of the development of functionally specific global legal horizons stresses constraints rather than opportunities, disincentives rather than incentives, second-best rather than optimal justifications. For the absence of a world state or of a centralised

---

[207] See e.g. Fischer-Lescano and Teubner, n. 30 above; Krisch, n. 122 above, chs. 1–2; and Koskenniemi, n. 30 above.

[208] That is to say, the key arguments are less to do with the natural or technologically constructed non-excludability and/or non-rivalrousness of the relevant public good in the classical economic sense, and more to do with considerations of efficient co-ordination or fairness and equal treatment in the context of a mutually implicated or common set of practices. These different possibilities, however, are better viewed as points on a spectrum rather than as categorical alternatives. For an incisive and wide-ranging consideration of the different types of global public goods and their amenability to legal treatment, see G. Shaffer, 'International Law and Global Public Goods in a Legal Pluralist World' 23 *European Journal of International Law* 669 (2012); and Barrett, n. 202 above.

system of world government, and the lack of the global common political cause and commitment necessary to generate such a central world order, patently poses significant problems of legitimacy and feasibility regarding the detailed provision of *any* response to the challenge of global public goods. It indicates that there is no world demos and no democratically supported world constitutional regime available to authorise the terms and conditions of supply of the various goods, still less – to recall the predicament of global legal pluralism – to decide the balance between them.[209] The language of risk and necessity, and of positive-sum benefits, can instead provide a baseline technocratic rationale for the regulatory enablement and control of such global public goods. And, indeed, global governance *is* often defended under the sign of politically disinterested efficiency and expertise.[210]

Yet significant value choices remain about the distribution of the costs and benefits of various global public goods, about their specification and internal emphasis, and about their optimal collective provision. In the context of domestic public goods all of these matters are resolved with the support of an additional layer of electoral justification that is not available on the global level. The lack of just such an integrated and representative world government places a premium on detailed systems of sectoral governance, but clearly does so under conditions that remain sub-optimal for their achievement. For if the political will to commit to common world government as a way of reconciling the deep diversity of national and regional interests in policy matters with global ramifications is lacking, the conditions of common political will formation in particular policy sectors, although somewhat less exacting, are likely to be deficient for the same reasons.[211]

The sheer variety and volatility of the institutional arrangements for incipient projects of functionally specific global government in the post-war period reflects and responds to these difficulties. One general periodisation of institutional models[212] draws a helpful distinction between the sectorally integrated international regimes of the immediate post-war period and the later emergence of 'regime complexes',[213]

---

[209] See section 3.4.1.2 above.
[210] See e.g. G. de Búrca, 'Developing Democracy Beyond the State' 46 *Columbia Journal of Transnational Law* 221 (2008).
[211] See e.g. Loader and Walker, n. 204 above, ch. 9.
[212] G. de Búrca, R. O. Keohane and C. Sabel, 'New Modes of Pluralist Global Governance' 45 *Journal of International Law and Politics* 723 (2013).
[213] *Ibid.*, at 733.

'orchestrated networks'[214] and other less hierarchical and more flexible and dispersed institutional forms, including the intense recent development of new modes of 'experimental governance'.[215] The early success of the integrated regimes that grew up alongside the United Nations, such as the International Monetary Fund, the World Bank and the General Agreement on Tariffs and Trade, owed much to the dominant position of certain leading states, or state coalitions, and their projected commitment to provide a coherent institutional response to a well-defined problem of global collective action. The hegemonic position of these forces and their capacity to frame the issue in terms of reasonably fixed and precise objectives for managing co-operation and redistribution in the world economy allowed them to sidestep the deeper questions of legitimacy and provide confidently hierarchical institutional responses.

However, as the number of issue areas in which global public goods are pertinent has multiplied, and as their complexity has deepened, the limitations of this kind of linear state-delegation model of institutional agency have become more exposed. And that challenge has been reinforced by the general amplification of the voice of the global South in the United Nations and other planetary political settings and their willingness to articulate different preferences to rich Northern powers. The arrested development of major integrated global initiatives of the last twenty years, from the failure of the WTO's Doha Development Round to the halting ratification and implementation of the Rio Convention on Climate Change and the Rome Statute establishing the International Criminal Court, shows an increasing failure to deliver grand settlements across significant interest divisions and across the broader set of sovereign states who assert a significant stake in these settlements. Instead, in areas as diverse as climate change, energy production, intellectual property and marine protection, the common response to heightened global interdependence tends to take the form of less unified and settled institutional structures with wider forms of participation and accountability, more decentralised forms of implementation and more iterative and reflexive styles of policy-making.[216] In their programmatic modesty, their broader and open-ended vision of relevant stake-holders and

---

[214] *Ibid.*   [215] *Ibid.*, at 738.
[216] See e.g. G. de Búrca and J. Scott (eds.), *Law and New Governance in the EU and the US* (Oxford: Hart, 2006); and C. Sabel and J. Zeitlin (eds.), *Experimentalist Governance in the European Union: Towards a New Architecture* (Oxford University Press, 2010). On experimentalism in the US, see e.g. M. Dorf and C. Sabel, 'A Constitution of Experimentalist Governance' 98 *Columbia Law Review* 267 (1998); C. Sabel and

their greater adjustability to changing circumstances and new knowledge, these new types of regime are more willing to acknowledge the problems of failed or delayed agreement and institutional blockage and inertia associated with larger and more permanent structures and instead emphasise dispersed influence and incremental policy development.

This analysis points to a growing tension between institutional coherence and global reach in the development of functionally specific regimes. The development of a global approach to the realisation or preservation of certain global public goods is increasingly unlikely to manifest itself in capaciously empowered, self-proclaimed instruments of world government. Instead, many new initiatives are breaking new organisational ground, entering 'under the radar' of a more conventional institutional mapping of globally ambitious structures.[217] In this area at least, the globality of global governance does not announce itself in headlines. Yet that modesty of profile is better understood not as a check on the progress of functionally specific global governance but as a condition of its gathering momentum.

3.4.3   New hybrids

Hybrid forms of global law supply new ways of conceiving of global legal order from the fusion of old legal disciplines based upon established functional distinctions. They share much in common with other approaches that draw upon the discursive resources of particular disciplinary traditions, whether the incremental adaptation of the conflicts approach[218] or the more pronounced global reconfiguration of the historical disciplines of state constitutional law and state administrative law.[219] Yet there are two key differences. First, while the past remains important as a resource base, the aim of the hybrid approach is to emphasise innovation rather than continuity and adaptation. We may venture, indeed, that while the historical-discursive approaches pour new wine into old bottles, with the label modestly amended, the hybrid

W. Simon, 'Minimalism and Experimentalism in American Public Law' 100 *Georgetown Law Review* 53 (2011). On experimentalism in the EU, see K. Armstrong, 'The Character of EU Law and Governance: From "Community Method" to New Modes of Governance' 64 *Current Legal Problems* 179 (2011).

[217] See e.g. Mazower, n. 6 above, ch. 14; and A.-M. Slaughter, *A New World Order* (Princeton University Press, 2004).

[218] Section 3.4.1.1 above.   [219] Section 3.3 above.

approaches set out to blend and bottle various old wines under an entirely new label.

Secondly, the hybrid approaches do not possess the same transversal quality as the various disciplinary traditions considered earlier. In their different ways, constitutional law, administrative law and even the conflict of laws in its most systemically ambitious formulation, each purport to cut across *all* functional or sectoral boundaries. And so each reframes the legal world as a whole in its own terms. Global constitutional law, in its convergent variants, invokes a common constitutional code of fundamental principles for all places and circumstances, or places constitutional norms or principles at the top of an all-embracing legal pyramid. Global Administrative Law treats all sector-specific regulatory strands as a single administrative cloth, and so amenable to treatment under a common set of principles. The conflict of laws articulates general legal rules or orientations capable of addressing and overcoming all particular clashes between legal orders, and, more specifically in the new approach, all sectoral collisions. The hybrid approaches, by contrast, claim to deal only with one strain of global legal order. In that regard, they display some similarities with the functionally specific approaches, but also certain important differences. Like the functionally specific approaches, they focus on the internal structure and distinguishing features of a special domain of global law, one that makes no claim to generality of scope. Unlike the functionally specific approaches, the hybrid approaches have a relatively expansive approach to jurisdiction. They aim to join rather than to divide, to provide more ambitious jurisprudential models of subject-matter coherence rather than to track detailed lines of functional segmentation. And in so doing, the hybrid approaches tend to treat law as active rather than passive, as generative rather than derivative. Rather than a mere instrumental response to changing functional imperatives, the new legal hybrids are more concerned with the capacity of law, drawing upon deep historical resources, to recast the ways in which it addresses some of the problems of an interconnected world. The defining image of global law here is one of *flow* – of the interfluence of various discrete streams to supply a stronger and more far-spreading new current.

A number of recent initiatives can illustrate this point. Ruti Teitel, for example, has made a case for a new 'humanity's law'.[220] This, she claims, reflects, endorses and encourages a profound normative shift in

---

[220] R. Teitel, *Humanity's Law* (Oxford University Press, 2011).

the global legal order from protecting state security to a more rounded notion of 'human security'.[221] Cumulatively, this normative shift, which is asserted to possess deep historical roots but to have achieved significant momentum only in the last fifty years, may be represented both as a new law *of* humanity – of those matters that are most fundamental in asserting the value and agency of all human beings – and as a new law *for* humanity as a whole.[222] It is a jurisprudence that spans the law of war, international human rights and international criminal justice. Teitel chronicles the way in which ideas about the deep rationale of these dimensions of law have gradually altered as courts, tribunals, advocacy groups and international actors and organisations have come to interpret and extend the Universal Declaration of Human Rights,[223] the Geneva Conventions and other documentary enshrinements of principles about rights and responsibilities relating to war and justice in ways that place certain universal principles of humanitarian consideration centre-stage.

Another, and substantively overlapping, example of the hybrid approach is Christine Bell's notion of a new 'law of the peacemakers', or *Lex Pacificatoria*.[224] The governing idea here is that state-centred constitutional mechanisms for recognising, negotiating and implementing peace agreements in periods of transition following sustained conflict operate in close interaction with international law norms in matters such as criminal law, human rights law and the law of humanitarian intervention. That interaction creates a new and dynamic mixed form which escapes the old discrete categories of internal and external – of constitutional law and international law. The relationship between the two is symbiotic, one of mutual dependence. But it is also highly creative. Legitimacy is a precarious and often elusive attribute of peace processes, and is achieved through a mix of highly particularistic, context-specific and audience-sensitive procedures and mechanisms, and of general, internationally endorsed disinterested standards. Neither state law nor international law is capable of providing the requisite authority on its

---

[221] On the history and prospects of the idea of human security, see M. Kaldor, *Human Security* (Cambridge: Polity Press, 2007).

[222] Teitel sometimes uses the term 'humanity law' instead of 'humanity's law'; the former rather suggesting 'humanity' and humanitarian concerns as the object of the law, and the latter rather suggesting 'humanity' as the subject.

[223] See also section 3.2.3.1 above.

[224] C. Bell, *On the Law of Peace: Peace Agreements and the* Lex Pacificatoria (Oxford University Press, 2008).

own, but each can supply the omission of the other. This interaction, moreover, can generate a significant epistemic dividend. The law of the peacemakers may evolve in an open-ended way both through particularistic reflection on international best practice and through international reflection on local experience. In this way the new law can develop a genuinely global resonance not by appeal to one overarching source and tradition but by reference to a productive relationship between different sources and traditions.[225]

A final illustration of the emerging hybrid species of global law is provided by Emmanuelle Tourme-Jouannet's new 'international law of recognition'.[226] According to Tourme-Jouannet, this describes an emerging 'set of legal institutions, discourses, practices and principles that had not previously been sufficiently theorised and brought together, although they have the same subject-matter which . . . arises specifically from the need for recognition'.[227] This 'need for recognition' reached an unprecedented contemporary pitch with the ending of the Cold War and its reawakening of dormant identities, and with the global spread of many new aspirations for the affirmation of distinctive forms of social and cultural belonging. Former colonies, indigenous peoples, ethnic groups, minorities and women have all sought new forms of legal acknowledgment of their sense of collective subjectivity. Whereas a narrow principle of state recognition, based upon common possession of a canonical set of attributes, has been central to international law in the dominant sovereigntist tradition, this new broader law of recognition is based upon the diversity of recognition-entitling identities. The new recognition jurisprudence can be found in the growth and intermingling of many strands; in the law recognising cultural diversity centred around

---

[225] Renewed interest in the category of *jus post bellum* is another example of innovative hybridisation around the areas of human rights, international criminal law and peace-making and peace-keeping norms. See e.g. the project of that name at the University of Leiden: http://juspostbellum.com. See also N. Bhuta, 'New Modes and Orders: The Difficulties of a *Jus Post Bellum* of Constitutional Transformation' 60 *University of Toronto Law Journal* 799 (2010).

[226] E. Tourme-Jouannet, 'The International Law of Recognition' 24 *European Journal of International Law* 667 (2013). See also the exchange with Jean d'Aspremont in the same volume: J. d'Aspremont, 'The International Law of Recognition: A Reply to Emmanuelle Tourme-Jouannet' pp. 691–9; and E. Tourme-Jouannet, 'The International Law of Recognition: A Rejoinder to Jean d'Aspremont' pp. 701–5. See, in addition, d'Aspremont, n. 37 above.

[227] E. Tourme-Jouannet, Guest Editorial, 'The Emergence of an International Law of Recognition' 9 *European Society of International Law Newsletter* 3 (February 2013).

the 2005 UNESCO Convention on the Protection and Promotion of the Diversity of Cultural Expressions;[228] in human rights law, and in particular in identity-preserving specific rights of individual and groups, especially those concerned with national, ethnic, religious or linguistic minorities;[229] and, more schematically, in the law concerning the reparation of historical wrongs.[230]

These various examples have certain significant features in common over and above their hybrid mixing of established disciplinary discourses. First, each has a transformative rather than a conservative aspiration. The exercise of re-imagination is mounted in aid of an agenda of change, the tendencies identified conceived of as the embryo rather than the mature expression of a new approach.

Secondly, each involves the decentring of a 'hard' doctrinal approach to disciplinary developments. Court judgments and treaties and their established *dramatis personae* remain important, but other actors, including the newly self-asserted principals of the politics of reparation, identity and recognition, a wider range of domestic civil society and other transnational non-state actors, and, notably, the academic sponsors themselves, are vital players in the process of reframing.

Thirdly, and most pertinently, in each case the catalyst for paradigm change is the shift from an international to a more expansively global legal warrant. For Teitel, states are no longer the exclusive subjects of the relevant hybrid field of law, and the regulated interests of states are no longer their exclusive object. Rather, humanity as a whole is the ultimate subject, and the standards and practices associated with a humanist ideal the relevant object. For Bell, the peacemakers are the new law makers, and peace is their governing object and purpose, with international law and constitutional law recast as contributory normative resources and supporting authorities rather than the exclusive vehicles of fixed and restrictive categories of the entitled. And, finally, for Tourme-Jouannet, the very categories of statehood and state recognition as, respectively, the generative framework and basic purpose of international law, are challenged as unduly limited and replaced by a more expansive warrant.

In each of these hybrid cases, therefore, international law remains an important platform, indeed springboard, for the emergence of a new

---

[228] The full text of the Convention is available at http://portal.unesco.org/en/ev.php-URL_ID=31038&URL_DO=DO_TOPIC&URL_SECTION=201.html. See also Tourme-Jouannet, n. 226 above, at 673–6.
[229] Tourme-Jouannet, n. 226 above, at 676–80. [230] *Ibid.*, at 680–6.

discourse. Yet, while none of these new variants of global law purports to replace international law in its entirety, each emerges from a critical confrontation of a narrow reading of the basis and purpose of some areas of international jurisdiction, and each proceeds on the basis of an aspiration to overcome these narrow limits. Once again, therefore, if from a more selective reading of its sources and areas of impact, international law is treated both as platform and as critical point of departure for the new global law.[231]

---

[231] See section 3.1 above.

4

The circuit of global law

4.1 Introduction

In the introduction to the previous chapter we referred to an underlying unity of concern across the quite different visions – convergence-promoting and divergence-accommodating – and the various species of global law. We also alluded to how that unity in diversity expresses itself as a relationship of mutual presupposition and mutual tension. Our subsequent exploration of the various species of global law now allows us to add meat to the bare bones of these propositions. We are able to identify the qualified basis upon which convergent and divergent conceptions, and the various species of global law bearing these conceptions, together with the various images associated with these conceptions – pyramid, umbrella, vessel, thread, chain, segment and flow – are able to co-exist and co-occur in principle.

In addition, we are in a position to demonstrate how that in-principle cohabitation among the different species of global law feeds into the close yet sometimes rivalrous interdependence of their embryonic practice. The incipient category of global law, in other words, possesses a self-generating and self-sustaining quality, but it is a quality that is also closely bound up with its self-critical and internally contested edge. This adds an important dimension to our understanding of the emergence of global law. We have seen in the previous chapter, in tracing the various pressures that shape the different species of global law, how much of its *foreground* impetus comes from the increased density and diversity of international and transnational regulation. Equally, we observed in Chapter 2 how much of its *background* influence comes from the occupational culture and practice of lawyers and jurists.[1] In addition, we are now able to claim, global law is a theme that both feeds and challenges itself, and so generates *forward* impetus, by dint of the very character and circuitous interplay of its discourse and practice.

---

[1] See in particular Chapter 2.2–2.3 above.

131

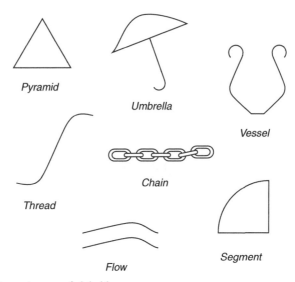

Pyramid

Umbrella

Vessel

Chain

Thread

Flow

Segment

Fig. 4.1   Seven images of global law

4.2   The double normativity of global law

Our argument here proceeds in three stages. In the first place, we should take note of the area of common ground occupied by the two positions. For all their apparent differences, neither the convergence-promoting nor the divergence-accommodating conception embraces the diversity of transnational law as an unalloyed good, just as proponents of both conceptions would readily accept that there are profound practical and ethical limits to any attempt to eliminate the diversity of transnational law. Rather, each type of approach sets out in its own way to recognise and regulate the underlying variety of transnational law *through* (more) law and to contain that variety *within* law. So understood, the convergent and divergent conceptions, rather than describing polar opposites, each refer to a cluster of positions tending from either direction towards the middle range of a continuum. Global law from either perspective – to repeat an earlier point – always assumes and contributes to a *double normativity*.[2] Each and every species of global law responds to the diversity of other forms of law by acting upon some of these diverse other forms of law. Each and every species of global law, therefore, is

---

[2] See Chapter 1.2.3 above and Chapter 5.2.4 below.

predicated on the existence of these diverse other forms of law, and would lack both orientation and traction in their absence. The most ambitiously directive of the abstract-normative positions in an area such as human rights, for example, assumes and still leaves much scope for local or otherwise special variations and applications just on account of its abstract character.[3] The most strictly hierarchical and broadly inclusive of the structural approaches to global law, too, still tends to fall far short of claiming or anticipating the emergence of a system of government, still less a parliament and legislature,[4] whose overall jurisdictional centre of gravity is planetary rather than local. Rather, under actually existing conditions of the distribution of legal authority,[5] global institutions such as the United Nations continue to presuppose and to require local or regional systems of law and administration to act towards and upon, whether with or against, in any and all areas that they possess material jurisdiction. Typically, for instance, the structural approach understands even the most coercive edge and even the most urgent and profound justification of institutionalised legal power at the global level, namely the use of force in response to an act of aggression or a breach of or threat to international security, as existing in tandem with more local forms of legal capacity based upon self-defence.[6]

---

[3] Consider, for example, the margin of appreciation doctrine: see Y. Shany, 'Towards a General Margin of Appreciation Doctrine in International Law?' 16 *European Journal of International Law* 907 (2005); and P. Schiff Berman, *Global Legal Pluralism: A Jurisprudence of Law Beyond Borders* (Cambridge University Press, 2012) pp. 161–3.

[4] Many, however, would advocate such a development: see e.g. D. Archibugi, *The Global Commonwealth of Citizens: Toward Cosmopolitan Democracy* (Princeton University Press, 2008). See also, for example, the work of the Campaign for the Establishment of a United Nations Parliamentary Assembly, established in 2007: http://en.wikipedia.org/wiki/Campaign_for_the_Establishment_of_a_United_Nations_Parliamentary_Assembly. See further Chapter 6 below.

[5] Recall that our definition of global law requires an element of grounding in and contribution to existing legal practice, and does not include ideal blueprints that are purely aspirational. See Chapter 1.2.3.2 above and Chapter 5 below.

[6] See UN Charter, Arts. 41, 42 and 51. The first part of Art. 51 reads: 'Nothing in the present Charter shall impair the inherent right of individual or collective self-defence if an armed attack occurs against a Member of the United Nations, until the Security Council has taken measures necessary to maintain international peace and security.' See further Chapter 3.2.1 above and Chapter 5.1 below. See e.g. Ş. Kardaş, 'Examining the Role of the UN Security Council in Post-Cold War Interventions: The Case for Authorized Humanitarian Intervention' 3 *USAK Yearbook of International Politics and Law* 55 (2010); E. de Wet, *The Chapter VII Powers of the United Nations Security Council* (Oxford: Hart, 2004).

The divergent positions, too, assume the existence of different levels of
normativity and a connection between these different levels, even if their
underlying dynamic tends to be 'bottom-up' rather than 'top-down'. All
but the most radical forms of legal or constitutional pluralism[7] recognise
that, in order to avoid or overcome collisions between different national
or transnational regimes, there need to be some standard forms of more
broadly encompassing legal connective tissue, even if we understand that
tissue as growing out of[8] or as grafted upon[9] each of these regimes' own
organic legal material. That is to say, the higher, potentially global level
of normativity remains a vital component, even if its adequacy depends
upon and is a product of its 'fit' with the local levels of normativity.
Equally, even the most specific functional vision of global public good
and even the most complexly decentred governance regime recognises
some ground, however narrow, on which a globally general convergence
of purpose and interest is possible. Whether we are talking about trade,
or international criminal law, or climate change, the articulation of the
regulatory good in global terms envisages a topsoil of general normativity for each sector – typically a set of guiding principles and a measure of
general institutional capacity – above a detailed and often quite differentiated substructure.[10]

[7] See e.g. N. MacCormick, 'Beyond the Sovereign State' 56 *Modern Law Review* 1 (1993).
See also N. Krisch, 'Who's Afraid of Radical Pluralism? Legal Order and Political
Stability in the Postnational Space' 24 *Ratio Juris* 386 (2011); N. Walker, 'Reconciling
MacCormick: Constitutional Pluralism and the Unity of Practical Reason' 24 *Ratio Juris*
369 (2011); and Chapter 3.4.1.2 above.
[8] See e.g. M. Maduro, 'Contrapunctual Law: Europe's Constitutional Pluralism in Action'
in N. Walker (ed.), *Sovereignty in Transition: Essays in European Law* (Oxford: Hart,
2003) pp. 501–37; and N. Krisch, *Beyond Constitutionalism: The Pluralist Structure of
Postnational Law* (Oxford University Press, 2010) pp. 285–96.
[9] See e.g. Schiff Berman, n. 3 above.
[10] See generally Chapter 3.4.2 above. On international trade law, see e.g. D. Z. Cass, 'The
"Constitutionalization" of International Trade Law: Judicial Norm-Generation as
the Engine of Constitutional Development in International Trade' 12 *European
Journal of International Law* 39 (2001); A. Lang, *World Trade Law after
Neoliberalism: Re-imagining the Global Economic Order* (Oxford University Press,
2011); and E.-U. Petersmann, *International Economic Law in the 21st Century:
Constitutional Pluralism and Multilevel Governance of Interdependent Public Goods*
(Oxford: Hart, 2012). On international criminal law, see e.g. J. Doria, H.-P. Gasser
and M. Cherif Bassiouni (eds.), *The Legal Regime of the International Criminal Court:
Essays in Honour of Professor Igor Blishchenko* (The Hague: BRILL, 2009); R. Cryer,
Prosecuting International Crimes: Selectivity and the International Criminal Law Regime
(Cambridge University Press, 2005). On climate change law, see e.g. D. Bodansky, 'The
History and Legal Structure of the Climate Change Regime' in D. Sprinz and
U. Luterbacher (eds.), *International Relations and Global Climate Change*, 2nd edn

If we move from the ends of the spectrum towards its centre, we observe, beyond this shared assumption and commitment to double normativity, even more telling evidence of common ground. For we find that the very boundary line that situates particular species of global law on one or the other side of the convergent/divergent divide is quite indistinct. This is true, for instance, within the broad historical-discursive church of global constitutionalism, and even the more modest parish of Global Administrative Law.[11] It is also the case, as we have seen, at the frontier between 'thick' forms of constitutional pluralism and abstract-normative forms of cosmopolitan law.[12] The general blurring between convergent and divergent conceptions of global law, then, is highlighted by the fuzzy categorical location of certain specific cases.

4.3   Global law's partial visions

In the second place, arising from their common general recognition and acceptance of the underlying diversity of transnational law, the various species arranged under the convergent and divergent conceptions of global law are far from being necessarily in conflict in the particular contribution they make to addressing that underlying diversity. They are, instead, in some measure complementary, or at least not mutually incompatible, and to that extent they operate as cumulative possibilities.

It was noted in the introduction to Chapter 3 that the contrasting images of the legal world fashioned by each conception and its various species are the product of different focal concerns. But these focal concerns are just that – *selective* forms of contemplation and treatment of what is of concern. And the adoption of these selective foci does not require the taking of a particular side, or sometimes, indeed, *any* side, in certain larger normative questions. To begin with, they do not them-selves encapsulate distinct and irreconcilable *comprehensive* moral or

---

(Boston, MA: MIT Press, 2013) pp. 11–31; and E. Morgera, 'Bilateralism at the Service of Community Interests? Non-judicial Enforcement of Global Public Goods in the Context of Global Environmental Law' 23 *European Journal of International Law* 743 (2012).

[11] See Chapter 3.3.2 above.

[12] See Chapter 3.4.1.2 above; and see e.g. D. Halberstam, 'Constitutional Heterarchy: The Centrality of Conflict in the European Union and the United States' and M. Kumm, 'The Cosmopolitan Turn in Constitutionalism: On the Relationship between Constitutionalism in and beyond the State', both in J. L Dunoff and J. P. Trachtman (eds.), *Ruling the World? Constitutionalism, International Law, and Global Governance* (Cambridge University Press, 2009) pp. 326–55 and 258–325 respectively.

political world-views on the part of their holders and sponsors.[13] That is to say, they do not represent and articulate competing visions of the global good life – of its proper ethical path, whether religious or secular. Equally, these different conceptions of global law do not seek to occupy the only somewhat less commanding heights of a global theory of justice.[14] They do not represent and articulate competing fully worked out conceptions of how it would be to achieve justice in a world inhabited by different visions of the good life, complete with prescriptions of how global resources should be distributed and basic rights reconciled between persons and peoples.[15] And finally, the different conceptions of global law do not supply the distinct and exclusive means towards any such distinct and irreconcilable comprehensive conceptions of the good life or of just global arrangements and institutions. That is to say, far from expressing the larger normative visions of the global good life or global justice, the different conceptions of global law do not even provide dedicated institutional or regulatory pathways towards these ends.

The various species of global law are unable to express or develop any such sharply competing visions, or dedicated pathways in pursuit of such visions, simply because as practical forms of endorsement or commit-ment to particular normative legal positions they cannot assume the institutional *tabula rasa* that would allow them the latitude to do so. Rather, just because, as we have seen, they take the underlying diversity of transnational law for granted, they must take the actually existing global institutional configuration in all its multipolar, interlocking com-plexity as their already engaged starting point and suggest any specific problem-solutions or associated forms of normative adjustments or reform from that baseline. The different conceptions of global law and

---

[13] See e.g. J. Rawls, *Political Liberalism* (New York: Columbia University Press, 1996) p. 13.

[14] Rawls famously developed his principles of justice as a form of common ground or overlapping consensus between those holding different comprehensive conceptions of the good. See e.g. J. Rawls, 'Justice as Fairness: Political not Metaphysical' 14 *Philosophy and Public Affairs* 223 (1985). For the view that a theory of justice implicates concep-tions of political morality that are just as difficult to reconcile as are comprehensive conceptions of the good, see e.g. J. Waldron, *Law and Disagreement* (Oxford University Press, 1999) ch. 7.

[15] On the difficult relationship between global ethics and contemporary conceptions of international law, and of global law more generally, see S. Ratner, 'Ethics and International Law: Integrating the Global Justice Project(s)' 5 *International Theory* 1 (2013). For a good primer on global ethics, but typically (and tellingly) with little to say about the ways and means of global legal organisation, see K. Hutchings, *Global Ethics: An Introduction* (Cambridge: Polity Press, 2010). See further Chapter 6 below.

the various species arranged under them are, therefore, only partial visions and perspectives. They supply specific angles of approach to the question of global legality, and correspondingly specific 'imagings' of global legality, that are compatible with, and potentially instrumental towards, many different overall conceptions of the global good or global justice. Their fitness for purpose, therefore, and the terms of debate concerning their fitness for purpose, are only indirectly linked to such larger questions, and sometimes, indeed, no such link will be made or at least explicitly acknowledged.[16] What counts as a good argument and as appropriate grounds for adopting this or that understanding of global law depends more immediately on the countless variety of factors contextualising their avenue of practical engagement – on the issue under consideration, the particular problem posed and question asked. In some contexts of apprehension and intervention, the focus is more likely to be on the encouragement of a convergent trend, whereas in others it is more likely to stress the accommodation and management of diversity.

It follows from the oblique relationship between global law and holistic considerations of political morality that it is possible and by no means incoherent in terms of those wider conceptions of the global good or global justice to adopt a position that subscribes, as the situation demands, to many, or indeed all, of the various species of global law within and across convergent and divergent conceptions. It follows equally, however, that it is no more incoherent to adopt a position that does *not* permit such wholesale or generous endorsement of global law. The clearest forms of complementarity and the strongest synergies, unsurprisingly, tend to occur *within* each general conception. Structural and formal variants of the convergent approach, for example, are often closely intertwined in a single narrative of global law, and frequently complemented by an abstract-normative vision such as that centred on human rights.[17] Equally, laterally co-ordinate approaches to global law are predicated upon the kind of segmented understanding of the world of transnational law most emphatically present in the functionally specific approaches or the more particularistic models of global constitutionalism, and so tend to 'hunt together' most naturally with these other approaches.[18] However, there are also many possible

---

[16] This is particularly so of divergence-accommodating conceptions of global law, which, by their very nature, are less likely to have an integrated conception of global justice in their sights. Although, see further Chapter 6.4.2 below.
[17] See Chapter 3.2.3.1 above.   [18] See Chapter 3.4 above.

combinations across the convergent/divergent divide. An endorsement of a structural model allowing for a modestly centralised framework of world governance within the established areas of United Nations jurisdiction such as peace-keeping and human rights, for instance, is perfectly compatible with the pursuit of a global approach within various functional specialisms, or a concern with basic rules of lateral co-ordination.[19] Sponsorship of a hybrid approach within one emerging substantive field, say the law of recognition or the law of peace, need by no means be inconsistent with a belief in a 'thin' formal overall integrity of a globalising international law.

By the same token, however, certain stances on global law may betray an overall background world-view of the means and the ends of the global good or global justice that does not permit the embrace of all species of global law. For example, an approach that concentrates on the limited possibilities of the legal cultivation of functionally specific public goods, or on the most modestly pragmatic or radically pluralist version of the laterally co-ordinate approach, may deny the kind of universal umbrella or vessel, however basic, of an abstract-normative approach, and vice-versa. Similarly, an approach which endorses a version of the historical-discursive vision of global constitutionalism based upon singularity or commonality may sit very uncomfortably with a historical-discursive approach predicated on the thin reconciliation of difference, as in constitutional pluralism or the conflicts perspective more generally.[20]

Of course, regardless of whether a 'full subscription' to the various species of global law is or can be taken out from any particular background perspective, significant choices will always remain in the pursuit of any overall profile of global law. In the absence of a fundamental contradiction – of a deep binary opposition with mutually exclusive effect – there is still, nevertheless, much scope for variation and contestation both within and between the two different conceptions and within and between their various different species of global law. And how this plays out, to repeat, is much

---

[19] Many of the approaches to international constitutionalism which do not accord the United Nations a dominant role would fit this description. See e.g. E. de Wet, 'The Constitutionalisation of Public International Law' in M. Rosenfeld and A. Sajó (eds.), *The Oxford Handbook of Comparative Constitutional Law* (Oxford University Press, 2012) p. 1224. See also Chapter 3.3 above.

[20] See Chapter 3.3.1 and 3.4.1 above. But see further Chapter 6.4 below on possible deeper channels of connection between singularist and pluralist conceptions of global law.

dependent upon circumstantial factors, a question of which issues arise where and when they manifest themselves in the complexly evolving architecture of post-national law. The possible combinations of approaches among the various species are many, a matter of nuance and rich complexity, rather than reducible to a specific and so restrictive series of settled formulae.

4.4   The mutual reproduction of global law

To argue, then, as we have so far, that the relationship among convergent and divergent conceptions of global law is not one of implacable opposition but reveals a contiguity of underlying perspective and a basic level of compatibility between particular species, is to propose that, statically conceived, much of what operates under the developing category of global law is capable of hanging together – of cohabiting. However, in the third place, in order to complete the picture we must thicken our account by adding a dynamic perspective. For the measure of the relationship between the various emergent species of global law is not only their forms and degrees of commonality and of fit, but also the terms of their mutual influence and the implications of their multidirectional causal links. The invocation of one type of conception is often at least partly *in response to* the invocation of the other type of conception, and this builds into a complex interactive circuit which is at once mutually supportive and mutually challenging.

The underlying element of commonality and fit, it bears emphasising, not only influences the pattern of this circular dynamic but also supplies its essential precondition. The relationship between convergent and divergent approaches could not reproduce itself *as* a relationship in which both approaches are sustained over time and, indeed, reinforced, if there was a fundamental antagonism between them. But if this tells us *why* the mutual reproduction of convergent and divergent approaches is conceivable, it does not yet explain *how* this actually transpires and with what consequences.

To take this last step, we must appreciate the way in which convergent and divergent tendencies operate as forms of mutual provocation and stimulation in various contexts of the invocation of global law. These contexts range across the relatively concrete and 'applied' and the relatively abstract and reflective. To take perhaps the best-known practical example from the contemporary politics of international law, we may cite again the protracted debate over unity and fragmentation. We noted earlier[21] how the sheer density and variety of contemporary transnational legal initiatives has given rise to an anxiety among some general international lawyers about the integrity of their discipline. It has spawned fears of the diffusion of certain of its general and long-standing normative commitments, and fuelled concerns about empire-building and systemic bias within particular regimes.[22] These considerations have led to efforts, spearheaded by the International Law Commission, to reinforce the formal unity of international law by reference to devices of ordering – jus cogens rules, erga omnes obligations, the supremacy clause of the UN Charter,[23] the obligation under the Vienna Convention on the Law of Treaties to take account of all relevant rules of international law applicable between the parties in the interpretation of particular treaties,[24] and the like – that imply the reinforcement of a globally integrative warrant.[25] Equally, however, those who defend the integrity and 'self-contained'[26] character of special regimes in areas such as environmental law, public health law or nuclear non-proliferation law, each with their functionally specific remit,[27] seek to resist the totalising embrace of formal unity by pleading the urgent particularity and distinctive policy logic of the global public good in the specific sector in question.[28] In this way, action and reaction combine to mutually reinforcing effect, practical questions driving an ever deeper and more conspicuous reflection on the nature of law's global warrant and an ever more marked insistence on different ways of grounding that claim.

---

[21] See Chapter 3.2.2 above.
[22] See e.g. M. Koskenniemi, 'The Fate of Public International Law: Between Technique and Politics' 70 Modern Law Review 1 (2007), particularly at 1–19; and P.-M. Dupuy, 'The Danger of Fragmentation or Unification of the International Legal System and the International Court of Justice' 31 New York University Journal of International Law and Politics 791 (1999).
[23] UN Charter, Art. 103.
[24] Vienna Convention on the Law of Treaties, 1969, Art. 31(3)(c).
[25] Fragmentation of International Law: Difficulties Arising from the Diversification and Expansion of International Law, Report of the Study Group of the International Law Commission, finalised by Martti Koskenniemi: 13 April 2006, UN Doc. A/CN.4/L.682 pp. 1–256; and 18 July 2006, UN Doc. A/CN.4/L.702 pp. 1–25.
[26] B. Simma and D. Pulkowski, 'Of Planets and the Universe: Self-contained Regimes in International Law' 17 European Journal of International Law 483 (2006).
[27] See further Chapter 3.4.2 above.
[28] See e.g. Koskenniemi, n. 22 above. On the tendency of formalism to be associated with an expansionist approach to the sources and scope of general international law, see J. d'Aspremont, Formalism and the Sources of International Law: A Theory of the Ascertainment of Legal Rules (Oxford University Press, 2011) ch. 7. See further Chapter 3.2.2 above.

A second example, even more directly engaged with practical questions, demonstrates how the revival of legal pluralism and the arrival of
its constitutional variant on the global stage both provoke and are
provoked by convergent counter-tendencies. The well-known *Kadi* litigation recently before the courts of the European Union[29] can be seen as
a contest over whether an entity such as the EU is entitled to come to an
authoritative decision on regionally applicable levels of human rights
protection without deference to the structurally more embracing authority of the United Nations.[30] Should the question of the legality of the
confiscation of the financial assets of a terrorist suspect be decided in
accordance with the lexical priority of UN sanctions, imposed by the
Sanctions Committee of the Security Council as part of its sanctions
regime targeted at Al-Qaeda and associated individuals? In that event,
the only control would be the self-discipline of the Security Council, and
perhaps[31] certain minimum jurisdiction-blind standards of human
rights based upon *jus cogens* and so consistent with the formal integrity

[29] See Joined cases C-402/05 P and C-415/05 P, *Kadi and Al Barakaat International Foundation* v. *Council and Commission*, Judgment of the Court (Grand Chamber), 3 September 2008, [2008] ECR I-6351 (*Kadi I*); and Joined cases C-584/10 P, C-593/10 P and C-595/10 P, *European Commission and Others* v. *Yassin Abdullah Kadi*, Judgment of the Court (Grand Chamber), 18 July 2013 (*Kadi II*). It is of significance that the Advocate General in *Kadi I* was Miguel Maduro, well-known in academic circles even before his elevation to the Court for his espousal of constitutional pluralism. See Maduro, n. 8 above. This blending of roles is a prime example of the fluidity of the global 'law-craft' continuum discussed in Chapter 2.3.4 above.
[30] 'One of the most discussed judgments in ECJ history': C. Murphy, *EU Counter-terrorism Law: Pre-emption and the Rule of Law* (Oxford: Hart, 2012) p. 115. A selection of the best commentary would include: S. Besson, 'European Legal Pluralism after *Kadi*' 5 *European Constitutional Law Review* 237 (2009); G. de Búrca, 'The European Court of Justice and the International Legal Order After *Kadi*' 51 *Harvard Journal of International Law* 1 (2010); C. Tomuschat, 'The *Kadi* Case: What Relationship is there between the Universal Legal Order under the Auspices of the United Nations and the EU Legal Order?' 28 *Yearbook of European Law* 654 (2009); J. Kokott and C. Sobotta, 'The *Kadi* Case – Constitutional Core Values and International Law – Finding the Balance?' 23 *European Journal of International Law* 1015 (2012); and I. Cameron (ed.), *EU Sanctions: Law and Policy Issues Concerning Restrictive Measures* (Cambridge: Intersentia, 2013). For early commentary on *Kadi II*, see e.g. M. Marakakis, '*Kadi II*: Fundamental Rights and International Terrorism', Oxford Human Rights Hub, 23 August 2013, available at http://ohrh.law.ox.ac.uk/?p=2680; and A. Tzanakopoulos, '*Kadi* Showdown: Substantive Review of (UN) Sanctions by the ECJ', EJIL Talk, 19 July 2013, available at www.ejiltalk.org/kadi-showdown.
[31] As was concluded by the General Court (then called the Court of First Instance) in *Kadi I* – a position not shared by the Court of Justice in its subsequent judgment. According to the Court of Justice, since the protection of fundamental rights formed part of the very foundations of the EU legal order, and as it was technically only concerned

of international law. Or, as the Court of Justice ultimately concluded, should the EU, as a self-proclaimedly autonomous supranational polity, be entitled to develop its own conception of appropriate rights protection by reference to its own constitutional framework, provided it does not claim complete autarky but instead continues to seek basic standards of 'pluralist' accommodation with other regimes and their normative perspectives?

Coded as a question of global law under the terms we have set out, we are faced with a contest between two sharply opposed positions. On the one hand, we have a version of the convergent conception which locates the structural superiority of the UN within a formally integrated global legal framework that acknowledges an abstract-normative floor of human rights protection. On the other hand, we have a version of the divergent approach which gives priority to the regional regime and its version of human rights universalism and which connects to other regimes only through a thin chain of lateral co-ordination.

What is instructive about this case, and what accounts for its remarkable profile as a widely and simultaneously experienced global legal 'event',[32] is in large part the manner in which deep questions of the disputed form, provenance and authority of global law in general are candidly articulated in a judicial setting, and by reference to substantive legal and political concerns that have themselves been highly topical and contentious. What is also striking, however, is the recursive nature of the underlying contest. *Kadi* built upon and anticipated a number of similarly high-profile cases in which regional or national systems have been confronted with the claims of planetary regimes or arguments from universal standards.[33] Indeed, the *Kadi* litigation was itself greatly extended over time, the Grand Chamber recently handing down a

---

with the legality of the EU regulation transposing the UN resolution, the relevant standards were to be found within EU law. *Kadi I*, n. 29 above, at paras. 303 ff.

[32] See Chapter 2.3.3–2.3.4 above.

[33] The recent jurisprudence of the European Court of Human Rights has provided a particularly rich seam of such cases. See e.g. *Bosphorus* v. *Ireland*, App. No. 45036/98, Grand Chamber, Judgment of 30 June 2005, ECHR 2005-VI; *Behrami & Behrami* v. *France* and *Saramati* v. *France, Germany and Norway*, Joined App. Nos. 71412/01 and 78166/01, Grand Chamber, Judgment of 2 May 2007; *Al-Jedda* v. *United Kingdom*, App. No. 27021/08, Grand Chamber, Judgment of 7 July 2011, at para. 102; and *Nada* v. *Switzerland*, App. No. 10593/08, Grand Chamber, Judgment of 12 September 2012. For discussion, see e.g. Kumm, n. 12 above, pp. 279–88; see also the US Supreme Court's consideration of the bindingness of an International Court of Justice judgment in *Medellin* v. *Texas*, 552 US 491 (2008). For instructive comparison of *Kadi* and *Medellin*, see de Búrca, n. 30 above.

judgment confirming the annulment of Mr Kadi's re-listing as a terrorist suspect some eight years after the decision approving his initial listing in the original Court of First Instance case. Yet this pattern of recurrence and re-engagement should not surprise us. The questions of universalism or global systemic coherence versus system particularism plus legal pluralism are and remain broadly controversial, replicable across many contexts of interaction of transnational legal orders[34] and in their deep authority-questioning structure inherently resistant to any authoritative 'last word'. And so once again, we observe how the profile of global law claims in general is raised by the mutual provocation and stimulation of different approaches.

A similar dynamic of claim and counterclaim between positions on either side of the convergence/divergence distinction is often evident in broader academic exchange which, while still practically engaged in questions of the proper frame and content of global law, stands at one remove from immediate contexts of judicial or other legal decision-making. For example, we have already discussed how the debate within global constitutional law can be treated as a microcosm of the broader controversy over global law.[35] In particular, with its emphasis on the singularity of the constituted legal order, constitutionalism in global perspective invites opposition between those who seek to emphasise and to celebrate the gathering unity or commonality of a world order and those for whom the relevant constitutional units are many and either territorially limited or functionally specific. The controversy here is over the legacy of a term that supports two quite different ways of thinking about the global legal landscape in holistically 'constituted' terms, with each reading a standing incitement to offer and defend the alternative.

Another well-established and iterative conflict lies between global constitutionalism more generally, whether of the one polity or of the many, and Global Administrative Law, where the emphasis is not upon the input and pedigree of transnational law and authority but on its susceptibility to general throughput standards of due process and accountability. Again each approach provokes the other, based upon a resilient distinction, adapted from the vocabulary and vision of national public law, between a perspective which seeks to engage seriously with

---

[34] See e.g. A. Fischer-Lescano and G. Teubner, 'Regime Collisions: The Vain Search for Legal Unity in the Fragmentation of Global Law' 25 *Michigan Journal of International Law* 999 (2004).

[35] See Chapter 3.3.1 above.

the terms of *constitutive* power and generative authority at the transnational level and one which dismisses such an orientation as unrealistic or irrelevant and instead begins by taking *constituted* transnational power in all its diversity for granted.[36]

Similarly provocative is the mainstreaming of the new conflicts or pluralist approach. The languages of conflict of laws or legal pluralism have always had a place within legal doctrine and legal scholarship respectively, but in both cases what has been emphasised is the marginal location of the discourse in question. Conflict of laws was something that took place at the edges between national legal systems, while legal pluralism typically focused on those forms of law that were peripheral to the state core. The idea that these marginal themes, globally updated, should assume a much broader role and a much more pervasive connecting influence in the global configuration stands conventional legal wisdom on its head, and in so doing encourages a reaction from two opposite standpoints: from a position that would favour a more hierarchical or integrated approach to global law, as well as from one that would favour restoring or re-emphasising a more modest state-centred role for a law of conflicts.[37]

It bears re-emphasising that in none of the cases is the tension we are talking about one of intractable conflict or mutually assured destruction.[38] It is vital for the capacity of global law to continue to insinuate itself into our legal understandings that each side of the various oppositions discussed shares a frame of reference with the other and allows some measure of mutual compatibility in most possible worlds. For the very exchanges, practical or theoretical, which irrigate the global law debate would not be possible if the discourses in question were simply incommensurable, each failing to use some of the same terms as the other or unable to occupy the same contentious ground as the other and address the same disputed questions as the other.

4.5   The relative autonomy of global law

We shall return to these relationship questions in the final two chapters, and in particular to how they dovetail with our sense of global law as an

---

[36] See Chapter 3.3.2 above. See also, in particular, Krisch, n. 8 above.
[37] See e.g. H. Muir Watt, 'Private International Law Beyond the Schism' 2 *Transnational Legal Theory* 347 (2011). See also Chapter 3.4.1 above.
[38] See e.g. J. H. H. Weiler, *The Constitution of Europe* (Cambridge University Press, 1999) p. 320.

'intimated' category – as something suggested but still contested and unsettled within our maps of legal authority, yet nevertheless widely understood as signalling an irreversible trend. For now, we conclude by acknowledging the 'loose fit' between the circuitous flow of global law and the wider dynamics of globalisation; let us do so by briefly considering how global law both reflects and reinforces these wider dynamics while developing a relatively autonomous trajectory.

Recall that in all spheres of social and economic life, globalisation, with its unprecedented compression of time and space in and across economic, political, cultural and technological registers, creates and amplifies new cross-border commonalities of practices, interests, identities and values; but at the limits and as the condition of these same commonalities, globalisation also makes and highlights new distinctions.[39] Law is no exception to this tendency. Law beyond the state articulates various different ways of simultaneously putting new areas of conduct in common and drawing new distinctions across national borders. In so doing it reflects and reinforces many of the new alignments and conflicts we find in and between transnational economic positions and interests, transnational cultural identities and dispositions, and transnational policy priorities and preferences. This transnational legal articulation, as we have seen, may occur in bilateral or multilateral accords, in regional institutions, in forms of transnational legal order among private parties, and in trans-jurisdictional but exclusive bonds of legal culture based upon factors such as religious or linguistic familiarity, or upon the legacy of imperial ties.[40]

Every species of global law is a response to the ways in which this ever-expanding multiverse of transnational law unleashes and places in dynamic tension these new forms of common legal engagement and new forms of regulatory differentiation. For global law sets out to contain 'unruly'[41] elements in this transnational mix. It does so in its

---

[39] See W. Scheuerman, 'Globalization', in *Stanford Encyclopedia of Philosophy*, available at http://plato.stanford.edu/entries/globalization/; A. Giddens, *The Consequences of Modernity* (Stanford University Press, 1990); and see further Chapter 1 above.

[40] See Chapter 1.2.3 above.

[41] See F. Johns, *Non-legality in International Law: Unruly Law* (Cambridge University Press, 2013). Johns is concerned with a rather different category of unruly elements in her study. Her focus is on the way in which law structures its relationship with non-legal elements of international practice more generally – including the pre-legal, the extra-legal and the illegal. My concern is more directly with 'unruly' elements within law itself – those caused by an excess of legality and manifest in the congested relationship between different legal orders and claims within transnational legal space.

convergence-promoting mode by advancing new forms of universal or global-in-general normative leverage, whether within peak planetary organisations, through multi-level and multi-institutional human rights standards, or in other claims to positive or pre-positive global normative order. And it does so in divergence-accommodating mode by refining or connecting the transnational fragments, whether within functionally specific global institutions of public, private or mixed provenance, through newly minted hybrids, or in thinner forms of lateral connection between local legal orders.

This pattern of response also serves, however, to highlight the relative autonomy of global law from the broader dynamics of globalisation. Global law always responds first and foremost to an existing register of *law*. In the first place, in its assumption of a framework of double normativity and its contribution to that framework, global law invariably acts upon existing transnationally expansive forms of law. Each and every species of global law seeks to contain or overcome forces of legal disunity or difference, therefore, but in doing so it will also reinforce existing divisions or create new ones. Each and every species of global law carries with it its own projection of how law should be shaped and 'cut' in global terms. In joining and connecting, global law will also inevitably divide and separate.[42] This is most readily apparent on the divergence-accommodating side of the divide. We may consider, for example, the cut that separates one functionally specific global legal regime from another, or that limits the scope of one of the new hybrid conceptions of global law, or that restricts the basis for pluralist or conflicts-centred reconciliation of different legal orders. But it is also true of the convergence-sponsoring side of the divide. An expansive conception of global human rights may challenge and cut across local or regional claims to legal autonomy, as too will a structural policy that concentrates legal use of force powers at the planetary level. Equally, an emphasis on formal global legal unity can challenge not just the autonomy but also the integrity of various specialist global regimes. And so the invocation of global law can contribute to the very tensions of transnational legal plurality and diversity it seeks to ameliorate, adding to the dynamic of commonality and difference, of inclusion and exclusion.

---

[42] See H. Lindahl, *Fault Lines of Globalization: Legal Order and the Politics of A-Legality* (Oxford University Press, 2013) ch. 1.

And in the second place, as we have shown in detail above, these various projections and incisions of global law, though sometimes perfectly compatible, may at other times be at odds with one another. Global law, therefore, may also respond non-harmoniously and competitively to other versions of itself. This kind of chain reaction fosters a new level of legal differentiation, competition and conflict – either convergence-promoting or divergence-accommodating – over the very means to manage transnational legal differentiation, competition and conflict.

In a nutshell, the emergence of global law announces the inauguration of a new 'meta' level of law's relatively autonomous capacity for both containing and compounding the global differentiation of its own forms. Not only does the regular invocation of global law in contemplation of how to resolve or compensate for some forms of transnational legal difference and division tend towards the production or reinforcement of other differences and divisions, but its interventions also occur in a manner that challenge global law's own diverse catalogue of convergent and divergent projections just as they rely upon and reinforce them.

5

Intimations of global law

5.1 Introduction

Our sense of global law as the concurrent emergence of a wide range of claims regarding law's worldwide warrant brings us to the idea of intimation. The very manner in which global law, or its functional equivalents, is approached, appreciated and engaged with as a distinctive modality of law, so signalling an epistemic shift among law's transnational community, tends to be tied up in one way or another with its 'intimated' quality. In particular, the intimated quality of global law connects closely with the particular kind of claim to authority that global law entails. Global law flows out of the decentring of a sovereigntist framework and the resulting challenge to conventional state-centred understandings of modern legal authority. Yet the form and process of global law's emergence reveal various special features of its own uncertain relationship to authority, a full appreciation of which requires a close examination of the role of all those who are involved in endeavours to fashion and to authorise global law.

The gathering intimations of global law, as we shall see, have particularly profound consequences for the academic study of law and for the study of the academy alike. For what we are experiencing is a twofold change in the nature of our focus on law as an object of study. On the one hand, and most obviously, the movement towards transnational law and, in turn, to the special type of transnational law we have specified as *global law*, implies a change in research and teaching priorities – with the balance tilting somewhat from the national to the post-national. On the other hand, the very legal quality of global *law* as 'intimated' is also somewhat different from other forms of law. The kind of material that counts as this new form of law is distinctive, as is the kind of argument and evidence that counts towards this new form of law. In turn, this distinctiveness includes a new emphasis on the academy as participants in producing, advocating or refining global law, with all its attendant difficulties and challenges, so highlighting a renewed requirement to focus on the academy itself as an object of study.[1]

Before we can proceed any further, however, we must pin down what we mean by the intimated quality of global law. The term 'intimation' has a cluster of interesting connotations for us, each pointing towards certain characteristics that global law, in all its species variety, holds in common. Defined most basically and most generally, an intimation is a suggestion or an indication of something that is not clearly evident or that is still in the process of becoming. In one specific strand of meaning – one, incidentally, well-known in 'legal English' when referring to the serving of notice in court proceedings – we use the term 'intimation' to convey the idea of an active suggestion or a giving of notice of a future happening or state of affairs; an advance declaration or disclosure. In another specific strand of meaning, however, intimation takes no such direct form and has no such explicit quality. Rather than the action of the referring subject, it concerns the object referred to. Here intimation consists not in the declaratory speech act itself, but in the indirect evidence of something unfulfilled or otherwise indistinct. If we pull these two strands together – active and passive, subjective and objective, express and implied, suggestion and suggestiveness – we can already point to a cluster of attributes that we are able to associate with global law.

First, to the extent that a conception or species of global law is expressly 'intimated' or declared, it acquires a projected character. As a forward-looking announcement, the very act or practice of intimating global law is intended to contribute to the realisation of the 'project'. Yet inasmuch as this involves a claim of self-authorisation rather than

---

[1] It is certainly not new for academics to investigate themselves as part of their study of the development of law. Often when doctrinal scholars examine expert authorities, this is part of a stock examination and exposition of sources. But often the investigation of scholars and scholarship is instead part of a critical inquiry – most closely associated with the Critical Legal Studies movement which became prominent in the last decades of the twentieth century – into the extent and nature of academic influence over the development of law and legal education. In critical international law scholarship, see e.g. M. Koskenniemi, *The Gentle Civilizer of Nations: The Rise and Fall of International Law 1870–1960* (Cambridge University Press, 2001). See more generally D. Kennedy, *The Rise and Fall of Classical Legal Thought*, orig. edn 1975 (Washington, DC: Beard Books, 2006). In the case of global law, for the reasons advanced in this chapter, there is simply more scope for academics to influence legal development: see in particular section 5.2.5 below. See also N. Walker, 'Beyond Boundary Disputes and Basic Grids: Mapping the Global Disorder of Normative Orders' 6 *International Journal of Constitutional Law* 373 (2008) at 373–96.

reliance upon a pre-existing source, the grounding of the projected claim remains insecure, even if, as we shall see, the legal past is often invoked as ballast for it. Secondly, however, and often closely intertwined with an approach of express projection, the 'intimation' of global law may also involve an implication, the drawing of a conclusion from hints or pointers, from basic and incomplete cues in the regulatory environment. That is to say, the suggestive background of global law will also include the reception or extraction of some rudimentary 'external' signs or evidence. The mature course or purpose of this externally detected activity often remains oblique, dependent upon the fuller development of the relevant trends as well as the creative 'insider' construal and endorsement of that evidence. Thirdly, it is on account of that doubly 'intimated' object – actively projected and obliquely sourced, and how this relates to the background tension between convergence-promoting and divergence-accommodating visions of how to contain legal variety – that the emergent category of global law retains a fluid and contentious quality. While already more than mere speculation or aspiration, it remains in an unsettled state and on a precarious footing.

Finally, however, even though largely projected, frequently oblique and persistently unsettled, the idea of global law as intimated also brings with it a sense, whether welcomed or feared, of inevitability. For we also understand an intimated object or state of affairs as one that is somehow preordained, or, more profanely, as unavoidable or at least as difficult to avert. This additional strand of meaning is thickened and rendered familiar by its literary resonance. When William Wordsworth wrote his famous *Intimations of Immortality* (1802–4),[2] and when a much later and less Romantic figure, the American beat generation poet Allen Ginsberg, wrote his *Intimations of Mortality* (1984)[3] in (critical) homage to his much admired predecessor, both were agreed on one thing at least. By invoking the term 'intimation', they were referring to the presentiment of a force beyond their control, and so to a sense of an inevitable presence, occurrence or unfolding. The intimation of global law on this reading, therefore, speaks to the ineluctability and inexorability of its becoming, or at least – if observed from a more critical distance – a sense that it is generally presented by its advocates and

---

[2] W. Wordsworth, 'Ode: Intimations of Immortality from Recollections of Early Childhood' in A. Quiller-Couch (ed.), *The Oxford Book of English Verse: 1250–1900* (Oxford University Press, 1918) p. 536.
[3] A. Ginsberg, *Collected Poems: 1947–1980* (New York: Harper & Row, 1984).

discussants in terms of its inevitability, or consistently with such a background assumption.

Projected yet oblique, unsettled yet inexorable: in what precise ways does this cluster of 'intimated' characteristics capture what is distinctive about global law and its prospects? Let us start with the ways in which how global law is 'suggested', both explicitly and implicitly, serves to reveal its complex relationship to the legal past and to the legal future and so to legal 'time' in general – as well as contributing to its unsettled quality and to a moderate bias in favour of aspiration over establishment, theory-driven orientation over embedded practice, the scholar over the practitioner. Then, in the second half of the chapter we address the final aspect of global law's intimated quality, and ask why and how its unsettled status and unrealised quality sit alongside a growing sense of its inexorability. This, in turn, sets the scene for our concluding discussion in Chapter 6, where we consider the broader context of critical challenge to the force of global law, and ask how global law might respond to that challenge.

5.2 Suggestions of global law

5.2.1 Projected features

First, then, let us assess the projected quality of global law. If we think of global law as an incipient development, as a legal form that is still coming to fruition and so largely future-orientated, we also draw attention to the fragility of its foundations. This is not a matter of the uncertainty or immaturity of a specific legal doctrine claiming a global warrant or of any particular pre-positive orientation associated with global law.[4] Rather, it speaks to the tenuous nature of the very claim to global law, under any of its various species, as a new general modality of law. No longer embedded in the state and so unable to rely on the recognised pedigree of state law as the internal expression of a sovereign authority, and no longer easily accommodated within the parallel category of international law understood in its dominant modern mode as grounded in agreement among sovereign state authorities, global law is uncertainly and insecurely founded. It is 'uncharted law',[5] not yet fully registered in any of our established maps of legal authority. Its projection, then, involves a

---

[4] See Chapter 3.2.3.2 above.
[5] N. Walker, 'Out of Place and Out of Time: Law's Fading Co-ordinates' 14 *Edinburgh Law Review* 13 (2010).

gambit, a calculated risk that its explicit self-sponsorship as a form of law should not be undermined by a lack of prior authorisation.

This complicates the relationship between global law and its antecedents, and, in particular, is apt to reveal a connection, but also to expose a tension and give rise to a trade-off between two quite different ways in which law derives authority from its past. On the one hand, global law is unable in its particular claims to present itself as the expression of an established legal order, or at least less able than our familiar categories of modern law to do so. It cannot, in other words, readily call upon a general standing authority to validate its particular legal propositions. On the other hand, however, global law often makes explicit reference to law's broader heritage, sometimes strong reference. Yet the two are linked. The very loudness of global law's appeal to the past is often a measure of the absence of a taken-for-granted structure of general authorisation. The reference to the past here, as we shall see, is part and parcel of the very establishment – or rather the attempted re-establishment – of law as a general authority, rather than the invocation of that general authority in one of its already established forms.

Global law, then, does not readily exhibit the typical 'traditionality'[6] that characterises the structure of modern law. Global law does not invoke any of our familiar past-oriented methods to support its own validity, or certainly does so with less confident presumption than we associate with conventional forms of legal order. In particular, it does not invoke the triad of, first, default orientation towards and contemplation of past legal processes and events as a basis for any new legal claim; secondly, selective specification of that past as an authoritative foundation for the present; and, thirdly, the conduct of that selective specification in accordance with a recognised transmission procedure or formula which consciously ensures continuity between past and present. These aspects of traditionality, as Martin Krygier reminds us, typically figure as a central feature of any modern state-based, or indeed any modern jurisdiction-specific and so jurisdictionally bounded legal system's generic claim to authority. This traditional structure and methodology is present whether law's authority is based upon the forms of selective specification and the transmission procedures and formulae associated

---

[6] *Ibid.*, at 21. Here I contrast 'traditionality' as a past-oriented methodology for identifying legal authority with 'traditionalism' as an ideology which accords value to rituals, customs and practices just on account of their actual or claimed venerable quality. We return to this distinction in the text below.

with case precedent, common law, custom, code, constitution or legislative history, or any combination of these.[7]

Global law, depending on the species in question, makes at best more questionable assumptions and more incomplete claims of this type. Here it is useful to pursue another distinction – or, more accurately, a spectrum of possibilities – introduced earlier between more or less endorsement-based or aspiration-based forms of global law.[8] We must grant that all global law, as a form of projection, is necessarily predicated upon the recognition of a gap between what legally is already settled and what legally ought to become but is still in the process of becoming, and so must in some measure be aspirational. We can nevertheless distinguish between those species of global law that are more about *reconstruction* than construction; between those that draw significantly upon existing bodies of legal doctrine, and in so doing present themselves as incremental extensions or natural progressions, and those that are more explicit and more candid in declaring their invocation of the past to be in support of the ongoing pursuit of novel legal horizons.

In the former category we find both structural and formal species of global law. Both depart from a strong reliance upon existing doctrine, and often present themselves as mere incidents and increments of the extant legal framework of international law. We may, for example, consider the intense recent history of arguments over the extension of the structural capacity of the United Nations, or of its member states, individually or collectively, to use force against other states on grounds of humanitarian intervention, or under what has lately begun to be termed 'the responsibility to protect'.[9] This is often treated by its supporters as a seamless development of the existing regime of coercive measures. The duty to avert a humanitarian crisis and protect civilian populations is deemed to flow from the same moral imperative of mutual care and responsibility within the international community as underscores the clear existing power to act against threats to international

---

[7] M. Krygier, 'Law as Tradition' 5 *Law and Philosophy* 237 (1986). See more generally H. P. Glenn, *Legal Traditions of the World: Sustainable Diversity in Law*, 4th edn (Oxford University Press, 2010) ch. 1; and J. Přibáň, *Legal Symbolism: On Law, Time and European Identity* (Brookfield, VT: Ashgate, 2007).

[8] See Chapter 1.2.3 above.

[9] See e.g. the work of the International Coalition for the Responsibility to Protect, founded in 2009, and relying on the commitments laid down in paragraphs 138–9 of the 2005 UN World Summit Outcome Document (UN General Assembly Resolution 60/1, A/RES/60/1): see www.responsibilitytoprotect.org.

peace and security. Yet any attempt to subsume this legal initiative under a prevailing framework of authority sits awkwardly with the conventionally – indeed, more traditionally – contractualist view of modern international law. For in claiming an overriding global authority to use force *in extremis* regardless of substantive or procedural scruples which are precisely designed and included in Chapter VII of the United Nations Charter to register the limited scope of our existing general compact or the weight given to the specific objection of state parties, the advocates of the new approach seek to replace, or at least supplement, a bounded *international* jurisdiction with an unbounded global one.[10] And whatever the merits of such a move, to present it as somehow merely consequential on the existing framework is to play down its significance.[11]

Similarly, formalist arguments in favour of emphasising and augmenting international law's hierarchy of norms from non-legislative sources, or insisting upon systemic unity and against fragmentation, are often based upon a particular type of belief in the integrity, autonomy and gradual perfectibility of the legal order of international law as a single order. They rest upon an assumption of the naturalness or intrinsic value of a certain template of legal order, and of the neutrality or evident worth of a certain idea of legal form. Again, this may be a less modest argument than it is often presented as.[12] The kind of 'joined up' authority it enjoins is more easily justified by the projection of a similarly holistic sense of world society or the 'international community' than by the historical record of international law.[13] The reach and co-ordination of jurisdiction contemplated, therefore, seem better served by the ambition of a globally exhaustive warrant, but once more this sits uncomfortably with the idea of the existing internationalist legal foundation supplying a sufficient platform of authority.

---

[10] See, in particular, Arts. 42 and 51, UN Charter. For sceptical views in light of recent international interventions in Libya and Syria, see e.g. P. Stockburger, 'Emerging Voices: Is the R2P Doctrine the Greatest Marketing Campaign International Law Has Ever Seen?', *Opinio Juris*, 23 August 2013, http://opiniojuris.org/2013/08/23/emerging-voices-is-the-r2p-doctrine-is-the-greatest-marketing-campaign-international-law-has-ever-seen/; and M. Nuruzzaman, 'The "Responsibility to Protect" Doctrine: Revived in Libya, Buried in Syria' 15 *Insight Turkey* 57 (2013), available at www.insightturkey.com/the-responsibility-to-protect-doctrine-revived-in-libya-buried-in-syria/articles/316.

[11] See further Chapter 3.2.1 and Chapter 4.2 above.

[12] See e.g. J. d'Aspremont, *Formalism and the Sources of International Law: A Theory of the Ascertainment of Legal Rules* (Oxford University Press, 2011); and M. Koskenniemi, 'The Fate of Public International Law: Between Technique and Politics' 70 *Modern Law Review* 1 (2007).

[13] See Chapter 3.2.2 above. See also the discussion of international constitutionalism in Chapter 3.3.1 above.

Functionally specific conceptions of global law in areas such as climate change or international criminal law also typically seek to situate themselves within an existing legal tradition, their point of departure supplied by the need to build upon or complete a particular legal regime.[14] Here, however, unlike the formal and substantive approaches, the continuity argument, just like the type of legal tradition to which it refers, tends to be driven by external rather than internal criteria. It is not a question of removing impediments to the full enforcement of a conception of global public order already enshrined in the UN system, or of following a familiar logic of legal system integration, but of pursuing further a set of extra-legal policy objectives gradually developed over the earlier stages of regime assembly.[15] In this case, therefore, for all the importance of the legislative past and present as a platform for global claims, the insufficiency of the existing framework in supplying the authority for further development of an encompassing conception of a sectoral public good is more apparent, more dependent for its resolution on the continuation of a stepwise process of development of externally driven policy rather than on the maturing of resources already present or latent within the system.

Whereas all of these approaches stretch – arguably overstretch – modern law's familiar template of authority as one of validation of new doctrine through subsumption under an existing normative code,[16] other more aspiration-based species of global law dispense with this kind of immediate link between tradition and justification. If we look, in particular, at how certain constructions of global law signal back to an existing discipline-based discursive narrative, we observe that the combination of inspiration and authorisation sought by their reference to the past rests upon a deeper but looser connection, a more fluid sense of continuity linked to more basic and more generic grounds of justification. The reference, say, to global constitutional law, involves looking back to what we have shown to be a highly disparate and in some respects internally conflicted set of themes centred on the constitution of the modern state, in support of a similarly wide-ranging set of arguments about the advent and direction of global law – including, incidentally, just these structural and formal conceptions of global law

---

[14] See the references in n. 10 of Chapter 4 above. [15] See further Chapter 3.4.2 above.
[16] See e.g. R. Alexy, 'On Balancing and Subsumption. A Structural Comparison' 16 *Ratio Juris* 433 (2003).

whose validation by reference to a more traditional understanding of international law we have shown to be precarious.[17]

On a somewhat smaller scale, Global Administrative Law, global human rights law, *jus gentium* or the conflict of laws offer a similarly open-ended set of historical connections.[18] Many of the abstract-normative frames of global law, such as those referring to the Rule of Law or to law as a universal code, likewise draw from a wider heritage of legal thought.[19] Similar considerations apply to the new hybrid global approaches such as the law of peace, or the law of recognition, or humanity's law. Far from discounting the past, they draw explicitly on a range of historical threads and upon arguments about the productive cross-fertilisation of legal traditions.[20] Tellingly, this kind of looser invocation of the past, further removed from the body of continuing practice under settled authority, instead taps into broader disciplinary or abstract-normative sources; in so doing, it involves a more explicit gambit of self-authorisation, and tends to fall more squarely within the domain of the academic expert – the knowledge consultant and ideas entrepreneur rather than the hands-on practitioner.[21]

In some part, to be sure, the link to the past will be a contingent feature of these justificatory narratives – a claim not to do with their 'pastness' as such but with the weight of legal doctrine and practice as a reservoir of good ideas and tried and tested experience capable of adaptation to new circumstances.[22] To that extent the authority sought is of an epistemic variety. It involves taking advantage of law's accumulated practical intelligence. This is also an approach, therefore, whose rationale tends to be non-jurisdictional, and so dovetails smoothly with a global outlook. To the extent that the test of the cumulative authority of law is its contribution to the fund of contemporary legal know-how, there is no more reason to discriminate on the basis of *where* the relevant knowledge arose than there is to do so on the basis of *when* it arose. This kind of justification, therefore, has an in-built propensity to look beyond national to transnational, and even to planetary horizons.[23]

In significant measure, however, this looser kind of invocation of the past is also ideologically oriented. Even as it purports to draw upon the

---

[17] See Chapter 3.3.1 above.   [18] See Chapter 3.2.3.1, 3.3.2 and 3.4.1.1 above.
[19] See Chapter 3.2.3.2 above.
[20] See Chapter 3.4.3 above. See also Glenn, n. 7 above, ch. 10.
[21] See section 5.2.2 below.   [22] See e.g. Krygier, n. 7 above.
[23] See e.g. J. Waldron, *'Partly Laws Common to All Mankind': Foreign Law in American Courts* (New Haven, CT: Yale University Press, 2012) ch. 4.

wisdom of the past – and often a jurisdictionally unbounded past – it plays upon a widespread cultural disposition to accord value to rituals, customs, to repeated claims and practices, and to expressly acknowledged traditions, just on account of their venerable quality. This ideological dimension of global law's attraction to its heritage is one that we might refer to as 'traditionalism' rather than 'traditionality' – a valorisation of the past for its own sake rather than as an element in a settled methodology of validation.[24] But it is also a traditionalism that trades on the familiarity to modern legal thought of the very traditionality that eludes global law. That is to say, the tribute that global law pays to the legal past in this looser ideological sense is all the more emphatic – and all the more explicable – on account of the intimacy, indeed quasi-automaticity, of the link between pastness and legitimate authority in the *standard* case of the validation of modern law, and the broader sense this deep-rooted standard practice radiates about the appropriateness of law's preoccupation with the past.

In summary, in none of the species of the genus 'global law' is there available an uncontentious path-dependent general authority to provide systemic undergirding for any particular new utterance and application. It follows that, much more than in the more settled forms of modern legal order, any particular project of global law tends to have to justify simultaneously both the general category and the particular case, both *langue* and *parole*. If the projection of global law involves a gambit, therefore, it is one that relies heavily on the venerability of law's many disciplinary and doctrinal roots. In this way, the debate over law's global future is in some measure bound to play out as a contest about its past.

5.2.2   Oblique character

Intimation, as we have noted, is as much about what is implicit in the world as it stands and as it unfolds, as it is about our explicit pronouncements on the world to come. It concerns what is hinted at indirectly as much as it indicates what we directly proclaim. In the context of global law, intimation in this additional sense is about what is present but oblique in the world, and requires, therefore, to be teased out and made explicit.

---

[24] See Walker, n. 5 above, at 21. See also e.g. A. Giddens, *Modernity and Self-identity: Self and Society in the Late Modern Age* (Stanford University Press, 1991) pp. 187–201.

This speaks to the other side of the coin to what was considered in the discussion of legal tradition. It tells us that the future of global legal authority depends not only on our capacity to draw upon the resources of the past but also upon our ability to extrapolate from the present. The projections of global law, therefore, are as much about anticipation as veneration. The theorist of global law has to be as adept at understanding and revealing the emerging distinctiveness of today as at harnessing and proclaiming the resilient authority of yesteryear.

The point here is a simple but important one. If those contemplating and addressing law's global reach and potential today encounter what appears to be an unprecedentedly fluid, diverse and complexly connected landscape,[25] that makes it more rather than less important, but at the same time more rather than less difficult, to start by gaining a good understanding of what is happening 'out there' at the coalface of social action and legal reaction. If we are to consolidate, refine or reshape the big picture of global legal authority, it is incumbent upon us first to document the many trends of transnational law precisely and insightfully, but to do so in circumstances where the rate and scale of change means that the overall pattern of legal ordering is shifting and elusive.

Often, indeed, we see the emphasis on the venerated past, the oblique present and the projected future in close juxtaposition. This is particularly so with regard to the historical-discursive approaches. In the founding editorial of the new journal *Global Constitutionalism* in 2012, for example, the oft-repeated insistence on the double nature of the project, as one of 'mapping' as well as 'shaping' new constitution-like global norms and institutions, is striking.[26] The project is intended, quite explicitly, to be both expository and aspirational, required to shed light

---

[25] See e.g. K. C. Culver and M. Giudice, *Legality's Borders: An Essay in General Jurisprudence* (Oxford University Press, 2010); and H. Lindahl, *Fault Lines of Globalization: Legal Order and the Politics of A-Legality* (Oxford University Press, 2013). Note, too, the significance of *the appearance of* complexity and diversity. One index of globalisation, and one part of the compression of time and space in the contemporary world, is increased awareness and knowledge of global complexity and diversity in various fields, and, indeed, this is just as important as objective evidence of such complexity and diversity. That increased awareness is an important aspect of the *Umwelt* of the outward-looking legal scholar, just as it is of scholarship across many disciplines in the humanities and social sciences: see e.g. A. Giddens, *The Consequences of Modernity* (Stanford University Press, 1990). See also Chapter 1.1 above, and Chapter 2 above generally.

[26] A. Wiener, A. Lang, J. Tully, M. Maduro and M. Kumm, 'Global Constitutionalism: Human Rights, Democracy and the Rule of Law' 1 *Global Constitutionalism* 1 (2012).

on the incipient tendencies of the present as a prelude and prerequisite to modelling the future. Yet in the very citation of the heritage of constitutionalism, there is, of course, also a powerful invocation of the past. Although it does not say so in so many words, therefore, the paradigm of global constitutionalism so presented is about 'mining' as much as it is about 'mapping' and 'shaping', but most of all it is about the close relationship between all these activities.

A story similarly connecting all three temporalities can be told in the more specific context of international constitutional law. Its embryonic present in the developing structures of the UN and in other 'world order' treaties[27] typically is both linked back to its roots in earlier ideas of 'international community' and carried forward in the projection of a more comprehensive constitutional mandate and a more explicit constitutional vision for the relevant constituent parts of a developed global society.[28] Global Administrative Law, too, seeks to connect past and future in the elusive flux of current development. A contemporary undercurrent of growing transnational administration and incipient legal recognition of its diverse forms becomes closely tied to the historical resource of state-centred administrative law on the one hand, and the projection of a generalised professional culture and practice of fuller administrative law-proofing of global governance on the other.[29]

If we look beyond these and other discipline-centred approaches, it is remarkable how many other analyses of the prospects of transnational law in general,[30] and global law in particular, are also about trendspotting. Here however, the stress is not upon the connection between

[27] See e.g. E. de Wet, 'The Constitutionalisation of Public International Law' in M. Rosenfeld and A. Sajó (eds.), *The Oxford Handbook of Comparative Constitutional Law* (Oxford University Press, 2012) p. 1224.

[28] See e.g. B. Fassbender, *The United Nations Charter and the Constitution of the International Community* (Leiden: Martinus Nijhoff, 2009); de Wet, n. 27 above; and B. Simma, 'The Contribution of Alfred Verdross to the Theory of International Law' 6 *European Journal of International Law* 33 (1995).

[29] See B. Kingsbury, 'The Concept of "Law" in Global Administrative Law' 20 *European Journal of International Law* 23 (2009); B. Kingsbury, 'International Law as Inter-public Law' in H. R. Richardson and M. S. Williams (eds.), *NOMOS XLIX: Moral Universalism and Pluralism* (New York University Press, 2009) pp. 167–204; and S. Cassese, 'Administrative Law without the State? The Challenge of Global Regulation' 37 *New York University Journal of International Law and Politics* 663 (2005). See also N. Carmouche, 'The Constructions of Global Administrative Law' (Ph.D. thesis, European University Institute, 2013); and Chapter 3.3.2 above.

[30] See e.g. P. Schiff Berman, *Global Legal Pluralism: A Jurisprudence of Law Beyond Borders* (Cambridge University Press, 2012).

the current trend and an established legal discourse. Rather, it is upon its suggestion of innovation. Proportionality analysis is an outstanding case in point. Over the last twenty years, many commentators,[31] and not a few judicial practitioners,[32] have commented on and encouraged the new tendency of appeal courts worldwide to weigh rights in the balance and to decide which way the scales tip on the basis of a contextual examination of comparative good and harm. And as we have seen, proportionality analysis is a key ingredient in different species of global law, figuring both in explicitly rights-based global discourses[33] and in other abstract-universal approaches requiring the mutual adjustment of various globally resonant desiderata.[34]

Many other examples could be given of this kind of 'trending', and of the proliferation of forms of authority that are 'liquid'[35] in terms of their patterns of emergence, mutation and circulation. The 'mainstreaming' of rights across different sectoral areas of legal policy is another tendency relevant to the development of rights discourse as a global vision.[36] Subsidiarity schemes, limited autonomy regimes and doctrines of toleration of diversity, as in the European Court of Human Right's 'margin of appreciation', provide resources from which new global themes of lateral co-ordination such as constitutional pluralism may be developed.[37] The development of global indicators as a new kind of rudimentary normative standard is significant for Global Administrative Law, but also for various functionally specific conceptions of global law.[38] Burden-sharing

---

[31] See e.g. R. Alexy, *A Theory of Constitutional Rights* (Oxford University Press, 2002); A. Stone Sweet and J. Matthews, 'Proportionality, Balancing and Global Constitutionalism' 47 *Columbia Journal of Transnational Law* 72 (2008-9); and D. Beatty, *The Ultimate Rule of Law* (Oxford University Press, 2004).

[32] See e.g. A. Barak, *Constitutional Rights and Their Limitations* (Cambridge University Press, 2012).

[33] See e.g. K. Möller, *The Global Model of Constitutional Rights* (Oxford University Press, 2012). See also Chapter 3.2.3.1 above.

[34] See e.g. M. Kumm, 'The Cosmopolitan Turn in Constitutionalism: On the Relationship between Constitutionalism in and beyond the State' in J. L Dunoff and J. P. Trachtman (eds.), *Ruling the World? Constitutionalism, International Law, and Global Governance* (Cambridge University Press, 2009) pp. 258–325. See also Chapter 3.2.3.2 above.

[35] See N. Krisch, 'Liquid Authority in Global Governance: An Anatomy' (unpublished paper, 2013).

[36] See e.g. P. Alston and J. H. H. Weiler, 'An "Ever Closer Union" in Need of a Human Rights Policy' in P. Alston, M. Bustelo and J. Heenan (eds.), *The EU and Human Rights* (Oxford University Press, 1999) pp. 3–66.

[37] See e.g. Schiff Berman, n. 30 above, particularly ch. 6.

[38] See e.g. G. Dimitropoulos, 'Global Administrative Law as "Enabling Law": How to Monitor and Evaluate Indicator-Based Performance of Global Actors' IRPA Research

in migration law[39] and emission-trading in climate change law[40] supply sector-specific but related methodologies for different global regimes. A new wave of compliance research in international law involves a kind of 'emergent analytics'[41] – an approach in which 'real world' testing is closely linked to normative adaptation. Similarly, new models of iterative normative reassessment and redesign under frameworks of 'experimental governance'[42] have pertinence across the range of global public goods as well as within and between more local or regional governance contexts. In addition, there is a range of other emergent tendencies in the legal world, from the growth of hybrid national/international courts[43] to the development of smart sanctions,[44] 'nudging' and applications of behavioural economics more generally,[45] that are not

Paper No. 7/2012 (20 October 2012), available at SSRN: http://ssrn.com/abstract=2167405; and K. Davis, A. Fisher, B. Kingsbury and S. Engle Merry (eds.), *Governance by Indicators: Global Power through Quantification and Rankings* (Oxford University Press, 2012).

[39] See e.g. V. Guiraudon, 'The Constitution of a European Immigration Policy Domain: A Political Sociology Approach' 10 *Journal of European Public Policy* 263 (2003).

[40] See e.g. J. Scott and L. Rajamani, 'EU Climate Change Unilateralism' 23 *European Journal of International Law* 469 (2012). This can shade into a boot-strapping self-referentiality in which the (real world) evidence that shapes and authorises normative development is little more than the emerging conviction of legal professionals or scholars themselves. We see this, for example, in the development of 'the responsibility to protect': n. 9 above. We also see it in the 'emerging' right to democratic governance, so vigorously sponsored by Thomas Franck: T. Franck, 'The Emerging Right to Democratic Governance' 86 *American Journal of International Law* 46 (1992).

[41] G. Shaffer and T. Ginsburg, 'The Empirical Turn in International Legal Scholarship' 106 *American Journal of International Law* 1 (2012).

[42] See e.g. C. Sabel and J. Zeitlin (eds.), *Experimentalist Governance in the European Union: Towards a New Architecture* (Oxford University Press, 2010). On experimentalism in the US, see e.g. M. Dorf and C. Sabel, 'A Constitution of Experimentalist Governance' 98 *Columbia Law Review* 267 (1998); C. Sabel and W. Simon, 'Minimalism and Experimentalism in American Public Law' 100 *Georgetown Law Review* 53 (2011). On experimentalism in the EU, see K. Armstrong, 'The Character of EU Law and Governance: From "Community Method" to New Modes of Governance' 64 *Current Legal Problems* 179 (2011).

[43] For example, in transitional justice settings in Kosovo, East Timor, Sierra Leone and Cambodia. See e.g. Schiff Berman, n. 30 above, pp. 171–80; see also C. Bell, *On the Law of Peace: Peace Agreements and the Lex Pacificatoria* (Oxford University Press, 2008); and Chapter 3.4.3 above.

[44] See e.g. D. Cortright and G. A. Lopez (eds.), *Smart Sanctions: Targeting Economic Statecraft* (Lanham, MD: Rowman & Littlefield, 2002).

[45] See e.g. R. H. Thaler and C. R. Sunstein, *Nudge: Improving Decisions about Health, Wealth, and Happiness* (New Haven, CT: Yale University Press, 2008); C. Jolls, C. R. Sunstein and R. Thaler, 'A Behavioral Approach to Law and Economics' 50 *Stanford Law Review* 1471 (1998).

exclusively matched to any particular template of global law. Instead they supply novel legal design resources that stand above any local context and may be adapted to a range of different visions of global law.

Both the plausibility and, in some measure, the legitimacy of what is proposed in the 'shaping' and projecting phase, therefore, depend crucially on what is discovered in the evershifting 'mapping' stage. What is oblique and circumspect must first be rendered transparent before it can be guided and reshaped in 'real time'. The image of 'rebuilding the ship at sea' has become popular in legal and public policy circles in recent years as a way of expressing the difficulties of 'grounding' a continuous process of reform, and indeed supplies the title of a well-known legal and political analysis of the post-Berlin Wall constitutional transformation of Eastern Europe.[46] The seafarers of global law, arguably, have an even more difficult task to perform, a multitask indeed. They not only have to rebuild the ship as it sails, but they have to do so in a shifting sea whose nautical charts are subject to continuous adjustment.

5.2.3   Unsettled quality

The two features of the intimated character of global law we have identified so far also contribute towards its unsettled quality. The range and insistence but tenuous authority of global law's appeal to the legal past in support of its various projected legal futures, as well as its intensive and extensive scanning for incipient trends in the legal present, are both evident and are both complicit in the precarious and fluid pattern of its emergence. In turn, global law's restless fragility also reflects and reinforces the element of contestation between the authority claims of its different species. As we shall see, there is an ironic circularity at work in the combination of these various factors[47] – an irresolution and awareness of the relativity of perspectives and partiality of solutions that breeds further unsettlement. And this is a dynamic that not only questions the fitness of each particular species of global law, but in so

---

[46] J. Elster, C. Offe and U. K. Preuss, *Institutional Design in Post-Communist Societies: Rebuilding the Ship at Sea* (Cambridge University Press, 1998).

[47] On the need for irony on the part of the scholar of transnational law, whose necessary inquiries into the evolving grounds of legal authority will inevitably disclose, and in so doing highlight and threaten to exacerbate, the precariousness of any and all legal understandings of the world, see P. Zumbansen, 'Defining the Space of Transnational Law: Legal Theory, Global Governance and Legal Pluralism', Osgoode CLPE Research Paper No. 21/2011 37 (2011).

doing also reinforces the challenge to the credentials of global law in general even as it feeds and sustains a self-reproducing momentum.[48]

In Chapter 4 we discussed the reasons for global law's self-propagating quality. We looked at how convergent and divergent conceptions of global law, as selective perspectives each acknowledging and accepting the complexly interwoven diversity of transnational law, find much scope for cohabitation. And we looked at how, even when practical conflicts and philosophical differences and oppositions do arise, they typically do so in a context of mutual provocation, each side acting as a stimulant to the other. Yet, for all global law's capacity to reproduce itself, its internal tensions and contentions compound, and are compounded by, its problematic relationship both to the legal past and to the legal present. As a result, global law is likely to remain a volatile currency, its value against all the other forms of national and transnational law that it seeks to complement and supplement uncertain and unstable.

Take first the question of legal tradition. How does the preoccupation of so many strains of an internally contested global law with the modern heritage of law exacerbate global law's unsettled quality? The key lies in the long and unflattering shadow cast by a central theme within that heritage, namely the state sovereigntist image of the legal universe. That Westphalian conception, to recap, assumes a pattern of mutually exclusive sovereign states, each with a sense of bounded legal ordering, which is challenged by the growth of so many new forms of transnational legal connection – the very growth pattern to which the emergence of a territorially 'unbounded' global law is itself a further response.[49]

It is important to appreciate not only the unique role that the state-centred sovereigntist conception has played in the modern age, but even more significantly, the place it continues to hold in the collective legal memory of that age. It is a conception which has offered itself as a ruling 'metaprinciple'[50] of legal authority. It has supplied an overarching order for all legal orders – a definitive general axiom to make sense of the relationship of all particular forms of legal authority in the world. Of course, this state sovereigntist conception, like much else that makes up the referential template of modern state-centred law,[51] is and always has been a highly stylised idea. It provides a reductive model of legal authority, one that has edited out massive asymmetries of sovereign power in an imperial and post-imperial world, has downplayed various sources and patterns of legal

---

[48] See section 5.2.1 above.   [49] See Chapter 1.2.2 above.
[50] Walker, n. 1 above, at 376.   [51] Ibid.

pluralism within and beyond the state, and has tended to screen off international law's claims to be more than a modest transactional addition to national legal authority.[52] And through this stylisation the state sovereigntist conception, like the projected images of global law that have followed it, has harboured and honed a constructive edge. Its presumptive mapping of legal space has been offered not merely for descriptive and explanatory purposes, but also as a means of 'making' and sustaining the world of law according to its own representation.[53] Despite its selective approach, therefore, but also partly because of it, the state sovereigntist approach did succeed in articulating a metaprinciple and associated 'black-box'[54] image of authority sufficiently plausible and sufficiently in harmony with dominant geopolitical interests to gain and retain traction over a long period.

Just as the state sovereigntist conception no longer dominates as it once did, or is recalled to have done, so none of the species of global law we have been considering can claim to supply an authoritative metaprinciple for a transnational age in a similar fashion and to a similar extent. As we have seen, each species of global law in its own more or less ambitious way seeks to contain the diversity of transnational law. Yet even the more ambitious models of global law – the convergence-promoting formal, structural and abstract-normative species – claim a less comprehensive framing effect than the state sovereigntist metaprinciple. While they provide a global corrective to some aspects of legal diversity, their pyramids, umbrellas and vessels[55] do not purport to capture and organise the entire planetary landscape of law in their own terms in the way that the 'box matrix' of the state sovereigntist model has sought to do. What is more, the very proliferation of candidate species of global law, their images of the legal world in some measure incompatible and rivalrous, further dilutes the authority of each. It is here that we begin to discern more clearly the ironic aspect of global law's pattern of countervailing claims. For if global law is understood as a compensatory response to the declining sway of the state sovereigntist model, then its very capacity to perform that function in a persuasive manner is

---

[52] See e.g. J. Tully, *Public Philosophy in a New Key: Volume II, Imperialism and Civic Freedom* (Cambridge University Press, 2008) ch. 7; and J. H. H. Weiler, 'The Geology of International Law – Governance, Democracy and Legitimacy' 64 *German Yearbook of International Law* 547 (2004). See also Chapter 1.2.1–1.2.2 above.

[53] See e.g. N. Goodman, *Ways of Worldmaking* (Indianapolis: Hackett, 1978); and M. Loughlin, *The Idea of Public Law* (Oxford University Press, 2003) chs. 1–4.

[54] W. Twining, *Globalisation and Legal Theory* (Cambridge University Press, 2000) p. 8.

[55] See Chapter 3.2 above.

impeded by the reactive urgency with which the task is often taken up, the speculative intensity with which it is pursued, and the competition this brings forth between its different species.[56] The lack of an agreed ordering relationship between legal orders, or 'disorder of normative orders',[57] then, is not only the salient circumstance to which global law responds; it is also a condition that becomes consolidated, even exacerbated, by the to and fro of the various species of global law seeking to engage with it seriously.

This is the danger that is strongly nourished by global law's traditionalist undercurrent. The still weighty contemporary resonance of the state sovereigntist approach and the tendency in some quarters to view its high water mark nostalgically as something of a 'golden age' – a tendency to which we return in Chapter 6 – is itself one key indicator of the significance ascribed to the legal past of the modern age within the contemplative horizon of late modern law. Another key indicator, however, namely the liberal use within global law of historical-discursive themes of a sort that are bound to recall this very state sovereigntist approach, only serves to encourage the kind of comparison from which global law is likely to suffer. The symbolic affirmation of constitutional law, and to a lesser extent international law, in the discursive narratives of global law, especially in support of the convergence-sponsoring species of global law, supplies a standing reminder of the Westphalian model and its similar reliance upon both constitutional law and international law. But while the state sovereigntist model played to the historical strengths of constitutional law as a state-centred discourse and of international law as an inter-state discourse, the models of global law must instead draw upon – indeed are required to *draw up* – versions of constitutional law and of international law that depart from the dominant state-derivative model. In so doing, they use a language that recalls older certainties in order to make new and far more tenuous claims to authority.

The internally competitive quality of the new global law further undermines its reliance on tradition. The ideological value of the call to the past always depends in some measure upon its claim to an authority that is held to be beyond question, or taken for granted, just on account of its venerable quality.[58] And as we have seen, this is all the

[56] See Walker, n. 1 above; Walker, n. 5 above; and Zumbansen, n. 47 above.
[57] Walker, n. 1 above, at 376.
[58] See e.g. Krygier, n. 7 above. See also, classically, Weber's discussion of traditional authority: M. Weber, 'Politics as a Vocation' in J. Dreijmanis (ed.), *Max Weber's Complete Writings on Academic and Political Vocations*, trans. G. C. Wells (New York: Algora Publishing, 2008) pp. 155–208.

more so with law, where past-orientation, or what we have called traditionality, is typically a standard methodological component in the claim
to validity. However, just like the various species of global law themselves, the historical discourses upon which these species rely are to some
extent at odds with one another. As we have seen, constitutionalist and
international law discourses may dovetail, but are often in tension,[59]
while the language of Global Administrative Law sits uncomfortably
with both of these.[60] Equally, the new language of a global law of conflicts
draws upon and significantly develops a private international law tradition in ways that, in their tolerance of a high level of self-containment of
each national or otherwise particular legal jurisdiction, do not easily gel
with more ambitiously convergent reconstructions of constitutionalist
or (public) internationalist approaches to global law.[61] Or, to take a final
example, the discourse of *jus gentium* speaks quite clearly to a more
ambitious strain of international legal thought than the familiar state-
centred one.[62] The point here is a simple one. If cashing out the legitimating claim of the past in contemporary currency depends upon the
presumptive or self-evident authority of that past, then the sheer diversity of global law's past reference and the scope it offers for rival lineages
of authority tend to cancel or reduce that dividend.

The internal contestations of global law are also apparent in how the
tendencies of the legal present are interpreted and extrapolated, and this
serves to reinforce its unsettled quality. If, as much as the respect-
conferring aura of tradition, persuasive trend-spotting is at a premium
in the making of the new global law, it is also quite as vulnerable to the
counter-suggestion of competing voices. Just as the value of the past as
an unassailable source of authority is eroded by the circulation of many
candidate pasts, so the value of one reading of current trends as a guide to
future focus is undermined by the persistent distraction of other readings. In the case of trend-spotting, the specific concern that contestation
brings is not the puncturing of a sense of long-established authority, but
the blurring of a sense of distinctive insight. The value of trend-spotting
lies in the capacity to read an incipient pattern into an oblique combination and complex sequence of movements. It offers a clarifying reduction, a way of reclaiming order out of noise, of penetrating 'the mystery

---

[59] Chapter 3.3.1 above.   [60] Chapter 3.3.2 above.   [61] See Chapter 3.4.1.1 above.
[62] See e.g. Waldron, n. 23 above, ch. 2; see also E. Jouannet, 'Universalism and Imperialism:
The True–False Paradox of International Law?' 8 *European Journal of International Law*
379 (2007).

of global governance'.[63] If, however, it is surrounded by other and competing clarifying reductions, the danger arises that the noise levels increase rather than decrease, and that the search for a bright line through a congested landscape merely leads to more clutter and confusion.

Let us revisit the case of proportionality. To some of its sponsors, proportionality is the new 'golden rule'[64] of law for an age in which fundamental legal values and objectives have never been more openly contested or in greater need of a method of reconciliation. For others, however, it is at best pleonastic, a term that adds nothing to our understanding of how to resolve hard cases. And at worst, it interferes with and detracts from the language of global basic rights[65] – itself still emergent – and so threatens to blunt a sharp weapon in the struggle for a universal language of justice.[66] Similarly, subsidiarity, a fragment of catholic social doctrine which entered the modern legal lexicon two decades ago as a way of justifying both the extent and limits of central authority in the European Union,[67] may be read two ways. It may be viewed as a suggestive neologism allowing us to make better sense of the proper allocation of legal authority between different levels and scales of government. Alternatively, it may be understood as a superfluous notion, one that adds nothing but terminological redundancy to our existing conceptual vocabulary of the devolution of power – in particular the family of concepts associated with federalism – and which is apt to confuse rather than enlighten our attempts to justify the global distribution of political capacity.[68]

Or, to take a final example, we may consider the notion of 'outcasting',[69] a recent candidate addition to the lexicon of international

---

[63] See D. Kennedy, 'The Mystery of Global Governance' in Dunoff and Trachtman, n. 34 above, pp. 37–68.

[64] D. Beatty, 'Law's Golden Rule' in G. Palombella and N. Walker (eds.), *Relocating the Rule of Law* (Oxford: Hart, 2009) pp. 99–115.

[65] C. R. Beitz and R. E. Goodin (eds.), *Global Basic Rights* (Oxford University Press, 2009).

[66] See e.g. F. J. Urbina, 'A Critique of Proportionality' 57 *American Journal of Jurisprudence* 49 (2012); G. Letsas, 'Rescuing Proportionality' in R. Cruft, M. Liao and M. Renzo (eds.), *Philosophical Foundations of Human Rights* (Oxford University Press, forthcoming).

[67] See e.g. P. D. Marquardt, 'Subsidiarity and Sovereignty in the European Union' 18 *Fordham International Law Journal* 616 (1994).

[68] See e.g. A. Estella, *The EU Principle of Subsidiarity and Its Critique* (Oxford University Press, 2002).

[69] O. A. Hathaway and S. J. Shapiro, 'Outcasting: Enforcement in Domestic and International Law' 121 *Yale Law Journal* 252 (2011).

law. Intended to account for how a plethora of international law instruments, from the World Trade Organization to the Montreal Protocol on the Depletion of the Ozone Layer, operate effectively *as* law by excluding the disobedient from membership and denying them the benefits of social co-operation, it is relevant to an expansive conception of global law inasmuch as it stands apart from a state-centred model of legal authority dependent upon the capacity to use coercion. It suggests a broader and more subtle sanctioning power for law, and in so doing it may allow us to reconsider the achievements and prospects of international law in a less restrictive and more flexible manner. Against that, however, a notion such as outcasting is as likely to continue familiar debates and revive old controversies in a new vocabulary as to secure a new and open-ended framework for understanding the trajectory of international politics. Rather than being welcomed as an agreeably supple device for harnessing old and new trends, it may be received questioningly by some as one more variation on the recurrent theme of 'soft power'.[70] It may be viewed sceptically as restating rather than resolving the problem of the relative impotence of much international law, as failing sufficiently to question a state-centred understanding of law between and beyond states,[71] and as sidelining rather than settling the key issue of locating the appropriate line and decisive distinction in transnational power relations between legal authority and other forms of orchestrated exhortation or reputational sanctioning.

Thirty years ago Jean Baudrillard coined the term 'hyperreality'[72] to depict what he claimed to be a special register of social reality that is created or simulated from models of the 'real'. His concern was with how certain culturally disembedded areas of contemporary social life are increasingly defined through a process of symbolic construction that conflates signifier and signified, and which may even lack a signified object. Most basically, the production of the hyperreal involves the practice of (re)representing certain representations of the world – or 'simulacra'[73] – as the only reality that counts. Baudrillard and other

---

[70] J. Nye, *Soft Power: The Means to Success in World Politics* (New York: Public Affairs, 2004).

[71] P. Spiro, 'The Sovereigntist Premise of Hathaway and Shapiro's Outcasting', *Opinio Juris*, 16 November 2011, http://opiniojuris.org/2011/11/16/the-sovereigntist-premise-of-hathaway-and-shapiros-outcasting/.

[72] See e.g. J. Baudrillard, *Simulacra and Simulation* (University of Michigan Press, 1994).

[73] *Ibid.*

post-structural theorists are concerned to stress the undesirable or unintended consequences of these developments, including a growing lack of cognitive appreciation of the distinction between the surface label and its underlying 'reality', and a broader cultural failure to seek value in, or to assign value to, human production in terms other than the 'signed' world. As a sociological thesis about the changing forms and uses of symbolic products, this seems overstated, or certainly as tending to overgeneralise from specific sectors of cultural life such as celebrity culture, virtual reality and the branding of consumer products.[74] Yet it does also contain insights that illuminate our understanding of areas of life subject to the acute forms of disembedding we associate with globalisation. In our particular case, it helps deepen the account of the unsettling effect of transnational legal thought's preoccupation with the exposure and repackaging of contemporary regulatory trends.

It is important to note that this is not simply a matter of individual choice or collective prejudice. The variously specialist inhabitants of the world of global law-craft are no more impervious to professional self-interest, ambition or vanity than anyone else, but the kind of symbolic work involved in sourcing and eliciting global legal trends is far from being reducible to a cynical or self-indulgent exercise in product marketing and placement. A key motivation for many doubtless remains the desire to re-engage with the complexity of contemporary transnational law in ways that will have tangible effects and, in their assessment, beneficial effects in terms of understanding and practical application. Yet the extent and range of thought and counter-thought, image and counter-image, that this brings forth, and which we have sought to illustrate in this and the previous chapter, does have significant unintended consequences in the realm of legal symbology. For it encourages an environment in which, regardless of underlying motivations, the competition between signifiers threatens to distract attention from the concrete prospects of the signified practice, and in which the discourse on global legal outlooks becomes less likely to be securely connected to extant forms of legal authority or grounded in widely affirmed emergent trends.[75]

---

[74] See e.g. A. Woodward, 'Was Baudrillard a Nihilist?' 5 *International Journal of Baudrillard Studies* (2008), www.ubishops.ca/baudrillardstudies/vol5_1/v5-1-article12-woodward.html.
[75] Kennedy, n. 63 above.

5.2.4   Realising global law

In Chapter 2 we introduced the idea of the continuum of global law-craft to grasp how the development of a global horizon of legal work has involved a new fluidity of location, event, office, role and professional organisation, and also of law-making sites and contexts. One key consequence of the absence of a rigid global division of labour and of organisational forms has been the greater involvement of the academic end of the occupational continuum in jurisgenerative activity, as regards both transnational law generally and global law in particular.[76] But this is no one-way street. It is not simply the case that the intermingling of functions, mobility of roles and intimacy of networks in the organisation and delivery of global law-craft has afforded the legal academy a greater opportunity to influence the content and tenor of global law than has been the case in the world of state law, with its more settled demarcation of the domains of theoretical knowledge and practical application. For it is also true, as we have sought to demonstrate above, that the very 'intimated' structure of global law invites a wider range of historical, comparative and prospective analysis and a greater level of speculative reason in its articulation and refinement. The channels of causality, therefore, run in both directions, and operate in a mutually reinforcing manner. The elaboration of global law implies a measure of reflection and theorisation that the transnational academy, already well placed and well connected on the law-craft continuum, is in any case well qualified to deliver.

In particular, it is the projected, oblique and unsettled quality of an intimated global law that is responsible for altering the general balance between the embedded and the unrealised aspect of its normativity. Legal normativity, indeed any type of normativity, necessarily implies both aspects in some measure, but the mix may differ. In specifying a required standard or form of behaviour, a legal norm or norm set refers to what is already established, or is at least arguable, as a rule, and what, therefore, may already apply or have been applied to regulate activity and resolve disputes. Yet the norm or set of norms also and simultaneously refers to the range of its possible future articulations and refinements in its various contexts of application. As we have already seen, global law tends more towards realisation and less towards

---

[76] See Chapter 2.2–2.3 above. See also Walker, n. 1 above; and G.-P. Calliess and P. Zumbansen, *Rough Consensus and Running Code: A Theory of Transnational Private Law* (Oxford: Hart, 2010) ch. 1.

consolidation.[77] Vitally, there must and there does remain an element of establishment in global law. Without some claim as to its current applicability – to its already possessing a rule-like quality – global law could simply not satisfy any meaningful operative definition of law. That is to say, the claim of global law would not be a *legal* claim, but simply an aspiration – a hope or prediction of what law might become. And, as we have also seen, global law *does* make claim to current applicability, and indeed does so through a process of what we have called double normativity.[78] Global law, of whatever species, always involves the operation of some general rule or other general dimension of law upon or through more particular rules. Yet global law's establishment as law always also remains precarious, both tentative in its emergence and fragile in its resilience.

In broad terms, as we have seen above, global law lacks the past-oriented authority of state-based law, and instead typically invokes more free-ranging narratives of legal pastness and speculative diagnoses of incipient trends in support of diverse and sometimes competitive images of law's emergent capacity for global containment. The shaping of law in the domain of global law, then, becomes somewhat more a question of prospection and construction and somewhat less one of retrospection and endorsement. And in that process of prospection and construction the emphasis shifts from custodianship of a state-based legal tradition to the reworking of old forms and recognition of new tendencies in realisation of emergent prospects. Such an orientation prioritises future over past, reframing over frame-filling, creativity over conformity, paradigm shifting rather than paradigmatic authority.

The forward-looking aspect includes both an epistemic component and an evaluative and advocacy component, although again the mix will vary. In the first case, it is a matter of the deployment of knowledge about how a legal approach adapted from our disciplinary traditions is likely to develop or how a current trend might unfold, both in terms of the unpacking and assembly of its internal normative logic and in terms of its likely relationship to, and reaction with, its wider social environment.[79] And in the second case, the forward-looking aspect is a matter of preferential forecasting, of advocating the pursuit of a general approach or the working of a new tendency in a particular direction because of the claimed or implied benefits of so doing.[80] In both components, however,

---

[77] Section 5.2.1 above. [78] See Chapter 4.2 above.
[79] See e.g. Shaffer and Ginsburg, n. 41 above. [80] See e.g. Walker, n. 1 above, at 376–85.

and in their interweaving, there is a significant element of schematisation involved, the building of a general model in terms of which a pattern of normative development may be anticipated and pursued.

If we take this unrealised dimension of global law fully into account, both in its epistemic and in its evaluative aspects, we might come to the conclusion that global law represents a category of law that, in order to include just this kind of anticipatory legal framing, is required to deepen and stretch our notion, or our range of notions, of what legal normativity, and legal doctrine as the expression of legal normativity, can cover.[81] Alternatively, if that is too much of a stretch, we might adjust our vocabulary to accommodate the novelty of global law. We might then hold that global law is a category of law that redefines, or at least refines, our very understanding of the scope of the operative domain of law. It does so in order to embrace not just doctrine or dogmatics but also the very schemes of legal thoughts or metaprinciples, including the relations of accommodation and competition between these schemes of thought, according to which we define the seven species of global law and through which we might frame, justify and seek to lend authority to the development of new doctrine.

This kind of second-order authorising framework, of course, is not itself a novelty, but has always been integral to modern law. But when that framework encapsulated an exclusive conception of state sovereignty, it normally sat in the settled background of positive legal doctrine. It provided the deep and typically unstated theoretical justification of that positive legal doctrine – its inarticulate major premise. And just because it was the subject of prior and independent establishment, the second-order sovereigntist framework could normally remain detached from the positive law that it framed on the occasion of the articulation

---

[81] What counts as doctrine is of course culturally variable. See e.g. A. von Bogdandy, 'The Past and Promise of Doctrinal Constructivism: A Strategy for Responding to the Challenges Facing Constitutional Scholarship in Europe' 7 *International Journal of Constitutional Law* 364 (2009); and responses in same issue from Mattias Kumm, Robert Post and Alexander Somek. See also the comparative work of M. Lasser on the different sources, weight and interaction of doctrine in three jurisdictions (France, the United States and the European Union): M. Lasser, *Judicial Deliberations: A Comparative Analysis of Judicial Transparency and Legitimacy* (Oxford University Press, 2004). More generally, of course, what counts as belonging within the operative domain of 'law' more broadly conceived is not only culturally variable but also controversial between different branches of legal philosophy (positivism, natural law, legal pragmatism, etc.). See e.g. R. Dworkin, *Justice in Robes* (Cambridge, MA: Harvard University Press, 2006), particularly the introduction and ch. 8.

and application of that positive law. But in our new circumstances alternative second-order frameworks are instead prominent in the unsettled foreground, and so their sometimes rivalrous formulations and framing justifications become inseparable from, and folded into, the very stuff of global law.[82]

5.2.5 The role of the academy

Under these new conditions, the relationship of all exponents of global law-craft to global law alters, but the role of the academy is particularly significantly affected. Legal scholars may become less the (relatively minor) keepers of a tradition and (more significant) refiners of its doctrine, and more a special case of the 'symbolic analysts'[83] that Robert Reich referred to when coining a new breed of social thinker for the contemporary age: namely, those who both comprehend and express the power of new problem definitions and framing ideas to harness those social technologies – including technologies of legal engineering – capable of achieving collective desirable ends in circumstances where the appropriate constituencies and plausible means of collective action become ever less clear. It is against this background that we can understand the especially prominent role of the legal academy in initiatives such as a global recasting of constitutional and administrative law, the blending of the new hybrid legal forms, or the development of new principles and techniques of lateral integration, not to mention the redeployment of more hierarchical models of coherence.

5.3 The inexorability of global law

Finally, we turn to the last of the 'intimated' traits of global law – to its seemingly inexorable quality. For all its unsettled status and precarious

---

[82] See e.g. Walker, n. 1 above, at 385–96; Walker, n. 5 above, at 36–44. Another practical example of this is the *Kadi* case law discussed in Chapter 4.4 above: see Joined cases C-402/05 P and C-415/05 P, *Kadi and Al Barakaat International Foundation* v. *Council and Commission*, Judgment of the Court (Grand Chamber), 3 September 2008, [2008] ECR I-6351 (*Kadi I*); and Joined cases C-584/10 P, C-593/10 P and C-595/10 P, *European Commission and Others* v. *Yassin Abdullah Kadi*, Judgment of the Court (Grand Chamber), 18 July 2013 (*Kadi II*).

[83] R. Reich, *The Work of Nations. Preparing Ourselves for 21st Century Capitalism* (New York: Knopf Publishing, 1991).

trajectory, and for all that it identifies a prominent role for the academy in the fashioning of new legal directions, an air of inevitability accompanies much of the discussion and debate over global law. Global law is here to stay. Or, at least, it is difficult to imagine otherwise. Why is that so? Let us begin by referring back to the broadest cultural measure of globalisation.

Across many dimensions of social and political life the gradual infiltration of our collective conscience by ideas of global scale and sweep – ideas such as global law itself – indicates a kind of process that is not easily rewound. As Manfred Steger has argued,[84] today we increasingly take for granted a global or planetary horizon of social and political prospect, potential and predicament alongside, and to some extent displacing, our national and other frames of reference. In so depicting the rise of the 'global imaginary',[85] he recalls the importance of the phenomenological dimension of globalisation.[86] He draws attention to the extent to which globalisation speaks to altered perceptions of the connectedness of the world as much as it does to objective indicators. And, of particular significance, he alerts us to the fact that once the relevance of the global-as-planetary has been 'imagined' and widely articulated in any particular context, however controversial some of the resulting visions are, it is difficult for it thereafter to become 'unimagined'.

The dissemination and widespread cultural embedding of different global themes takes many forms. It embraces the utopian and the dystopian, the exotic and the mundane. It covers contemporary political themes and movements such as feminism, environmentalism and nuclear disarmament, all of which were 'born' in global rather than national political 'space' and which are organically transnational in their organisation and all-encompassing in their discursive range. It embraces global 'bads' such as climate change, pandemic disease and 'terror' – borderless collective action problems whose apparent urgency, as we have already noted,[87] tends to reinforce their planetary credentials. It includes global political ideologies, movements and orientations that contemplate and seek to achieve transformative results or consolidate gradual worldwide trends, and which in so doing come to strike attitudes of mutual engagement and competition: from market globalism to a left-leaning 'global justice' orientation and 'jihadist globalism', and from the

[84] M. Steger, *The Rise of the Global Imaginary: Political Ideologies from the French Revolution to the Global War on Terror* (Oxford University Press, 2008).
[85] *Ibid.* [86] See the references at n. 25 above. [87] See Chapter 3.4.2 above.

very idea of a globally open 'cosmopolitan' politics to a similarly widely disseminated and globally connected anti-globalisation movement, and an almost equally widespread and well-networked revanchist nationalism.[88] And, finally, the rise of the global imaginary also refers to forms of consciousness that are parasitic on already existing global practices, forms of consumption, events and institutions, from celebrity culture, health and lifestyle regimes, social networking, gaming and other virtual fashions, to peak sporting events such as the Olympic Games and the football World Cup, and even global political entities such as the United Nations and the G8.

All of this means that thinking globally takes on both a headline and a quotidian significance. Indeed, it can become so taken for granted and so 'natural' to think globally in certain areas of social and political life, the occasional highlights corroborated by the low thrum of everyday reference, that we can lose sight of how far and how quickly orientations have changed and how rapidly the category of the global has insinuated itself into our social consciousness. In many cases, moreover, as we have seen with the rise of global law-craft itself,[89] even though core transnational practices are led by narrow elites with privileged access to resources, knowledge and networks, these very forms of privilege also amplify their capacity to disseminate, to shape and to influence, and so to infiltrate broader spheres of popular consciousness. In addition, this widespread set of globalising changes has a cumulative – indeed, encompassing – effect. Just as national consciousness has an inbuilt connector – the very category of the nation suggesting a roundly identified 'way of life' and roundly identifying 'way of seeing' rather than something functionally and experientially discrete[90] – so, too, the category of the global has a transversal quality. As a stratum of consciousness and referent of experience, it is also in principle boundless in its referential scope, with advances in global awareness and encounter in some domains encouraging an atmosphere of invitation and expectation in others. It is much more than glib sloganeering, therefore, to suggest that the more we have and the more we experience 'global institutions', a 'global economy', 'global politics', 'global communications' and 'global culture', the more we will also expect to have and to experience something like 'global law'; or, indeed, to suggest any causally sequential variation on the above.

---

[88] Steger, n. 84 above, particularly chs. 5–6; and C. Calhoun, *Nations Matter: Culture, History and the Cosmopolitan Dream* (New York: Routledge, 2007), particularly chs. 1–3.
[89] See Chapter 2 above.   [90] See e.g. Steger, n. 84 above, pp. 8–10.

Rather, it speaks precisely to the way in which the global, however much it may continue to play second fiddle to other levels and forms of belonging and communities of practice, and however diversely and unevenly it is experienced within and between different communities, is itself gradually becoming understood as a holistic category – as something which achieves purchase across the expanse of collective living and experience.

Beyond these general ways in which global law is nurtured and naturalised by the background culture of globalisation, there are also far more specific factors that contribute to its accompanying sense of inexorability. The projected, oblique, unsettled and emergent qualities of global law mark it out as a novel paradigm of constructive legal thought and practice, but also as one that feeds its own development. Our discussion of the circuitous character of global law in Chapter 4 sought to show the twofold character of this. We observed how global law responds, first, to the remorselessness of transnational law and to the insistent pressure to provide convergence-promoting and divergence-accommodating approaches to its containment. This, indeed, is the other side of global law's double normativity. Global law responds through its various images and schemes of containment to actually existing forms of normativity, whether in the form of particular legal initiatives, or specific cases or disputes, or concrete tendencies. In so doing it does not control the generative context, and so does not dictate either the content or the pattern of occurrence of the various instances of transnational normativity that it acts upon. Instead, it is compelled to react to that content and pattern of occurrence. Secondly, however, global law also responds to the mutual contestations and provocations of its own various second-order solutions to the ever-emergent problems and opportunities of the containment of transnational law. This process, as we have seen in the previous section, is dogged and further stimulated by the way in which the competition of authority claims between the various species of global law dramatises and underlines a general erosion of a sense of settled authority.

Global law, then, reflects the progressive normalisation of a general movement of 'acting up' in the culture of globalisation, as well as the intensity and synergy of the fluidly interacting elites of global law-craft. But it is also caught in a dynamic of internal competition that it can neither avoid nor resolve. The net effect is one in which the apparent inevitability and irreversibility of global law in general is as resistant to questioning as its detailed trajectory is unclear and controversial.

The players in the drama of global law, like many others on the global stage, find themselves faced with a terrain as seemingly inescapable as it is inscrutable. On the one hand, their point of departure is an acceptance of, and confrontation with, the world as it is, with all its path-dependencies and in all its evolved complexity. On the other hand, their point of projection is to a different world, but one as elusive, contested and insusceptible to resolution as their point of departure is fixed and taken as given. This, indeed, is why we hear much talk of the post-national in the circles of legal analysis, but also why, now, and in the foreseeable future, we are likely to hear little or nothing of the post-global. That is the case even though global law seems destined to continue to offer a series of obliquely connected angles of legal intervention and an intermittent theatre of contestation, as much as it does a shared and cumulative framework for addressing and reconciling the diversity of transnational law.

6

Confronting global law

6.1 Reconsidering global law

Our sense of global law as a contemporary trend that is as insistent as it is unresolved brings us, finally, to the question of how we might consider its future development.

We should begin, however, by sounding a note of caution. Perhaps there is simply nothing more we can say, and, in fact, nothing further *to* be said about the intimations of global law. In the opening chapter the primary aim of our inquiry was stated to be diagnostic rather than prescriptive. Our priority was to specify the nature and forms of global law and to assess its condition, as well as its preconditions. We set out, in particular, to examine the various species of global law organised under the two general convergence-promoting and divergence-accommodating conceptions, to consider why and how they have emerged, and to investigate how they relate to one another. Yet nothing we have said from this analytical and investigative standpoint has sought to take sides between the two conceptions, and the various species arranged under the two conceptions, or to argue that some should be ranked higher than others in order of preference or significance. And, arguably, nothing we might say could make a difference, or even should seek to make any difference, to the approaches taken.

The promoters of convergence, armed with a measure of general cosmopolitan vision and optimism, will continue to make formal, structural and abstract-normative arguments in favour of a certain type of global law, and will do so with or without the help of one of law's grand historical discourses, such as constitutional law or international law. The accommodators of divergence, preoccupied with the problems rather than the opportunities of devising global legal forms in the face of such an array of sharply differentiated and often contending transnational legal regimes, each with its own priorities and domain interests, will display the more selective commitment of a functionally specific approach or a hybrid approach, or the more modestly reconciliatory ambition of the laterally co-ordinate approach, again with or without the help of one of the grand historical discourses. And to a greater or lesser degree, the various advocates and bearers of the arguments of global law, regardless of their point of departure and angle of engagement, will seek to merge or combine the various species where they judge it possible, and to differentiate and choose between them where they consider it necessary.

If anything, the analysis provided in the previous chapter would simply reinforce in the various theorists and practitioners of global law a sense of the appropriateness of the course they have taken. For if our assessment of its intimated quality is correct, global law in all its diversity flows naturally, and in a powerful current, from a committed concern with the condition of transnational law. And if this leads to an environment of sustained, even irresolvable, tension between different approaches and the value commitments which underpin them, then perhaps that is only as it ought to be. Law has always been an arena of disputation as much as a framework of common action.[1] If the coming of global law announces a new site of contestation, then, even if that contestation seems in some ways more basic and intractable than in the state-centred paradigm of modern law, is this not only to be expected, and, indeed, accepted as an extension of law's normal socio-political condition?

But this conclusion is surely too quick and too neat. It is too ready to treat the contemporary path of development of global law as *in fact* inevitable or irresistible, as opposed to merely persistent and exhibiting a strong tendency towards self-reproduction. And it is too ready to accept that the script of the terms and conditions under which the global law debate will continue to unfold has already been written. For, even if the broad course of development of global law cannot easily be reversed, its detailed trajectory would surely repay closer and more critical consideration. We should not be so easily satisfied, therefore, that a study that does not take sides between the various species of global law cannot nonetheless offer insights or possess lessons for future practice – not least the future practice of theory.

In order to take this further and final step, we must begin by alerting ourselves to what might be said *against* global law at a more fundamental level than we have so far considered. This is so for two reasons – one external, the other internal. First, we cannot make a fully informed assessment of what is at stake in the future of global law, and how the continuation of the present pattern of practice might be defended or

---

[1] See e.g. J. Waldron, *Law and Disagreement* (Oxford University Press, 1999).

moderated, unless we know what its basic drawbacks and shortcomings are, or what alternatives exist. What criticisms might be offered to the idea of global law in general, as opposed to its particular manifestations, and what might be suggested in its place? Secondly, this perspective, as we shall see, not only offers a standard of evaluation, but also provides part of the political backdrop against which global law is shaped and part of the cultural milieu within which global law operates. As such, the critical attitude also supplies a set of forces that acts upon and sharpens the particular limitations experienced and challenges faced by various species of global law even as they sustain a circuit of self-reproduction; and, indeed, the critical attitude becomes part of that circuit of self-reproduction.

6.2   Two platforms of critique

Scepticism towards global law, or at least towards the kind of conceptions and images of the world of law that global law endorses and to which it responds, flows from two quite distinct general platforms and world-views, although there may be some overlap between them. Each offers its own critique, its own accompanying attitude, and its own more or less constructive set of responses. In the first place, scepticism can be mounted from the *statist* perspective. The critical message about law here concerns a loss or erosion of certain valued properties of law associated with the state. The accompanying attitude is one of preference for, even 'nostalgia'[2] towards, a world that is in danger of disappearing. The response is, more constructively, one of re-emphasising and restoring state-centred legal precepts and structures; less constructively, it involves either the denial or downplaying of the degree of denationalisation of law already achieved and of any need to respond restoratively, or, by contrast, resignation in the face of loss. In the second place, scepticism can flow from what we might call, under the broadest of umbrella labels, the *radical* perspective. The critical message about law here concerns its support for or complicity in unjustified economic and political power structures. The accompanying attitude is one of critical exposure and condemnation. The response is, more constructively, one of wholesale transformation, or, less constructively, structural fatalism, with various intermediate points available between these two positions.

---

[2]   M. Kumm, 'The Best of Times and the Worst of Times: Between Constitutional Triumphalism and Nostalgia' in P. Dobner and M. Loughlin (eds.), *The Twilight of Constitutionalism?* (Oxford University Press, 2010) pp. 201–19.

The aim here is not to develop these platforms in any depth or to say anything about the many positions and countless nuances that can be accommodated within each. The literatures are massive, and it would take two additional books to do them justice.[3] Rather, our much more modest objective is to understand the broad limits within which the global law paradigm operates and the critical edge and attendant suspicion and hostility that lurks at either margin. For that restricted purpose we make do with a highly stylised and inevitably reductive account of the two platforms.

The statist platform, which incorporates much conventional 'sovereigntist' wisdom within both constitutional law and international law,[4] tends to emphasise the democratic credentials of the modern state, its capacity to speak to 'national' bonds of affinity and common voice, and its ability to count on the underlying sympathy of 'losers' consent'[5] to deliver solidaristic forms of public policy.[6] It is a stance that favours moral particularism over moral universalism – or at least is prepared to give a strongly particularistic slant to moral universalism.[7] It is also a

---

[3] For a flavour of the statist platform, see essays by Dieter Grimm, Martin Loughlin and Rainer Wahl, in Dobner and Loughlin, n. 2 above: Grimm, 'The Achievement of Constitutionalism and its Prospects in a Changed World' pp. 3–22; M. Loughlin, 'What is Constitutionalisation?' pp. 47–72; and R. Wahl, 'In Defence of "Constitution"' pp. 220–44. See also my review of some of these positions in the same volume: N. Walker, 'Beyond the Holistic Constitution?' pp. 291–308. For a flavour of the radical platform, see J. M. Beneyto, D. Kennedy, J. Corti Varela and J. Haskell (eds.), *New Approaches to International Law: The European and the American Experiences* (The Hague: Springer, 2013).

[4] See Chapter 1.2.2–1.2.3 above. There is a significant parallel state- or nation-centred literature in political theory: see e.g. D. Miller, *Justice for Earthlings: Essays in Political Philosophy* (Cambridge University Press, 2013); D. Miller, *Citizenship and National Identity* (Cambridge: Polity Press, 2000). There is also a parallel 'intergovernmentalist' literature in international relations: see e.g. A. Moravcsik and F. Schimmelfennig, 'Liberal Intergovernmentalism' in A. Wiener and T. Diez (eds.), *European Integration Theory*, 2nd edn (Oxford University Press, 2009) pp. 67–88.

[5] C. J. Anderson, A. Blais, S. Bowler, T. Donovan and O. Listhaug, *Losers' Consent: Elections and Democratic Legitimacy* (Oxford University Press, 2005).

[6] See e.g. Grimm, n. 3 above; and Miller, *Citizenship and National Identity*, n. 4 above.

[7] See, for example, the debate concerning 'constitutional patriotism' (*Verfassungspatriotismus*), the much-discussed theory associated with Dolf Steinberger and, then, more famously, with Jürgen Habermas, which seeks to reconcile national political and cultural identity with an attachment to universal constitutional principles: see e.g. J.-W. Müller, *Constitutional Patriotism* (Princeton University Press, 2007); and also N. Walker, 'The Place of European Law' in G. de Búrca and J. H. H. Weiler (eds.), *The Worlds of European Constitutionalism* (Cambridge University Press, 2011) pp. 57–104. See also, more generally, Chapter 3.3.1 above.

stance that supports a delegation or 'editorial'[8] model of international law and relations in which states keep the last word, and one which retains a sense of the value of non-state law as merely aggregative, dependent on the sum of the benefits it delivers for each of the states considered discretely. Where it does not adopt a tone of resignation, the statist position, together with its various 'thin' internationalist and 'intergovernmentalist'[9] accomplices, is often quick to downplay the extent to which the relevant units of collective action in an interconnected world are becoming increasingly identified as transnational, and frequently reluctant to accept the extent to which the sovereign prerogative of states might have already been sacrificed or compromised to take account of this.[10]

The radical position includes much of the thinking in the transnational literatures inspired or informed by Critical Legal Studies, Marxist theory, critical race theory, feminist theory, post-colonial theory and other New Approaches to International (and transnational) Law.[11] It focuses on the original sin and continuing blind spot of international law, and transnational law generally, as a framework authorising, giving 'apology'[12] for, and extending the hegemony of Western political and economic power. The flaws in the transnational power structure, according to this view, lie both in the resilience of its imperial foundations and in the continuing tendency of global legal arrangements and political voice to track the prevailing asymmetries of economic, political and military power. The first aim of the radical perspective is to provide the means for critical confrontation, and so to disseminate knowledge and understanding of law's implication in global injustice. Beyond this, the radical perspective, in dramatising the size and stubbornness of the

---

[8] P. Pettit, 'Democracy, National and International' 89 *The Monist* 301 (2006).

[9] See Moravcsik and Schimmelfennig, n. 4 above.

[10] Much of this argument is pursued in the specific context of the European Union. For a recent well-developed example, see P. Lindseth, *Power and Legitimacy: Reconciling Europe and the Nation-State* (Oxford University Press, 2010).

[11] See e.g. Beneyto et al., n. 3 above; and H. Charlesworth, 'Feminist Methods in International Law' 93 *American Journal of International Law* 379 (1999); J. Tully, *Public Philosophy in a New Key: Volume II, Imperialism and Civic Freedom* (Cambridge University Press, 2008); B. S. Chimni, 'Third World Approaches to International Law: A Manifesto' 8 *International Community Law Review* 3 (2006); M. Koskenniemi, 'The Politics of International Law' 1 *European Journal of International Law* 4 (1990); B. Bowring, 'What is Radical in "Radical International Law"?' in J. Klabbers (ed.), *Finnish Yearbook of International Law, Vol. XXII, 2011* (Oxford: Hart, 2013); T. Pogge, *Politics as Usual: What Lies Behind the Pro-poor Rhetoric* (Cambridge: Polity Press, 2010).

[12] M. Koskenniemi, *From Apology to Utopia: The Structure of International Legal Argument*, 2nd edn (Cambridge University Press, 2006).

gap between the current condition of transnational law and any imaginable system of global social and political justice, may strike a melancholic note. Or it may suggest basic institutional reforms or social and political initiatives as a way to begin bridging that gap.[13]

For all their differences, these positions provide the basis for a combined challenge to global law, four elements of which stand out. Just as the two platforms are often at odds, so these four heads of challenge are not necessarily mutually supportive or even mutually consistent. They nevertheless belong together as part of a front that provides both a basis for critique of global law and a living and shaping challenge.

In the first place, there is the charge of *elitism*. The statist position, as we have seen, tends to display its democratic credentials prominently, and makes the absence at the transnational level of democratic community and of its attendant intensity of political engagement, or even of its feasible prospect, central to its critique. The radical position tends to depart from a less fixed and stylised template of democracy, but is equally critical of the weakness of representation and narrowness of voice in transnational legal circles. Both positions are broadly critical of the use of expertise and other purely output-oriented criteria in transnational policy circles as substitutes for input-based legitimacy.[14] Importantly, the role of the lawyer, jurist or academic commentator as a source of expertise – so central to the condition of global law – is also vulnerable to this critique, even if it is one that tends to be articulated more strongly from the radical perspective than from the statist perspective.[15] The charge of elitism, then, is one that can be laid against many of the institutional arenas of global law, from the United Nations Security Council to the privileged networks of appellate court judges.[16]

---

[13] See e.g. A. Buchanan, *Justice, Legitimacy, and Self-Determination: Moral Foundations for International Law* (Oxford University Press, 2003).

[14] For an overview of these criticisms, see G. de Búrca, 'Developing Democracy Beyond the State' 46 *Columbia Journal of Transnational Law* 221 (2008).

[15] See e.g. M. Koskenniemi, 'The Fate of Public International Law: Between Technique and Politics' 70 *Modern Law Review* 1 (2007); and S. Marks (ed.), *International Law on the Left: Re-examining Marxist Legacies* (Cambridge University Press, 2008).

[16] See e.g. O. Schachter, 'The Invisible College of International Lawyers' 72 *Northwestern University Law Review* 217 (1977); S. Villalpando, 'The "Invisible College of International Lawyers" Forty Years Later', Conference Paper No. 5/2013 (4 December 2013), available at http://ssrn.com/abstract=2363640; M. Koskenniemi, *The Gentle Civilizer of Nations: The Rise and Fall of International Law 1870–1960* (Cambridge University Press, 2001); and M. Koskenniemi, 'The Politics of International Law – 20 Years Later' 20 *European Journal of International Law* 7 (2009).

But it can also be levelled against the very persons – the symbolic analysts of academia and the wider academic environment – who have done so much to develop, refine and argue (and sometimes contest) the case for global law.[17]

In the second place, by accepting the world as it is as its point of departure, global law stands exposed from the perspective of the two critical platforms to the charge of historical *obliviousness*. Whether by active suppression, or by inattention due to the distractions of the new, the various species of global law tend to cut off close consideration of either the historical legal structures or the deep social and economic forces from which the new law has begun to emerge. On the one hand, the statist perspective expresses a concern that the achievements of national constitutional democracy have been forgotten or obscured in the new preoccupation with transnational law, even if, as we have seen, the conceptual language of the statist past has been heavily and often ostentatiously borrowed in pursuit of that new preoccupation.[18] On this view, global law can be criticised for tending to underestimate the *discontinuity* of the new legal setting, and so to gloss over or understate the difficulties of translating solutions fit for one state-centred type of global configuration to another state-decentred type.[19] On the other hand, the radical perspective is concerned much less that the new vocabularies of global governance and global law fail to do justice to the successes of the past, and much more that they sanitise its failings, and, in consequence, that they are unable or unwilling to appreciate the extent to which the legacy of these earlier failings remains inscribed in the problem-framing formulations and solutions of today. On this view, global law can instead be criticised for tending to underestimate the *continuity* of the causes and sources of global injustice.[20]

---

[17] See e.g. D. Kennedy, 'The Mystery of Global Governance' in J. L Dunoff and J. P. Trachtman (eds.), *Ruling the World? Constitutionalism, International Law, and Global Governance* (Cambridge University Press, 2009) pp. 37–68; and Koskenniemi, 'The Politics of International Law – 20 Years Later', n. 16 above.

[18] See Chapter 5.2.1 above; see also D. Grimm, 'Types of Constitution' in M. Rosenfeld and A. Sajó (eds.), *The Oxford Handbook of Comparative Constitutional Law* (Oxford University Press, 2012) pp. 98–132; Grimm, n. 3 above; Wahl, n. 3 above; and Loughlin, n. 3 above.

[19] See e.g. N. Walker, 'Postnational Constitutionalism and the Problems of Translation' in J. H. H. Weiler and M. Wind (eds.), *European Constitutionalism Beyond the State* (Cambridge University Press, 2003) pp. 27–54; and P. Capps and D. Machin, 'The Problem of Global Law' 74 *Modern Law Review* 794 (2011).

[20] See e.g. Chimni, n. 11 above.

In the third place, it can be further claimed from our alternative critical platforms that this closing off of the old, except as a resource in the rhetoric of renewal, can lead to a *detachment* from the lost opportunities and resilient difficulties in which a more candid awareness of where we have come from would instruct us as we confront and address the new circumstances of global law. That detachment born of obliviousness, however, can take sharply differing forms. It may manifest itself as a form of excessive idealism, even of 'triumphalism'[21] in its celebration of a law-led journey to the Promised Land. Arguably, for example, some of the more ambitious forms of abstract-normative global law, such as those centred around human rights, and some of the more progressive forms of global constitutionalism, gain much of their purchase from their decontextualisation and deracination; from a position that tends to float free of and away from the historical constraints of a state-centred political configuration and a market-centred economy and to imagine new cosmopolitan structures released from these confines. Here the elitist critique comes back into focus. The standing temptation is for the brave new world of post-national law to be viewed as an opportunity to write a new script unencumbered either by past political constraints or by past political priorities and accomplishments. What is more, precisely because of the absence of many of the familiar cues of state-centred governments – legislatures and executives, elections and democratically responsive forms of accountability – it is a script that academics and judges might be tempted to develop in their own self-empowering and self-legitimating image.[22]

Equally, however, detachment may take a more limited and limiting form. The sealing off of the perspective of global law from the deeper forces and antecedents of globalisation may lead to a narrowly legalistic reflex, to a concentration on legal symptoms rather than deep socioeconomic causes. It may, in turn, foster a preoccupation with technical questions, say of formal integrity in public international law, or the precise terms of translation of national administrative law models to transnational entities, or fine distinctions between different gradations of constitutional pluralism in conflicts between national and transnational courts; as if these questions, however much at issue in any

---

[21] Kumm, n. 2 above.
[22] See e.g. Koskenniemi, *The Gentle Civilizer of Nations*, n. 16 above; and R. Hirschl, *Towards Juristocracy: The Origins and Consequences of the New Constitutionalism* (Cambridge, MA: Harvard University Press, 2004).

particular case, were the nub of the matter and the extent of what was at stake in the debate over law and globalisation. The danger here is that the narrow confines of such an approach reflect, or breed, a professional myopia – an imperviousness and indifference towards wider causes and consequences, or even a complacent disregard for these.

Finally, there is the charge of *disillusionment*. Here we are concerned not only with the critical insight afforded to us by the two platforms, but also with the second reason we gave for drawing upon these platforms. We shift our attention to the manner in which, as alternative living ideologies inhabiting the same political space as the emerging global law, the two critical platforms *in fact* combine to affect the cultural climate and framework of political possibility in and through which global law operates. On the one hand, the shadow of the state-centred approach serves as a political reminder, in however nostalgically ideal-ised a fashion, of a diminishing world of national political self-determination. It offers a lingering rebuke to a post-national or global position which, for all its many and varied forms and formulations, perennially struggles to re-aggregate voice, community and effective common action. On the other hand, the shadow of the radical approach brings with it a persistent whisper of the unsatisfactory nature of the present global configuration of law when measured by any standard which fails to accord significant weight to imperial and post-imperial path-dependencies. It treats the gulf between global law and global justice, and the absence of a programmatic commitment to overcoming the profound difficulties involved in closing this gap, not as a tribute to the grounded realism and versatile pragmatism of global law, but as a standing indictment of a culture incapable of contemplating institutional transformation rather than mere adaptation.[23] Together, these two posi-tions can operate as a kind of ideological pincer movement, a simulta-neous reminder of the desertion of one set of options and the remoteness of another – of a lost past and an unattainable future.[24] Global law, in this

---

[23] See S. R. Ratner, 'Ethics and International Law: Integrating the Global Justice Project(s)' 5 *International Theory* 1 (2013); and A. Peters, 'Realizing Utopia as a Scholarly Endeavour' 24 *European Journal of International Law* 533 (2013). See also S. Marks, 'Law and the Production of Superfluity' 2 *Transnational Legal Theory* 1 (2011). See also Chapter 4.3 above.

[24] See, for example, the melancholic analyses of T. Judt, *Ill Fares the Land: A Treatise on Our Present Discontents* (New York: Penguin, 2010); T. Judt, *Thinking the Twentieth Century* (New York: Penguin, 2012); and J.-W. Müller, *Contesting Democracy: Political Ideas in Twentieth-Century Europe* (New Haven, CT: Yale University Press, 2011), particularly ch. 6.

perspective, is not only exposed by its alternatives, but engloomed and perturbed by them.

Elitist, oblivious, detached and disillusioned: these are wide-ranging claims, but their own unsure credentials should also be kept in perspective. They are far from offering a compelling charge-sheet against global law as it stands, or even specifying trends for which we can provide unimpeachable empirical confirmation. They derive from positions that are themselves contentious and elusive, from platforms that also offer only a partial view, and which indeed, as we have seen, stand in significant mutual tension.[25] Rather, then, these counterclaims should be offered more modestly and with greater circumspection, as indications of global law's possible shortcomings and pitfalls and as evidence of the source and shape of some of its external pressures. They introduce new and wider tendencies that contribute to the volatile mix of global law. They are, if you like, intimations of its pathological possibilities, just as we have also sought to understand its normal state as 'intimated'.

How, then, might these charges be acknowledged in a way that treats their concerns seriously, yet still be addressed in a manner that avoids the conclusion that 'making the best' of global law is a forlorn or meaningless task?

6.3   Charging global law

First, there is the charge of elitism. This can be answered in two ways, though both answers come with significant reservations. In the first place, there is an argument from necessity. Global law, as we have seen, stems from treatment of real disputes as much as it does from contemplation of moot cases or from appreciation of deeper second-order legal questions in the abstract. Consideration of global law often

---

[25] Of course, occupants of these positions are often very aware of their limitations and vulnerabilities. For example, as regards the statist platform, Grimm (nn. 3 and 18 above) is very reflective about the particularity of his position, and the dangers of descent into 'golden age' nostalgia. As regards the radical platform, MacDonald, for example, offers an interesting and instructive account of the tendency for the critique of the epistemic foundations of the present global system to spill over into a posture of general epistemological doubt, including doubt about the credentials of the critic's own radically subjective outlook. This position can, of course, reinforce the pattern of disillusionment described in the text: see E. MacDonald, *International Law and Ethics After the Critical Challenge: Framing the Legal within the Post-foundational* (Leiden: Martinus Nijhoff, 2011). See more generally D. Kennedy, *A Critique of Adjudication (Fin de Siècle)* (Cambridge, MA: Harvard University Press, 1998) ch. 1.

becomes of first and immediate relevance in those areas of remote or congested jurisdiction, and, by the same token, uncertain and precarious jurisdiction that are so typical of the transnational legal environment.[26] It is frequently introduced in contexts where a legal issue is live before a court or tribunal or other dispute resolution body and a decision must be forthcoming. As the adjudicative branch, judges and their fellow decision-makers cannot deny their part in conflict resolution, and to that extent simply cannot be denied their position as co-architects of global law.[27]

In the second place, and somewhat linked to the first, there is the argument from specialist knowledge. As we argued in Chapter 5,[28] there is undeniably an epistemic dimension to the intimations of global law – to its various processes of adaptation, discovery, abstraction and projection. This argues for a more central role, or at least a more diversely influential one, for a range of forms of professional expertise than may be the case for juristic knowledge in other ages and contexts. Awareness and understanding of the roots, conditions of possibility and applicable range of grand historical legal discourses, of the capacity to discern and extrapolate from emergent underlying trends, of the ability both to perceive the problems of contestation involved in the presence of diverse sources and streams of law before a particular context of transnational norm-making or issue settlement, and to see the potential of law's planetary variety in the fashioning of new solutions to these problems: all of these capacities, the requirement for each of which stems from the intimated quality of global law, involve skills which those trained in legal argumentation, the justification of legal authority, legal history, comparative law, transnational legal doctrine and so on, possess in comparative abundance.[29] Moreover, as one of the distinguishing features of global law is the way in which first-order questions of immediate validity and persuasive argumentation and deeper second-order questions of authoritative framing tend to become folded into one another,[30] there is a particular need for the integration of these various forms of expertise – of close links between the overlapping knowledge bases and orientations of practitioners, judges and academics. The fluid continuum of global

---

[26] See e.g. Chapter 4.4 above.
[27] See e.g. N. Walker, 'Beyond Boundary Disputes and Basic Grids: Mapping the Global Disorder of Normative Orders' 6 *International Journal of Constitutional Law* 373 (2008) at 391–6.
[28] See Chapter 5.2.2, 5.2.4 and 5.2.5 above.
[29] See Walker, n. 27 above; and Chapter 5.2 above.   [30] See Chapter 5.2.4 above.

law-craft,[31] in other words, becomes as pertinent to the 'joined-up' relevance of legal expertise in the nurturing of global law as it has been to the generation of the conditions under which global law emerged in the first place.

Yet it should not be forgotten that the new prominence of judges and jurists on the global stage is in significant measure a consequence of the *disorientation* of certain long-standing perspectives on the legal world. It is a product of change and the declining relevance of old problem-solving paradigms, as viewed from the statist platform, or the continuing and exacerbated inadequacy of these old problem-solving paradigms, as viewed from the platform of radical critique. It is, in short, a prominence, however unavoidable, which is born of the relative lack of other forms and sources of the generation of legitimacy at the global level, and it cannot compensate for that lack. Rather than the formidable project of replacing other forms of authority, the more practical and more instructive and, therefore, also the more legitimate purpose of the deployment of the continuum of legal expertise in the causes of global law, must be to provide a context of *reorientation* in which the broader questions of the negotiation and contestation of multiple partial claims to authority can be kept alive, brought into focus and addressed anew.

Here the critique of global law's elitism becomes closely linked to the critique of its obliviousness, and, in turn, to the critique of its detachment. What is crucial if the key role of legal expertise is not to congeal into an increasingly globalised version of 'juristocracy'[32] is that global law's focus on the new, and the growing consciousness of jurists of the prominence of their own role in the debate over global law's proper direction, does not obscure the significance of the wider and deeper historical context. Here, the rhetorical concern of the users of global law with the traditions of state-centred law assumes a delicately double-edged significance in terms of its effects upon the self-understandings of the user community.

On the one hand, calling upon the legacy of constitutional law, international law and various other venerable and venerated traditions, can bring false or exaggerated comfort to particular approaches in the short term, however much, as we have seen, this may feed into a longer competitive process of diminishing authority.[33] Of course, the endorsement of the familiar trademarks of our legal heritage might imply that, at

---

[31] See Chapter 2.3.4 above.   [32] Hirschl, n. 22 above.   [33] See Chapter 5.2 above.

least within the perspective of a particular global law position, the difficult lessons of the past have, indeed, been taken on board, and that a persuasive case has been mounted for the acquisition and adaptive application of such legitimating credentials as the most eligible paradigms of modern legal authority still possess. But the reference to grand legal traditions may in fact be mainly or entirely gestural. It may involve a borrowing of labels rather than a serious engagement with substance. And in that event there is a standing danger that the invocation of law's disciplinary heritage be treated as a cue for forgetting rather than for remembering; that a raid on the conceptual language of the past, however token, be treated as sufficient reason to draw a line under that past, thence to forge ahead armed with its normative dividend yet weighed down by none of its burdens.[34]

On the other hand, the traditions of law can also be educational. They can assume a more modest but also a more precautionary significance. To begin with, the legal models of the past, as we have noted,[35] can always serve a sober and closely focused pedagogical purpose. They are and always will be capable of being cannibalised for their vast range of present and future useful applications. There are countless instances of particular legal rules and devices that figure within one model, and operate effectively in the context of that model, being adapted to other contexts, without necessitating the larger claim that the models themselves retain wholesale relevance. To take but two isolated examples, state constitutional law can offer many particular lessons to the architects of any possible legal future about the separation of powers or their federal dispersal,[36] just as modern international law has much to teach any projected regime about the range of human rights protection or the relationship between special and general jurisdiction in pursuit of that protection.[37]

However, it is the precautionary significance of the past that is of most immediate purchase here – that provides the key contrast to tradition-as-placebo. Rather than offering the blanket of false comfort, the retention of the normative language of the past may strike the opposite note, supplying a salutary, and doubtless uncomfortable, reminder of what

---

[34] See e.g. Wahl, n. 3 above; and Koskenniemi, n. 15 above.
[35] See Chapter 5.2 above. See also N. Walker, 'Constitutional Pluralism in Global Context' in M. Avbelj and J. Komárek (eds.), *Constitutional Pluralism in the European Union and Beyond* (Oxford: Hart, 2012) pp. 17–38: in particular, discussion of the distinction between 'constitutionalism as doctrine' and 'constitutionalism as imagination', pp. 32–6.
[36] See Chapter 3.3 above.   [37] See Chapter 3.2.3.1 above.

remains stubbornly at stake even as circumstances rapidly change. In this alternative perspective the normative language of the past, and in particular the language associated with influential visions such as constitutionalism, Rule of Law and internationalism, predicated upon an idea of progress, however romanticised, and of law's contribution to the gradual amelioration of the human condition, is preserved and functions as a 'placeholder'.[38] That is to say, it operates as a kind of proxy or holding position – an orientating or, rather, re-orientating 'mindset'[39] – while new solutions are sought and worked out, rather than as a passing off of old solutions as adequate to the new.

Whether and to what extent global law's rhetoric of tradition is *in fact* likely to feed one kind of attitude rather than the other is an open question, dependent on the perspective of the user, the priorities and prior commitments of the audience, and the kind of issues at stake.[40] In general terms, however, a tendency to find false comfort is underscored by the predisposition of global law to accept the law as it now stands as its starting point, and so to seek to detach itself from the kind of counterfactual reading of the past that would expose the frustrated possibilities of a different point of departure.[41] And detachment, as we have seen, can take two forms. It can be naïve and tending towards the hubristic, determined to remake or renew the world through law. Or it can be narrowly self-regarding, simply restricting itself to the letter and immediate practice of the law as if the legal domain could be adequately addressed and appraised in its own terms, sealed off without reference to other forces of globalisation.

Yet if, alternatively, the lessons of global law's past are taken seriously, as they will be where the better standards of the legal past are treated as no less but also no more than placeholders for global law's own standing problems of legitimacy, and where, in any case, awareness of the diminishing returns of competing traditionalist ideologies may gradually become internalised, there is a danger here too. For this is how we may end up, not with mere discomfort and disenchantment, but instead with their descent into disillusionment. In this perspective, the message of history, from both its statist and radical emissaries, may in contrast be *too* well received. Global law will be regarded as diminished, as basically

---

[38] Koskenniemi, n. 15 above, at 30. See also Walker, n. 3 above.
[39] M. Koskenniemi, 'Constitutionalism as Mindset: Reflections on Kantian Themes about International Law and Globalization' 8 *Theoretical Inquiries in Law* 9 (2007).
[40] See Chapter 4.4 above.   [41] See Chapter 4.3 above.

an epiphenomenal production, one that is largely cosmetic in appearance and effect and incapable of disturbing the deep structures of global power and injustice.

6.4   Recharging global law

6.4.1   Putting global law back together

Triumphalist, compartmentalised or disillusioned? These, of course, are stylised positions, just like the statist and radical platforms in whose shadow they grow. Yet however broad-brush, and however tentatively developed, they do speak to real tendencies in the culture of global law. But are these the only attitudes available to global law's participants with regard to broader questions of global justice? If they were to be, then it would be difficult to see how we might reconsider global law in a more positive light. We would be left with an unpalatable menu. Global law makes a literal and triumphalist claim to 'rule' the world, or it commands its own narrowly compartmentalised domain, or it stands buffeted and disillusioned at the mercy of larger forces; the last position, indeed, amounts to little more than an insider recognition and reflection of the statist or radical critique, and resonates strongly with their more negative conclusions – whether the nostalgic rewind or resignation of the statist, or the radical resort to structural fatalism.

On closer examination, however, there does remain a horizon of possibility beyond triumphalism, compartmentalisation and disillusionment. The key to this lies in recognising that, however different they may be in mood and motivation, each of these three positions involves a similarly incomplete assessment of the relationship between the pursuit of global law and the making of the social and political world. Each tends to make an assumption that leads to an unduly restrictive focus. Specifically, each supposes that the relationship between the emerging manifestations of global law and the making of the social and political world is a *singular* one; and, more particularly, that in its singularity, this relationship implies one (and *only* one) measure both of the degree of *autonomy* that law enjoys from wider social and political forces and of the level of *influence* it exercises over these forces.

In the case of the triumphalist approach, global law is deemed to possess a significant measure of autonomous standing together with widely dispersed influence. Global law, conceived of in its more robustly universalist and convergence-sponsoring modes, is seen to operate as a single self-standing stream of normative authority with some impact across a wide range of different sites and levels of social and political power. In the case of the compartmentalised approach, global law is once again seen as somewhat autonomous from larger social and political forces, but in this case its remoteness is also a measure of its operational modesty and a signal of its limited relevance and influence. It can make a difference at the micro-level of particular cases or even through modest reframing of somewhat broader legal areas, but it hardly disturbs global society's higher range of steering forces and mechanisms. In the case of the disillusioned approach, finally, in the inverse image of the triumphalist approach, global law possesses neither autonomy nor influence in any significant measure. Rather, it is a product of, and dependent upon, larger social and political forces and mechanisms, and its contribution remains parasitic upon, and reflective of, these larger forces and mechanisms.

Two objections may be raised against the singularity of these perspectives, and the starkly different views of autonomy and influence they support. To begin with, they do not sufficiently appreciate the different ways in which global law makes, or should make, a contribution at each of the macro- and micro-levels of social intervention. Secondly, and of deeper significance, they do not pay sufficient heed to two different basic templates through which law seeks to intervene in the social and political world, nor to the relationship within and between these different templates. The second issue we will address in the following subsection, but let us first deal with the micro–macro question.

It surely paints a less reductive and more balanced picture, and one more consistent with our background sense of law's relative autonomy,[42] to view global law neither as operating purely at the micro-level of social intervention, as the compartmentalists would have it, nor as incapable of making a difference at that level notwithstanding its relationship to macro-level global steering forces, as the disillusioned would have it. Instead, global law can and should engage both the deepest and widest steering mechanisms of our global constellation and the countless immediate and detailed contexts of social conflict and decision-making, but will inevitably do so with different forms of purchase and levels of influence. On the one hand, global law cannot only concern itself with the coalface of existing disputes and normative arrangements where its occasional interventions and incremental arguments can make a decisive

---

[42] See Chapter 1.1 above.

difference. It would, at one and the same time, display undue diffidence about the capacity of the legal imagination at least to contribute to the broader steering pattern of global society, and be complacently neglectful of the wide-ranging and deeply penetrating influence of the 'real world' of global economics and politics, to conclude otherwise. On the other hand, and as a caution against the triumphalist tendency, global law's contribution to that broader steering pattern cannot be anything other than modest and dependent on its close articulation with other basic factors. It would be both naïve as to the capacity of law to affect the world and neglectful of the steering power of other forces to conclude otherwise.

This advice should not be regarded as a cry in the wilderness – as one bound to fall on deaf ears. It is not a plea to those who participate in global law to separate out that which they have obdurately left unseparated, or to complement that which they have myopically left in isolation. It by no means implies that the bearers of global law have uniformly failed to face up to the problem of how to deal with the here and now without entirely neglecting its responsibility or compromising its contribution to larger questions of social and economic justice; or, conversely, that they have entirely avoided the issue of how to address the large questions without neglecting the myriad more urgent and detailed ones. Recall that when we invoke the tendency towards triumphalism, compartmentalisation and disillusionment we *are* just talking about tendencies – about tentative trends and future possibilities rather than hardened patterns. For it is also the case that some of the global law we have discussed, both in convergence-promoting and in divergence-accommodating perspective, does seek to distinguish micro- and macro-levels and does strive to complement the former with some consideration of the latter.[43] Indeed, the unsettled authority of global law often challenges its sponsors to do something of both – to 'dig in' and respond to the world as it is at the coalface and simultaneously to 'drill out' in search of a narrative of broader justification, authorisation and ongoing normative guidance.

But this is precisely where the deeper difficulty of the reconcilability of the different strands of global law takes hold. For it lies not so much in the lack of reflexivity of particular positions within global law, and more in the overabundance of such reflexivity if we consider the field of global law as a whole. It is a difficulty which derives from the often urgent need

---

[43] See generally Chapter 5.2.4–5.2.5 above.

to start from the here and now, and from the very frequency and variety of the tendency to extrapolate from the particular case across the diverse range of global law's species-specific narratives of justification, with their limited record and perceived prospect of reconciliation. Once we take this into account, indeed, our three stylised positions may be seen to be as much a product of heightened awareness of the tenuous condition of global law as they are of its insufficient consideration. The triumphalist temptation may be as much about a staunch refusal to compromise a particular macro-position or qualify its range of application in the face of other and equally implacable views, as it is a failure to appreciate the penetrative limits, fragility and contestability of all positions.[44] The tunnel vision of compartmentalisation may be as much about carving out and defending a manageably modest set of objectives in the face of a wide terrain of unmanageable difference and unassailable macro-level forces as it is about imperviousness to that difference and these forces.[45] The spectre of root-and-branch disillusionment may be as much about frustration at the failure to find and pursue coherence between a range of different global visions and their legal indicia as it is about a flat sense of the in-principle impossibility of such a development.[46] In other words, the difficulty is not just about finding the proper balance between micro and macro and about the different senses of global law's autonomy and influence this calculation reflects, but also, and more fundamentally, about how the development of normative positions across micro- and macro-levels of legal intervention inevitably exposes and highlights the stubborn species-diversity of global law.

6.4.2   Overlapping horizons: between ratio and voluntas

But what, if anything, can we indicate by way of counter-trends in global law that would answer the deeper concerns and more basic differences of perspective that underpin these three positions and encourage their corrosive tendencies? It bears repeating what we developed at length in Chapter 4. Much that is diverse in global law does not necessarily lead to deep incompatibility and conflict. There is at least a floor of agreement

---

[44] See e.g. the reflections of Kumm at n. 2 above, particularly at pp. 201–4.
[45] At least some versions of the formalist response to the fear of fragmentation in international law betray this tendency: see Chapter 3.2.2 above; see also Koskenniemi, n. 15 above.
[46] See e.g. Koskenniemi, n. 15 above; and MacDonald, n. 25 above.

across the different species of global law about the irreducible variety of the world of transnational law. In addition, consistent with the fact that global law always takes the world of law as it stands, each point of departure gives rise to a partial perspective, a particular and limited angle of comprehension and interception of the legal world, and one, therefore, that is not self-evidently incompatible with others and need not be viewed as such.

Building on this fragile outline of a common set of background assumptions, can we look beyond internal differences and rivalries and find any basis for the fashioning of a second-order consensus for global law in general, one that may overcome the various tendencies to singularity reported above; sufficiently modest to stay the hand of premature triumphalism but sufficiently assertive to resist compartmentalisation and disillusionment alike? Can we discover an emerging common sense – or set of common senses – of global law, however narrow, that might provide common ground and stand as a common juridical offering at the level of general global steering mechanisms, while also informing the resolution of particular cases? In a nutshell, from the kaleidoscopic variety of global law perspectives – the seven species and their various sub-species – is there discernible any significant overlap between their horizons and the visions and images of global law with which they fill these horizons?

In addressing this question let us look, in conclusion, at a number of more promising lines of thought, and at the relationship between these. Before doing so, however, in order to provide the key to their significance, we must, as we undertook to do, introduce another and final conceptual distinction: namely, between the two basic templates of law's mode of intervention in the world. This is a distinction that runs even deeper than the divide between convergence-promoting and divergence-accommodating conceptions of global law, and that in some measure cuts across it. It is the distinction, profoundly inscribed in legal history, which holds between law as *ratio* and law as *voluntas*,[47] and which draws a line between an understanding of law as possessing a general and

---

[47] See in particular K. Tuori, Ratio *and* Voluntas: *The Tension between Reason and Will in Law* (Farnham: Ashgate, 2011). See also M. Loughlin, *Sword and Scales: An Examination of the Relationship between Law and Politics* (Oxford: Hart, 2000) ch. 1; G. Palombella, 'The Rule of Law and its Core' in G. Palombella and N. Walker (eds.), *Relocating the Rule of Law* (Oxford: Hart, 2009) pp. 17–42.

presumptively universal rationality of its own, and law as an expression and instrument of human will.

Of the convergence-promoting species, the majority of approaches – namely all the formal and abstract-universal types – fall within the template of law as *ratio*. Only the structural approach, with its invocation of the United Nations as the expression of some kind of planetary collective, falls within the *voluntas* template. Of the divergence-accommodating species, the laterally integrative approaches, at least in those of their iterations that avoid radical pluralism, display a thin sense of universal *ratio*, and the hybrid approaches, too, display an emergent sense of general rationality, albeit within a materially restricted jurisdiction. The functionally specific approaches, however, are driven by a logic of common will – in this case sectorally differentiated. And finally, the historical-discursive approaches, just as, in their wide variety, they straddle the convergence–divergence divide, so too they straddle the *ratio–voluntas* distinction.

Global law, therefore, clearly sounds in both basic templates – both as *ratio* and as *voluntas* – but more often as *ratio*. What is more, global law, given its dimension of double normativity, also necessarily *acts upon other law* that must itself fall predominantly within one or other template. Most obviously, global law as *ratio* acts upon a wide variety of forms of law as *voluntas*. Formal, abstract-universal, laterally integrative and hybrid approaches are clearly largely concerned to address the widespread diversity of sub-global common wills, including – and still most significantly – the common wills inscribed in state law, but so too are the global 'common wills' of the structural and functionally specific species. Yet finally, to complete the mixed picture, it is also the case that many of the sub-global laws that the various species of global law act upon, from national constitutional laws to regional human rights regimes, are themselves as much a statement of *ratio* as they are a product of *voluntas*.

What this complex pattern suggests, then, is a tendency in global law towards the universalism of *ratio*, but also a close relationship between the two templates. How, then, does this help us to develop a sense of global law's overlapping horizons? Our argument here builds upon three elements.

In the first place, given the preponderance of *ratio* within global law, the richness and serious engagement of the debate about a universal register of law is in some respects an encouraging sign.[48] Patently, the very density of transnational law and the very visibility of the emergent

---

[48] See in particular Chapter 3.2.3 above.

ratio of global law is typically predicated upon an idea of law as a joint construction, as a collective accomplishment. Whether the universal code, or a set of widely shared cosmopolitan principles, or a catalogue of commonly affirmed rights, or a thin model of coherence, or a gradually confluent flow of previously disparate strands, the idea is of a global law that is possible only because of a profoundly *social* process and endeavour – of common experience, common learning, common commitment and common potential and construction at levels of generality up to and now including the global – rather than an appeal to an external source of morality.[53]

The significance of this is twofold. First, these conceptions all bear a family resemblance, in each case success turning on a self-fulfilling argument about our ability to persuade ourselves and each other of what we hold in common and of the value of holding that in common. Secondly, and crucially, just because each of these arguments has the same constructivist success conditions, they also tend to speak to one another, or at least to be open to that possibility. If persuasion of the very terms of our common normative heritage and horizon is the common litmus test of each, then these various universal register arguments are likely to be drawn into a process of common engagement. In this way the argument about the oneness of law in a world of increasingly constructivist conceptions of law may then gradually become the *one argument*, and so a common project of contestation and resolution for global law.

Our second line of argument focuses on a dimension of the divergence-accommodating conception which is most frequently contrasted with the convergence-accommodating conception, but which in fact also tends to subscribe to the same basic template of universal reason. If one particularly busy and creative centre of discussion of the terms of global law has been the overt universalism of the various abstract-normative approaches, it is telling that the other has concerned

conceptions of legal universalism: J. Waldron, '*Ius Gentium*: A Defence of Gentili's Equation of the Law of Nations and the Law of Nature' in B. Kingsbury and B. Straumann (eds.), *The Roman Foundations of the Law of Nations. Alberico Gentili and the Justice of Empire* (Oxford University Press, 2010) pp. 283–96.

53 See famously J. Rawls, *Political Liberalism: Expanded Edition*, 2nd edn (Columbia University Press, 2005); see also G. Klosko, 'Political Constructivism in Rawls's *Political Liberalism*' 91 *American Political Science Review* 635 (1997). On the constructivist nature of modern political thought, see e.g. P. Roberts, *Political Constructivism* (New York: Routledge, 2011); and see more generally C. Taylor, *Modern Social Imaginaries* (Durham, NC: Duke University Press, 2004).

the terms and conditions of global legal pluralism.[54] What kind of relationship holds between these two prominent clusters, often seen as in manifest opposition? Is the universalism of the chain, predicated on the acceptance of diversity, so much thinner than the universalism of the umbrella or the vessel, primed to absorb difference, that there is little scope for overlapping horizons? Or is there more common ground than their cultivation and continued occupation of such distinct 'camps' suggests?

On closer inspection, one of the striking features of the new global legal pluralism, constitutional and otherwise, is how continuous it is with techniques and mechanisms we often find within settled single legal orders. Many of the ideas that we find at the cutting edge of inter-systemic co-ordinate arrangements, from subsidiarity schemes to conditional forms of mutual recognition, from proportionality doctrines to margins of appreciation, from forms of institutional autonomy to general conflict of jurisdiction rules, and from the protection of minority forms of collective voice to basic rights protection,[55] are adaptations of notions with a long pedigree in state and other relatively closed legal systems. Clearly, important differences remain. In the kind of inter-systemic relations with which global legal pluralism concerns itself, the absence of a common hierarchical framework of rules to provide authoritative resolution in the case of conflict or disagreement sets them apart from the infra-systemic case: in particular, underlining the significance of legal techniques geared towards agreement or compromise. Still, a decentralised legal order can operate in a remarkably similar fashion to a plural configuration of legal orders. It is often observed, for example, that federal state systems, with their multiple levels of internal authority, exhibit some of the same characteristics of heterarchical authority within the four corners of a single legal order as do looser post-national confederal relations, such as the state–EU nexus, that operate in transnational legal space.[56]

Beyond this particular analogy, a more general point can be made of any modern legal order. Modern state law is charged with achieving

[54] See Chapter 3.4.1 above.
[55] See e.g. P. Schiff Berman, *Global Legal Pluralism: A Jurisprudence of Law Beyond Borders* (Cambridge University Press, 2012).
[56] See e.g. M. Maduro, 'Contrapunctual Law: Europe's Constitutional Pluralism in Action' in N. Walker (ed.), *Sovereignty in Transition: Essays in European Law* (Oxford: Hart, 2003) pp. 501–37; and D. Halberstam, 'Constitutional Heterarchy: The Centrality of Conflict in the European Union and the United States' in Dunoff and Trachtman, *Ruling the World?*, n. 17 above, pp. 326–55. See also M. Avbelj, 'Theory of European Union' 36 *European Law Review* 818 (2011).

abstract 'system' integration rather than concrete 'social' integration.[57] It is concerned with the relations within large populations whose interests and beliefs may diverge strongly and clash, perhaps even their broader regional or national identities. They are communities bound together as much by proximity as by affinity,[58] and so modern law from the outset is concerned as much with overcoming recurrent difference as with articulating common cause. The unity of modern legal order, in other words, is very much premised upon the idea of a 'second-best' morality. It provides the basis for generating agreement – typically 'incompletely theorized'[59] – where substantive consensus is absent or sparse.[60] What this means is that modern state-centred law, even before external legal pluralism became a prominent issue, had in any case been innately predisposed to recognise and deal with its own *internal pluralism*. Its techniques and mechanisms for overcoming or negotiating differences of value or interest are built into its DNA, as likely to figure on any checklist of fundamental characteristics as anything else. In a nutshell, the techniques for dealing with pluralism in the transnational age have long been folded into our very sense of the universal character of law.[61]

From both ends of the spectrum of universalism, therefore – thick and thin – we see the potential within the conversations and debates of global law for a partial convergence of horizons. Crucially, however, it can and should be seen only as a partial convergence. To the extent that pluralists accommodate rather than seek to transcend different legal orders, they are

---

[57] M. Archer, 'Social Integration and System Integration: Developing the Distinction' 30 *Sociology* 679 (1996).

[58] See e.g. J. Waldron, 'The Principle of Proximity' NYU School of Law, Public Law Research Paper No. 11-08 (17 January 2011), available at http://papers.ssrn.com/sol3/papers.cfm?abstract_id=1742413.

[59] C. R. Sunstein, 'Incompletely Theorized Agreements' 108 *Harvard Law Review* 1733 (1995).

[60] M. Rosenfeld, 'Rethinking Constitutional Ordering in an Era of Legal and Ideological Pluralism' 6 *International Journal of Constitutional Law* 415 (2008).

[61] As regards the close connection between some forms of constitutional pluralism and certain abstract-universal positions, recall in particular the role of certain procedural norms in both, discussed at Chapter 3.4.1.2 above. See in particular Kumm, n. 2 above. See also G. Teubner, 'Substantive and Reflexive Elements in Modern Law' 17 *Law & Society Review* 239 (2006); G. Teubner, *Constitutional Fragments: Societal Constitutionalism and Globalization* (Oxford University Press, 2012); and P. Kjaer, 'The Under-Complexity of Democracy' in G.-P. Calliess, A. Fischer-Lescano, D. Wielsch and P. Zumbansen (eds.), *Soziologische Jurisprudenz: Festschrift für Gunther Teubner* (Berlin: De Gruyter, 2009) pp. 531–42, on the way in which the 'procedural turn' in modern law predates, but is amplified by, the recent intensification of global trends.

clearly more concerned with the prerogatives of *voluntas* than the sovereignty of universal *ratio*. And this diversity of core concerns is much more the case where we bring into the frame those species of global law – structural, functionally specific and in some measure historical-discursive – that directly embrace the idea of *voluntas* and collective will.

At this level of remove, the contrast seems much starker, the scope for reconciliation much less. The universalist insists that some part of global law's contribution, however ambitious or modest in effect, involves an assertion of those ways in which law, in its distinctive oneness, can supply or enable a single grid of practical reason or *ratio*. Here, then, the emphasis is on law as making an independent contribution, however limited, to the substantive structure of debate about global social, political and economic relations. Law, to recall our earlier discussion, is an autonomous point of departure in this vision, though a price for that autonomy may be paid in the likely thinness of its commonly endorsed contribution. For her part, the defender of the idea of *voluntas* insists on a quite different dimension of the historical functionality of law. She requires that some part of global law's contribution, however immodest in effect, involves an acknowledgment of the ways in which law, in its diverse dependence, is both a product and a conveyor of so many different expressions of social or political will. Here the emphasis is on law as a servicing form and instrument, a means of rendering possible, and effective, the articulation of different and differently representative voices, and of managing the relationship between these. Law is heteronomous rather than autonomous in this vision. It depends upon and accompanies the settled political process rather than supplying its independent frame or control. And as the dependent variable it is often quite distant and delayed – and quite remote in prospect – from the very underlying social and political struggles over voice and interest representation that it might seek to structure in (more) equality-respecting terms.[62]

---

[62] See e.g. N. Fraser, 'Reframing Justice in a Globalizing World' 36 *New Left Review* 69 (November–December 2005). See also J. Tully, 'The Crisis of Global Citizenship', *Radical Politics Today* (July 2009), available at http://research.ncl.ac.uk/spaceofdemoc racy/word%20docs%20linked%20to/Uploaded%202009/Tully/The_Crisis_of_Global_ Citizenship_James_Tully.pdf. In this article, Tully contrasts 'modern citizenship', which tracks the legal and political structures of the modern state, with 'co-operative citizenship', which is practice-based rather than status-based, and which concerns all informal relations of governance and common cause in the 'here and now' (section 3). Tellingly, it is the forms of co-operative citizenship which Tully believes have the more radical potential to redistribute global political power, but which remain the more detached from the support and structuring influence of law – whether through existing or incipient legal institutions.

Yet this is where we can catch a third and final glimpse of overlapping horizons. For even between those cases that represent the two conceptually quite distinct basic templates, there is some scope for a common outlook. Collective voice, whether that of the demos or other group, is no more *self*-defining at the global level than at the national level. Its articulation requires decisions about its conditions of origin and termination, its membership, its representative forms, its decision-making processes and accountability channels, and its material (if not territorial) limits to jurisdiction.[63] Democracy and other contexts of collective will, in other words, need their own meta-democratic modes of regularisation and normalisation of practice, and typically they have recourse to their own law as the proper medium of this.[64] But as soon as the idea of a law of, and a law *for*, democracy is conceded, then the possibility of universalism again rears up. As the advocates of Global Administrative Law remind us,[65] the idea of good legal *process* in contexts of collective will formation and monitoring is as susceptible to universal specification and regulation as is good legal *content*. And to the extent that much global law as *ratio* is already concerned, as we have seen, with the 'second best' means of managing and negotiating unavoidable difference, and so with treating the voices of difference seriously, the scope for connection becomes apparent. For global law as process, in directly tracking global law's other and secondary template as *voluntas*, should nevertheless remain closely linked to law as *ratio*, not just in terms of patterns of interactive and combinatory compatibility, but also in terms of possessing in common certain core moral concerns, often articulated in the language of basic rights,[66] to respect autonomy and protect diverse life chances wherever these desiderata are at issue or under challenge.[67]

[63] See e.g. N. Walker, 'Constitutionalism and the Incompleteness of Democracy: An Iterative Relationship' 39 *Rechtsfilosofie & Rechtstheorie* 206 (2010); and J. Waldron, 'Can There Be a Democratic Jurisprudence?' 58 *Emory Law Journal* 688 (2009).
[64] See in particular J. Habermas, *Between Facts and Norms: Contribution to a Discourse Theory of Law and Democracy* (Cambridge, MA: MIT Press, 1996).
[65] See Chapter 3.3.2 above.
[66] For example, rights of freedom of expression and association are both significant in procedural terms as protecting voice and participation in collective decision-making, and independently and universally valuable dimensions of human freedom. See e.g. Walker, n. 63 above; Waldron n. 63 above.
[67] On the overlapping concerns of process and substance more generally, see e.g. J. Gledhill, 'Procedure in Substance and Substance in Procedure: Reframing the Rawls–Habermas Debate' in J. G. Finlayson and F. Freyenhagen (eds.), *Habermas and Rawls: Disputing the Political* (New York: Routledge, 2011) pp. 181–99; R. Forst, *The*

6.4.3   Summing up

We are now in a position to summarise our findings on the possible emergence of overlapping global horizons from significant species-diversity of perspective as follows. If global law is to hope to overcome and move beyond the mutually incompatible but also mutually provocative styles of triumphalism, compartmentalisation or disillusionment, it must set aside a singular framework and instead attend to both reason and will and their associated legal templates. It must involve a distillation and attempted reconciliation of the various strands of law's own global *ratio*, aided and abetted by the 'constructivist' turn in transnational legal and political thought, as well as re-engagement with the myriad forms and combinations of law as *voluntas*. In addition, cutting across the core theoretical domains of the convergence-promoting and divergence-accommodating conceptions of global law, and in particular between abstract-normativism and legal and constitutional pluralism, we also see some common subscription to a pluralism-accommodating dimension of universalism, and so a further space within which relations of mutual support or complementarity might be developed. And, finally, extending the common window still further across the most basic divide between global law as *ratio* and global law as *voluntas*, even here we see some prospect of intersecting fields of vision in terms of the substantive moral commitments implicit in process values.

Yet we should, in conclusion, remind ourselves that all that will be achieved if these new overlapping horizons open up is that global law will less likely be unduly and divisively singular in its outlooks. The gap between global law and a concerted and effective framework of global justice will not shrink by dint of this. But, at least, as a preliminary to that, there could emerge a clearer sense of the diverse limits and potential of global law – both as the medium of a generally reasoned refinement of power in social relations and as a vehicle of collective voice – and of the relationship between these two mutually irreducible templates in the overall pursuit of global social and political forms through law. However, we should equally note, even these modest foundations remain jeopardised by the potentially viral effect of some of the pathologies of competition we have discussed. If it is the case, as we have argued in Chapter 5, that rivalry between traditional sources of authority as a legitimate basis for global law can undermine the very idea of traditional

Right to Justification: Elements of a Constructivist Theory of Justice (New York: Columbia University Press, 2011).

legal authority in this context,[68] and if it is equally the case that competition between different forms of trend-spotting can undermine the salience of any and all trends,[69] then the participants in the global law debate may see their skirmishes breed negative sum consequences for the authorising potential of global law in general. If global law descends into constant academic conflict, in other words, then its protagonists should be aware that their conflicts are in danger of themselves becoming merely 'academic'. Global law is at its best, and at its most generally resonant, to the extent that it offers a broadly persuasive basis and effective methodologies for the transnational spread of particular laws and legal orders to contain and condition its own otherwise unmanageable diversity. But if its own containing approaches were to become as unmanageably diverse as that which they seek to contain, then global law would be on course to undermine itself. Awareness of these dangers may just help concentrate some minds upon emphasising and seeking to develop the measure of common ground sighted above.

The new global law, then, describes a trend which, in viewing law as a less grounded and less embedded form, a more malleable and more precarious category, captures and expresses nothing less than a new shift in the legal analyst's relationship to law itself. The hard work of settled doctrinal analysis will, of course, remain central to much law teaching and research, and most of transnational legal practice. But, alongside this, the global jurist as symbolic analyst must become, and is becoming, more adept at trend-spotting, more engaged in challenging or rethinking our very ideas of legal order, more reflexively aware of the role of the legal analyst herself in the mapping and making of legal authority, and more reconciled to this new world as a steady state of unsteady post-national authority. More particularly, the new world of the global jurist is one in which the problem of connecting law to the global pursuit and resolution of public affairs in a manner that responds to larger considerations of social and political justice, while far from beckoning a new era in which law can be the primary global steering mechanism, is neither so intractable that we must be resigned from the outset to failure nor so beyond a narrow occupational focus as to be simply edited out of our contemplation. Rather, joining global law to global justice offers a challenge of perennial significance requiring ever new forms of address and treatment.

Interesting times lie ahead.

---

[68] See Chapter 5.2.2 above.   [69] See Chapter 5.2.3 above.

INDEX

abstract-normative versions of global
law, 70–86, 133, 156, 178, 196,
198, 204
  framed positivity, 77–86
  and human rights law, 71–7
  layered positivity, 71–7, 85, 116
American Lawyer journal, 32
Association of Transnational Law
  Schools, 37

Baudrillard, Jean, 168
Bell, Christine, 127–8, 129

Center for Transnational Legal Studies,
  37
collective action problems, 182
common law, 39, 48
communities of interest and practice,
  8, 41, 65
conflict of laws, 106, 107–14, 126, 144,
  156
  double deformalisation, 114
  and global governance, 108
  and regime collision, 114
  scope of, 109
constitutional law, 47, 70, 181
  and international law, 127
  legacy of, 189
constitutional pluralism, 115, 118, 134
constitutionalism, 87, 126, 146, 165,
  166
  antinomies of, 88–91
  as commonality, 94–7
  cosmopolitan, 80–1, 85
  democratic, 89
  global, 87, 101, 137, 141, 143, 155
  and governing capacity, 91, 100

Janus-faced aspect of, 100–2
national, 100
oppositions in, 100, 105
as plurality, 97–100
and political community, 101
relationship between the particular
  and the universal, 90, 91–4, 100
sectoral constitutionalisation, 95
semantic roots of the concept, 88
as singularity, 91–4, 100
societal, 97–100, 104
and states, 95, 101
transnational, 98
as universal, 90, 100
versions of, 91
constructivism, 48
contrapunctual law, 117
convergence-promoting approaches to
  global law, 55, 58–86, 135, 178,
  198
  abstract-normative versions, 70–86
  and divergent approaches, 87, 138,
    139, 150
  formal versions, 63–70, 196
  and hierarchy, 58
  structural versions, 59–63, 196
  and transnational law, 132
cosmopolitanism, 80–1, 85, 93
Critical Legal Studies, 182
criticisms of global law, 180–7, 192
  compartmentalisation, 192, 193,
    194, 195, 204
  detachment, 185–6, 189, 191
  disillusionment, 186, 191, 192, 193,
    194, 195, 204
  elitism, 183–4, 185, 187
  historical obliviousness, 184, 189

forms of global law have had some effect in re-awakening attention and re-opening minds to the idea of law as something more than a patchwork of difference and a collection of particulars. As we have observed, the majority of both convergence-promoting and divergence-accommodating approaches favour a universal approach. Global law in all these cases is endeavouring somehow to refine and condition the variety of law in accordance with some dimension of universal rationality – whether envisaged and presented as chain, umbrella, vessel, thread or flow. In all these approaches, global law, however thinly cut, is predicated upon a belief in the oneness of law in some aspect of its referential domain. What is more, none of the other approaches to global law – structural or functionally specific – is necessarily out of sympathy with such an approach. They simply bracket off a more basic sense of the ontological oneness of law as a separate concern, rather than necessarily ruling out such a possibility. Indeed, we have already observed the close synergy between the structural 'will' of a UN-centred architecture and the unifying formal 'reason' of international law.[49] And in the case of the various functionally specific species, their sense of the incipient common ground of a segment of transnational law, for example in matters of international criminal law or climate change law, may, notwithstanding the instrumental drive of a common legislative will, be seen as a precursor and preliminary contribution to the idea of a more broadly conceived unitary dimension within global law.[50]

The clearest evidence of the lure of the possibility of law's universal register, however, can be seen in the range and density of possibilities within what we have called the abstract-normative position, and also those incorporating many of the sub-species of global constitutionalism. From Klaus Günther's universal code of legality[51] to the thickest form of human rights universalism, and various formulations of a global Rule of Law, we see a multitude of ways of thinking about legal oneness. What is perhaps most striking about this debate, however, is how little it depends on earlier dogmas of legal universality – such as those associated with natural law and other objectivist theories of the good law.[52] Instead the

---

[49] See Chapter 3.2.1–3.2.2 above.   [50] See Chapter 3.4.2–3.4.3 above.

[51] K. Günther, 'Legal Pluralism or Uniform Concept of Law? Globalisation as a Problem of Legal Theory' 5 NoFo – Journal of Extreme Legal Positivism 5 (2008).

[52] See e.g. J. Waldron, 'Partly Laws Common to All Mankind': Foreign Law in American Courts (New Haven, CT: Yale University Press, 2012) ch. 2. See also Waldron's perceptive essay on Alberico Gentili as a bridging figure between a natural law and a positive law foundation of international law at the end of the sixteenth century, and as an example of the blurring of boundaries between metaphysical and progressive-empirical